THE BEGINNINGS
OF GRADUATE EDUCATION
IN AMERICA

THE BEGINNINGS
OF GRADUATE EDUCATION
IN AMERICA

BY

Richard J. Storr

THE UNIVERSITY OF CHICAGO PRESS

The University of Chicago Press, Chicago 37
Cambridge University Press, London, N.W. 1, England

Copyright 1953 by The University of Chicago. All rights reserved. Published 1953. Composed and printed by The University of Chicago Press, *Chicago, Illinois, U.S.A.*

To

MY FAMILY

Preface

A LIVELY university is a work of art, a product of imagination and of command over material. For a university to come into existence, someone must become aware of a new opportunity or a fresh need for higher education. For a university to endure, many men and women must master the resources which make higher learning possible. This book is a record of the awakening which led to the first American experiments with graduate education in the arts and sciences and of many efforts to secure and organize the requisite talent and funds.

The subject with all its ramifications in intellectual, social, economic, and political history is too large for one book. I have therefore restricted my investigation to those proposals and projects which anticipated modern graduate schools of arts and sciences in their institutionalized forms. This limitation may appear to belittle the very real contributions to graduate education made by a wide variety of schools and individual instructors outside formal graduate departments of arts and sciences. These qualifications may also seem to impose modern distinctions upon an age in which such distinctions were only beginning to crystallize. To recognize these possibilities is, however, sufficient protection against the misconceptions they breed. To seek to avoid them altogether by refusing to place any restriction on the subject would be to embark upon an endless search, which might produce an extraordinary mass of factual material without necessarily throwing a concentrated light on the ideas and activities of the men who first sensed the need for graduate education in the arts and sciences as we know it and who initiated the struggle to create institutions to meet the need.

There may seem to be something ludicrous in a book devoted to the pre–Civil War history of a kind of education which failed to make a deep impression on the American mind until long after the war. "Why, graduate education meant little or nothing until Johns Hopkins burst upon the country!" The best answer to a remark of this sort is a reminder that a work of art, whether a poem or a university, does not just happen; it is not produced by spontaneous generation. It used to be said that Coleridge created "Kubla Khan" in one dreamlike moment; but John Livingston Lowes showed how long was the road to Xanadu.

The evolution of graduate education toward clarification in idea and success in operation was an even longer process. Its early history lends perspective to the academic world of Daniel C. Gilman, Charles W. Eliot, and the other university-builders of their generation, to whose work we attribute so much of the good or evil in education and the life of the mind today.

To thank all those who have enabled me to write this book is beyond my power. The broad subject, academic life, is one which my instructors and other friends illuminated in the past and which colleagues, students, and still more friends continue to illuminate in numberless ways today. These men and women have contributed to my knowledge of university affairs, knowledge which is as truly essential to the writing of the book as is the historical research which went into the preparation of it. I must pass over the company of my teachers and helpers with this inadequate recognition of my indebtedness and name only Professor Arthur Meier Schlesinger, under whose guidance the work was begun and with whose aid and understanding counsel I have completed it. I am deeply grateful to Harvard University for fellowship assistance during the year when most of my research was under way and to these institutions for allowing me to use their libraries and collections of documents: the American Academy of Arts and Sciences, the Boston Public Library, Bowdoin College, Columbia University, Georgetown University, Harvard University, the Library of Congress, the Massachusetts Historical Society, the New-York Historical Society, the New York Public Library, New York University (Washington Square and University Heights Libraries), the New York State Library, the New York State Museum, Union College, the University of Chicago, the University of Michigan, the University of Pennsylvania, the University of the South, the University of Virginia, Western Reserve University, and Yale University. I also wish to thank Mrs. Louis Faulkner for permitting me to use papers in her possession, and to express my gratitude for permission to quote from these books: Russell H. Chittenden, *History of The Sheffield Scientific School, 1846–1922,* 1928, published by the Yale University Press; Roy J. Honeywell, *The Educational Work of Thomas Jefferson,* 1931, published by the Harvard University Press; Charles M. Perry, *Henry Philip Tappan, Philosopher and University President,* 1933, published by the University of Michigan Press; and *The Diary of George Templeton Strong,* edited by Allan Nevins and M. Halsey Thomas, 1952, published by the Macmillan Company. To my wife, my final word of gratitude!

R. J. S.

University of Chicago

Contents

I

The Shortcomings of the College

WHAT fired the imagination of the men who began to advocate graduate education in the late eighteenth and early nineteenth centuries?
There had once been a time when the Bachelor's diploma truly represented a "first degree" of academic life rather than the completion of
formal study; but that time was long past when the history of graduate
education, as we know it, began. Many Americans did, of course, take
the Master of Arts degree, qualifying for it by staying alive and out
of trouble for three years after graduating from college and by giving
very modest evidence of intellectual attainments. Residence as a student
in a university was not ordinarily required.[1] Did a desire to rescue the
M.A. from complete decay motivate reform? Where it existed at all, this
concern was apparently incidental. The medieval tradition of exacting
study in a university for the second degree and then for a doctorate
had grown too feeble by 1800 to be the inspiration for change. Instead,
academic men were aroused to action by what they found when they
scrutinized the established system of higher education in the United
States and measured it by standards appropriate to the times. The
American college of the decades just before and immediately after 1800
may well have been more effective in an unassuming way than its
critics admitted, but it did have limitations which became increasingly
intolerable.[2]

College studies had become almost entirely undergraduate; and yet
this curriculum offered the most advanced instruction in the arts and
sciences available in the United States. Occasionally Bachelors of Arts
did linger on about the campus; but these "resident graduates" are
scarcely to be considered graduate students in the modern sense. Their
title suggests the provision made for them as well as their academic
status: they were permitted to reside in the college community, but
they received little or no attention. At most they could expect that a
class would be formed "if a sufficient number present themselves."[3]

The deterioration of the Master's degree removed old incentives for advanced study, and the Ph.D. had yet to be introduced into the country. Any American desiring this mark of learning or the systematic guidance with which it was associated was obliged to expatriate himself temporarily.

Financial incentives to remain at one's books were meager and did not continue beyond the taking of the M.A. when they extended even that far. In 1643 Lady Anne Mowlson founded a scholarship at Harvard for "some poor scholler" to enjoy until he became a Master of Arts; but the gift was absorbed into the capital funds of the college.[4] Bishop George Berkeley gave to Yale some property, the income from which was to be used to assist three "scholars of the house" during the interval between the first and second degrees.[5] By the mid-nineteenth century, however, the money available provided only about $46 for each recipient, a sum even then "too small . . . to have any special influence upon the student's mind or purpose."[6]

The undergraduate course was largely or entirely prescribed, the boy being expected to adjust to the curriculum, not the curriculum to the boy. For this reason the college was often called a Procrustean bed. Bachelors of Arts possessed sufficient knowledge of the classics to appreciate the allusion, and they would probably be acquainted with academic philosophy, orthodox religion, mathematics, and the rudiments of the social and physical sciences; but they did not necessarily love good literature, recognize their own special talents, or command any profound knowledge of things outside the limits of conventional learning. "I am astonished sometimes," wrote a college boy in 1847, "to discover what *little* knowledge & information I have, and have come to the conclusion that it will not be increased much by studying (shut out from the world 4 yrs) latin & greek [*sic*]. Yet these may exercise the mind & prepare for the reception of other things hereafter."[7]

This judgment simply reflects the fact that the colleges of the period emphasized mental exercise and relegated knowledge to a place of secondary importance. "The two great points to be gained in intellectual culture, are the *discipline* and the *furniture* of the mind; expanding its powers, and storing it with knowledge. The former of these is, perhaps, the more important of the two."[8] The Yale authorities, who made this statement, believed that the mind possessed certain faculties, all of which had to be brought into play in laying the foundation of a thorough education; and they implied that such an education required understanding of essential subjects so numerous as to permit no option to the student.

The primary considerations were general intellectual ability and familiarity with an established body of learning. When a Bowdoin College undergraduate asked his father if it was more to a student's advantage to puzzle over geometry and dig out Greek roots than to pay attention to current literature, to study history, and, in general, to acquaint himself with subjects of practical value, the father replied: "if the studies of College [the classics and mathematics, in particular], are not mastered at College, they will be never mastered;—and an ignorance of them will hang like a dead weight round the neck of any man, even if he should be equal to Daniel Webster. But thorough-paced scholars, when they leave College, can soon master all the light literature of the day, and they can be just what they please in any profession."[9] Such ideas were defensible; but they were not calculated to create an atmosphere or to shape a system of education wholly satisfactory to the inquisitive searcher after new truths, particularly if he were a natural scientist. The common belief that piety was even more important than intellect in college life did not improve the situation for the student in pursuit of secular knowledge.[10]

The unattractive features of the accepted undergraduate program must have been accentuated by the customary method of instruction by recitation. Occasionally college presidents or professors of great learning and personality made a deep and favorable impression;[11] and when the textbook material had been covered, there might be an opportunity for disputation. President Jeremiah Day, of Yale, called this "an important part of our course of exercises";[12] and Professor James L. Kingsley, also of Yale, was convinced that something very like direct and vigorous action of the professor's mind on that of the student did take place.[13] Yet drill was the rule: "the root of the matter is to be found in the humble and simple, old-school, tedious business of recitation."[14] This device was used "from necessity, consequently listened to with but little pleasure, and its termination diffuses joy over the faces of most of those who are present."[15] To the latter half of this statement one recorded reaction was a brief, "c'est vrai."[16]

A college with a prescribed course taught by recitation did not need a great variety of specialists, who, after receiving the Bachelor's degree, had studied systematically for academic careers. A few young teachers, Benjamin Silliman and Edward Everett, for example, were enabled to study abroad; but foreign preparation became common only as the nineteenth century advanced. The typical campus figure was the general scholar with a B.A. degree and, perhaps, some theological training. He might possess wisdom as well as scholarship, ripened during many hours of midnight work; but the student could not assume that the professor was prepared to offer advanced courses. Even the alert teacher may have found that a constant routine of hearing undergraduate recitations often deadened the impulse or forestalled the opportunity to convert his personal learning into courses suitable for graduates.[17]

Religious sectarianism, local pride, and the size of the country also inhibited the growth of institutions of the highest learning by encouraging the founding of many weak colleges rather than the development of a few strong universities.[18] The United States did not lack able men; but they were scattered over a wide land. Its inhabitants in general came to know many of them as missionaries of education; but its gifted sons could not benefit from a union of intellectual forces which did not exist.

Moreover, even long-established colleges lacked the wealth required to support more than a handful of scholarly teachers or to purchase and maintain a modicum of equipment. Colleges might run bills with the butcher, the baker, or even the builder, or secure loans from their own professors by delaying salary payments; but fundamental innovations in American education called for larger funds than petty borrowing could supply. Although public support furnished by some state governments helped a few institutions, the amounts were too small to meet the full demands of educational leaders. The day of great private benefactions had to wait until enormous personal fortunes became relatively common. Between the Revolutionary and Civil Wars, Harvard received less than a quarter of a million dollars in large gifts, exclusive of funds raised by subscription,[19] although its alumni and friends must have included many of the richest college men in the country. As one professor said, "most men really cannot afford to build colleges among us."[20]

Critics of the American colleges were inclined to apply several tests, in all of which the colleges did badly. As the number of scholarly men familiar with European universities grew, it became increasingly common to quiz the college on its ability—or more often its inability—to do what was being done abroad. The most significant body of men to examine the college in the light of European accomplishments was made up of Americans who knew English and Continental universities at first hand and Europeans who were living in the United States. Americans who stayed at home could become acquainted with European academic institutions through a growing shelf of books on foreign education. Some of this material was gathered by special observers like Alexander D. Bache and some by students abroad, one of whom gave his fictionalized reminiscences the significant subtitle, *Memoirs of a Provincial*.[21] Such writing did not supply a simple prescription for reform, since general agreement on the exact character or meaning of European education did not exist in this country. The perceptions of the observers differed, and the things perceived were neither uniform nor static. Nevertheless, acquaintance with European universities did draw attention to academic attainments compared with which those of the American college appeared to be painfully slight.

A very different standard of criticism was "the spirit of the age." This phrase and variations on it appeared repeatedly before 1861 in connection with an intense and widespread concern for education. One Yale professor remarked that the demands of this spirit were so numerous and discordant that it was not easy to ascertain them distinctly;[22] but even though exact definition was lacking, the connotations of the phrase usually were democratic and utilitarian. Invocation of "the spirit of the age" was in effect a call for something more immediately practical than the liberal arts.

"A few only [said Albert Gallatin in 1830] are destined for the learned professions, or calculated to follow the pursuits of science and literature. But all want such degree of practical and useful knowledge, which can be acquired during the earliest years, of life. It is that want which is generally felt; for which there is a loud and well founded clamor, and which ought to be satisfied."[23]

Opening the college to new courses and new classes of students could lead to provision for advanced study, or reaction to an apparent debasing of the arts curriculum might produce a university department designed to forestall change in the college proper. In either case, tradition was broken.

The college was also judged inadequate when its curriculum was compared with the entire body of knowledge. At a time when all fields of learning, from chemistry to philology, were expanding at an extraordinary rate, the college course changed slowly. To be well-informed in many subjects, a student would have had to go far beyond the limits of the Bachelor's attainments. Contrary to an impression general today, however, the curriculum was not invariable in content, although it was rigid in its prescriptions. The colleges did sometimes incorporate new material into the established course, but they did so at the risk of treating no subject thoroughly. With liberal arts education in danger of becoming either archaic or superficial, college authorities were forced to justify their old ways or to invent methods of adjusting the curriculum to the growth of learning. One result was experimentation with courses for graduates.

Chronologically, the first test to be put to the colleges stemmed from patriotism. It is common knowledge that, once political independence was gained, there developed a desire for cultural independence which found expression in everything from textbook revision through Noah Webster's work on American language to Emerson's *The American Scholar*. This address did not, of course, deal with graduate studies as such, but it revealed the spirit of men who could not be reconciled to the modest, if solid, achievements of the ordinary college. In 1837, the year of Emerson's address, President Philip Lindsley, of the University of Nashville, pointed out the absence in the United States of any institution comparable to the universities of Europe. He went on to specify America's needs: professors of every language, dead and living, and of every science in all its branches and subdivisions, in all its bearings and applications. "There should be schools, in short, for all the sciences, arts, languages and professions. So that no youth need ever cross the ocean to study and learn what ought to be taught much more safely and advantageously at home."[24] Evidence of this dislike for dependence on European education had appeared before. Not long after the War of 1812, when protective tariffs were under debate, the *North American Review* suggested that foreign principles might creep in as easily as foreign goods and argued against those who thought it dangerous to freedom to be clothed in British garments while they were indifferent to having British philosophy, poetry, morality, and politics poured into the American mind from the moment it began to have an idea.[25] What the United States needed was the creation of a literary profession and authors and books of its own—"fine, chaste writers, historians, whom the world should read, sweet poets and sensible critics."[26] A university offering more than undergraduate studies and professional preparation for medicine, divinity, and law, was the most efficacious means to that end.[27] It would elevate the national spirit. Nor was this academic nationalism new. It had emerged in the troubled times when the Constitution was being framed.

II

"The Revolution Is Not Over"

D R. BENJAMIN RUSH was a patriot in education as well as in politics.
For him the American Revolution was something more than a war to
secure independence from Great Britain; it meant also the establishment
of republicanism. Until this was accomplished, the Revolution was not
over.[1] To complete it, he believed, Congress must not only restore the
public credit, provide for defense, and revive commerce; it should also
appropriate money to found a national university. Perhaps this was even
more urgent than the other activities, for they would have to wait upon
the time when the citizenry became inspired with federal ideals, "which
can only be effected by our young men meeting and spending two or
three years together in a national university, and afterwards disseminating
their knowledge and principles through every county, township, and
village of the united states [sic]."[2]

This sentiment, which Rush voiced in the year of the framing of the
Constitution, was echoed by the Federalist editor, John Fenno, in the
year of its first operation. "As we have taken our station among the other
nations of the world, it is highly proper we should form on national principles, which can be best done by promoting such institutions as have a
tendency to remove local views and habits, and beget mutual confidence,
esteem, and good fellowship between those who are embarked in the
same bottom, and must rise or fall together. . . . [A federal university]
will be happily calculated to answer those valuable purposes, and have
the most beneficial effects, in a political view."[3]

Both Rush and Fenno made a distinction between a college and a
university. So also did Samuel Knox, president of Frederick Academy
in Maryland, and Samuel Harrison Smith, a Jeffersonian journalist, who
divided a premium offered by the American Philosophical Society for
essays on liberal education adapted to the American genius of government.
For all these men the college was a steppingstone to the university. In
1786, while still thinking in terms of Pennsylvania alone, Rush produced

7

a plan calling for free township or district schools, county academies, four colleges, and a university which would admit holders of the Bachelor's degree for a season or two of lectures.[4] Some such outline was presumably in his mind the following year when he advocated the founding of a federal university for young men who had completed their studies in the colleges of the states.[5] Knox, too, envisaged a four-part system of parish schools, county schools or academies, state colleges, and a national university, where a student, usually at the end of his twenty-first year, would receive an M.A. degree after three years of work at the highest level.[6] Smith's program was made up of only three divisions—primary schools, colleges, and a university; and he set no limit to the final course.[7] Fenno did not propose a graded scheme of any sort, but he did suggest that the university should accept college graduates for two or three years of additional study.[8]

Knox recommended public support of a few university students, and Smith touched prophetically upon the practical question of supplying an incentive to young scholars to continue their education. He recommended that a student be permitted to remain in residence at the university "so long as he please on a salary, in consideration of his devoting his time to the cultivation of science or literature, in which last case, he shall become a fellow of the University."[9] Time was to show that, in the absence of a law, such as Rush suggested,[10] closing federal office to all but university graduates, financial encouragement might be necessary for the success of graduate education.

Had Congress undertaken to found a national system of education, a crisis might well have developed. If Rush's outline of 1788 had been followed, the university would have taught predominantly useful and vocational subjects. Mathematics would have been limited to phases relevant to the division of property, to finance, and to warfare; natural philosophy (physics) and chemistry would have been studied in connection with agriculture, manufacturing, commerce, and war. The classics and the cultivation of the intellect for its own sake had no place in his curriculum.[11]

By contrast, Knox gave first thought to "elevating, enlightening, and dignifying the human mind."[12] In his opinion, the university's primary aim must be "to accommodate such as wished to indulge their literary genius to the greatest possible extent, and who were in such circumstances as to account no part of their life spent more agreeably or to better advantage, than in receiving the highest possible improvement in Arts and Sciences."[13] In practice, this would have meant a strongly humanistic offering of courses, with little of Rush's utilitarianism.[14]

But a great national university, whether dedicated to utilitarianism or humanism, whether poor or endowed with rich fellowships, did not materialize. In spite of the support of men like Washington and Jefferson, the idea never became sufficiently popular to be embodied in legislation. Perhaps the project was "too federal"[15] for the times; perhaps the cost, although possibly as low as $125,000,[16] frightened a people who shied at taxation.

Although the schemes just discussed may in retrospect appear hopelessly utopian, they are signs of a significant attitude toward educational reform; and they illustrate a related mode of action. Both attitude and mode characterized the founding of the University of Virginia, which was originally conceived of as a graduate institution. The attitude is best exemplified by Thomas Jefferson's unwillingness to confine academic reform in Virginia to alteration of his Alma Mater, William and Mary College. At one time he did attempt such reform; but later and more persistently he worked for the creation of a wholly new institution. Impatience with gradualism was natural to a generation which had executed a successful revolution and had changed the central government by supplanting, rather than by amending, the Articles of Confederation. If governments could be founded on written constitutions, why should not educational systems be similarly based? If the first step toward a proper ordering of political society was the framing of an instrument indicating its parts and their articulation, why should men not begin reform in education by drawing up a constitution for it? The question was: What ought the whole educational mechanism to be? The answer: a system completed by something more advanced than the colleges.

The initiator of the legislative activity which produced the University of Virginia was Charles Fenton Mercer, a member of the House of Delegates, champion of internal improvements, and author of the bill which had created the Virginia Literary Fund for the encouragement of learning. On February 15, 1816, the Delegates' finance committee, of which Mercer was chairman, submitted a report, which Mercer had written, to the effect that means for a system of public education might be found in funds due from the federal government. This recommendation having been approved, a resolution, also drawn up by Mercer, was passed by the House and, within two hours, concurred in by the Senate. The resolution requested the president and the directors of the Literary Fund to digest and report a system of public education. It was, the resolution suggested, to embrace a university, colleges, academies, and schools. No more details than these were indicated, but this much sufficed to distinguish between university and undergraduate work as parts of an over-all scheme. Both the distinction and its incorporation into a system of education were to appear again.[17]

What precisely Mercer was thinking in 1816 is not a matter of record; but an address on popular education which he wrote ten years later suggests what he may have had in mind. Certainly, the grades of education laid down in his resolution of 1816 correspond to the parts of the system which he described in some detail in 1826. In that year he advocated four levels of formal education. Elementary schools should supply those means of intellectual and moral culture which all members of society should command. Instruction in the academies should begin precisely where that of the primary schools stopped. Colleges succeeding the academies should accommodate their course of study to advances already made by pupils of the academies and should fit them for entering upon the study of the learned professions and of the arts and sciences in all their higher branches. "An university [Mercer continued] at the head of each system of education, should adapt its instruction to the natural and easy extension of the collegiate course, prepare its youth for the practice of the liberal professions which they have respectively chosen; and be capable of teaching, moreover, all that man can learn in the existing state of human knowledge, whatever be his intended occupation; and whether he designs to enter on the theatre of active life, or to devote the residue of his days to the culture and pursuit of science."[18]

These specifications may not, of course, be an accurate picture of Mercer's ideas in 1816. Yet, in order to see the inception of the University of Virginia in true perspective, one must note that Mercer may have entertained such thoughts at the time when he was a chief mover for educational reform in Virginia. Since he was not a member of the circle centering about Thomas Jefferson, which was ultimately to organize the University, his interest in a university distinct from the colleges is evidence that the idea of the university as a graduate institution was not the sole possession of the man who is commonly—and rightly—supposed to have given substance to proposals for a University of Virginia.

After seeking advice, the president and director of the Literary Fund reported in favor of primary schools, academies, and a university to rescue young Virginians from the necessity of leaving their home state or even the United States for general or professional education, at the risk of alienation from the customs and principles of their parents and ancestors.[19] The report also specifically recommended fellowships for "such young men, who, though destitute of the means of obtaining an education, have been selected for their talents, and instructed and supported at the public expense."[20] These would form a seed-bed of future teachers and professors. "Besides, it is a consideration of great importance, that you create a corps of literary men, who, enabled by receiving a decent competence, to devote their whole time to the pursuits of science, will enlarge its boundaries, and diffuse through the community a taste and relish for the charms of literature."[21]

Once this report was made, a bill or bills were in order; but none passed the House of Delegates until Mercer prepared one calling for a university and a number of colleges, academies, and schools.[22] The House of Delegates passed this bill, but it miscarried in the Senate. There Mercer let the matter rest, as he was elected to the United States Congress.[23]

Jefferson, who believed that Mercer's proposal overburdened the Literary Fund,[24] had a measure of his own. Known as a "Bill for Establishing a System of Public Education," Jefferson's plan was based on an idea he had held for many years: the division of a public school system into three parts.[25] The bill provided for ward schools, colleges, and a university, in the last of which all branches of useful knowledge would be taught: "history and geography, ancient and modern; natural philosophy, agriculture, chemistry and the theories of medicine; anatomy, zoölogy, botany, mineralogy and geology; mathematics, pure and mixed; military and naval science; ideology, ethics, the law of nature and of nations; law, municipal and foreign; the science of civil government and political economy; languages, rhetoric, belles lettres, and the fine arts generally."[26] These subjects should be combined into not more than ten appropriate groups, with a professor in charge of each.

Although the bill did not make graduation from college a prerequisite to the university, Jefferson's provision that state-supported students move from college to the university certainly implied that the latter was to be more advanced than the former.[27] As he had written to Governor Nicholas a short time earlier, the colleges "are intended as the portico of entry to the university";[28] and later, in 1822, he spoke of existing colleges of the South as preparatory to the university.[29] Clearly, he meant to make a distinction between "college" and "university"; but in the Nicholas letter he displayed some uncertainty as to the role of the schools of intermediate or college level, suggesting that they might be considered grammar schools. This ambiguity introduces some vagueness into his system. Yet in the absence of positive evidence to the contrary, one must assume that Jefferson ordinarily meant by a "college" what that institution was generally accepted as being.[30]

From the general trend of Jefferson's thought, it is apparent that, however low the portico of the university, its ceiling was to be the limits of knowledge itself. Such an institution, he was convinced, should keep abreast of intellectual progress.[31] While he had strong utilitarian principles, his view of the curriculum was far from narrowly vocational. He wished to encourage the study of Greek and Latin and explicitly opposed Rush's negative attitude toward the classics.[32]

The Bill for Establishing a System of Public Education precipitated a hot debate, in which Joseph C. Cabell served as Jefferson's principal spokesman. As in most legislative discussions on education, the financial question proved crucial. Since the Literary Fund was too small to maintain a complete system of schools, the bill's supporters proposed that the lowest schools be sustained by direct taxation. After much argument in the House of Delegates, Jefferson's plan was rejected in favor of an amendatory bill providing schools for the poor only. When this measure came to the Senate, it was referred to a committee of three, of whom Cabell was one. He proposed that the college and university sections be restored to the bill; but the other members of the committee prevailed upon him to withdraw the college recommendations for the time being because of the practical difficulties involved and because of the danger of losing all by attempting too much. The committee did agree to insist upon a university. On that ground the two houses reconciled their differences.[33] The sill and pediment of Jefferson's educational structure were approved; but the pillars between them were neglected.

Once the university project was enacted into law, a Board of Commissioners, of which Jefferson was a member, was appointed to decide on matters of organization. Meeting at the Rockfish Gap of the Blue Ridge in August, 1818, the Commissioners set high purposes for the university: individual happiness and comfort, good government, and the prosperity of society. Failure to establish a sizable institution "would leave us . . . without those callings which depend on education, or send us to other countries to seek the instruction they require."[34] The nature of knowledge demanded something more elaborate than existing colleges: "each generation succeeding to the knowledge acquired by all those who preceded it, adding to it their own acquisitions and discoveries, and handing the mass down for successive and constant accumulation, must advance the knowledge and well-being of mankind, not *infinitely,* as some have said, but *indefinitely,* and to a term which no one can fix and foresee. Indeed, we need look back half a century, to times which many now living remember well, and see the wonderful advances in the sciences and arts which have been made within that period."[35]

The breadth of this concept was matched as nearly as was feasible by the course offering. In brief, this was to consist of ancient languages, the modern languages, pure mathematics with naval and military architecture; physico-mathematics (such as mechanics); physics (meaning, in the Jeffersonian sense, chemistry and mineralogy); botany and zoölogy; anatomy and medicine; government, political economy, law of nature and nations, and history; municipal law; and ideology, or "the doctrine of thought," general grammar, ethics, rhetoric, belles-lettres, and fine arts, with the subjects to be grouped according to the professorships of those who were to teach them.[36]

This was, however, only a paper project. Seven years of the most trying labor elapsed before the University of Virginia actually offered instruction to students. Still, Jefferson did not lose his ambition for the University. At the time of its opening a college instructor wrote to ask if education at Charlottesville was to be *"really* profound and extensive—up to the level of the learned institutions in France & Great Britain . . . especially as regards the important branch of philology, and those useful sciences which are increasing our small acquaintance with the earth & air."[37] Jefferson answered: "With respect to the degree in which the sciences will be taught here, I think I may say in as high an one as in the universities of Europe, should any of the students propose to pursue them so far."[38]

But would students so propose to study? The University would in practice rise to the level of Continental institutions only if students asked for the highest instruction and were prepared to receive it. John A. Smith, once a student at St. Thomas' Hospital, London, and after 1814 president of William and Mary, may have been moved by jealousy to some extent; but he was positive that there existed in America no demand for science which did not contribute to moneymaking. Those few who wished to study natural history and allied fields should go abroad, "where these subjects are better taught than it is *possible* (I speak literally) they can for ages be taught here."[39] Even Jefferson himself, in spite of his aspirations for the University, used the subjunctive when he spoke of elevating its curriculum. As early as 1821 he talked, not of rivaling Oxford and Göttingen, but of admitting to the University those who were then going to Harvard, Princeton, Columbia, and the University of Pennsylvania.[40] As the southern counterpart of these colleges, the University would perform a notable service; but it would not be a graduate school.

The friends of the University did not immediately surrender their conviction that education in Virginia was incomplete without colleges. In 1818 the Commissioners at Rockfish Gap noted the need for schools or colleges to supply students to the University;[41] and, in the following year, Jefferson indicated his eagerness for the opening of a classical school to serve as a reliable nursery for the University.[42] When the removal of William and Mary to Richmond was discussed, he suggested that its funds be used to found preparatory colleges.[43] But hope had to be deferred.

In 1816 President Timothy Dwight, of Yale College, had written: "If my experience has not deceived me, such a scheme of a *College* in the *American* sense, and still more of a *University* in the *European* sense, as will fairly promise extensive utility to the public, must involve many important parts; all of them nearly or absolutely indispensible [*sic*]."[44] Virginia's experience simply proved the crucial role of the colleges. Before the United States could have great universities, it had to possess facilities for good undergraduate preparation.[45]

III

German Influences

I

JUST before the aging Jefferson undertook his last great work, he was visited by George Ticknor, a young New Englander about to set off for Europe and whatever education he could find there. The parting of these two men, so different in many ways and so like in others, has a meaning which must have been missed at the time. Both were deeply interested in learning; both were to make great, but somewhat abortive, contributions to higher education. Yet their approaches to their work and the material with which they dealt differed widely. Jefferson, standing in the tradition of grand projects, planned an entirely new institution; Ticknor, representing the influence of the German universities, did his work as an educational reformer within the limits set by an established college. At Harvard he kindled a light, which, Jefferson predicted, would draw an empire to it;[1] but he could only set in motion a process of growth which in the end could not be considered the product of a single plan.

Before leaving home, Ticknor had not been predisposed in favor of German methods. Writing in 1815 to another of Jefferson's young friends, who was thinking of travel, he had asked: "what will you do . . . ? Shall you sit yourself down amidst the literary society of Paris and pass there in solitary study or intellectual intercourse the greatest part of the time you can allow yourself to be absent? Or shall you trouble the pools of stagnant learning in Germany & England and visit with a classical eye and a classical imagination the curious remains of art and antiquity in Italy? Methinks I can almost see you in a delightful hesitation between the Coliseum and the Institute—between Port Royal on the one hand and Göttingen and Oxford on the other."[2]

By 1816, after he had seen German learning at first hand, Ticknor's attitude toward its alleged stagnation had changed. Impressed by the admirable facilities for study and inducements to it offered by a German university, he renounced an interest in the law and prolonged his stay in

Europe so that he might make himself a scholar. Inclined toward literature, he only wondered where he could best prepare himself for a career in it. The vigorous spirit of youth had fled from England, he felt, although he found there a green and honorable age. In France, literature, buried under the ruins of national independence, had become the sport of political revolutionists; in the south of Europe, it had lain in its grave for centuries. In Germany, however, where the spirit of letters had first begun to be felt about a half-century before, all was still new and young: "the workings of this untried spirit starting forth in fresh strength & with all the advantages which the labour & experience of other nations can give it are truly astonishing."[3] Much was to be hoped from the Germans, not because of what they had done or were doing but because of "the free, & philosophical spirit with which they do it[,] the contempt of all ancient forms considered as such, and the exemption from all prejudice—above all, the universal activity with which they push forward, & the high objects they propose to themselves."[4]

While still a student at Göttingen, Ticknor grew exceedingly anxious to have transplanted to the United States this spirit "of pursuing all literary studies philosophically—of making scholarship as little of drudgery & mechanism as possible."[5] The further progress of learning in America depended, he was persuaded, on a thoroughgoing revision of the educational system.[6] Writing to Stephen Higginson, Steward of Harvard College, Ticknor raised the question of improving college libraries in this country;[7] and he apparently enlarged on his view of academic reform in a letter to James Savage, who must have passed it on to President John T. Kirkland.[8] Kirkland replied to Ticknor: "I agree with you in the main parts of your discourse on education & on us. We are however poorer than you think. But we apply our time & direct & distribute our instruction to great disadvantage. I am sorely troubled at the loss of time, produced by our system or no system. The school discipline must be continued longer. Still the pupils must not be detained from active life, professions &c longer than now, nor may the expenses of our education be much increased. But if we throw back our elements, such as are taught the two first years & part of the second upon the Schools we shall lose our pupils or at least not have them but two years instead of four, unless we make a part of their College term of four years go towards their professional preparation. To have a gymnasium & a University together on the same ground is not good. We cannot well keep two classes close & the others at large."[9] Despite his doubts, however, Kirkland anticipated a time when "we bring here students of maturer minds, that is, divide our Seminary into gymnasium &

university";[10] and in a draft of the same letter he went so far as to suggest that eventually Harvard might have "a school for the *three* faculties . . . & philosophy[,] that is to say[,] be a gymnasium & a university, [as] in Germany."[11] Reorganization along this line was presumably one of the recommendations which Ticknor had made to Savage: Harvard should become a university in the Teutonic sense.

Ticknor's interest in a college which was not his own is explained by his appointment, in 1819, to the Smith professorship of French and Spanish languages and literatures and the professorship of belles-lettres at Harvard. In accepting the post, he stipulated that he must have the means for preparing as good lectures as his talents and industry would permit, that students should have an opportunity to hear him, that he should not be obliged to drill them in the elements of language, and that he should be permitted to live in Boston. These conditions made his position unique; for they enabled him to examine the college from the inside and, at the same time, to speak with some detachment.

One of Ticknor's Harvard colleagues was Edward Everett, professor of Greek literature, who also had recently returned from study abroad and was accordingly inclined to judge academic institutions by Continental standards. Measured by these criteria, Everett found Harvard narrow[12] and American education incomplete, crudely organized, and poorly supported. Although European universities, Everett said, cultivated some branches of knowledge for their own sake, these institutions were, properly speaking, professional schools where young men who had perfected themselves in classical studies at the gymnasium or high school came to prepare for careers in the law, medicine, divinity, or teaching. In the United States, he went on, teaching was scarcely recognized as a profession, and the number of schools offering training in the other fields was inadequate. Still worse, these few often stood isolated from one another in spite of the fact that learning, a living body, could not retain all its properties if cut in pieces. Only a fraction of the corporate spirit of a university, in which all parts of a finished education were brought together "to emulate . . . , to illustrate, to adorn, to aid each other,"[13] survived when the parts were divided. Moreover, separate schools could provide neither a fine library nor the subsidiary branches of knowledge which belong to all professions but are not peculiar to any single one. That the state and national governments had done little or nothing to remedy the situation was "a sore point in our history":[14] "Our mouths are filled with the praises of our own illumination, we call ourselves happy, and we feel ourselves free, but content with a vulgar happiness, and an inglorious freedom, we leave it to despots, to build universities as the toys and playthings of their slaves."[15]

Using the vocabulary Ticknor and Everett had learned, Tutor George Otis got down to cases. Was it the purpose of Harvard College, he asked, to form perfect scholars or to be a preparatory school for liberal professions, "as affording only the elements of knowledge;—as furnishing a Gymnasium for the prolusions, or first essays of mind?"[16] Otis' question was answered by Ticknor in 1821. In a year and a half of teaching, he said, he had found much idleness and dissipation among the students and had become disillusioned with the work in his own field. He talked to the President, who did nothing, and to Professors Andrews Norton, Levi Frisbie, and Henry Ware, who agreed with him that great changes were necessary. Two of the latter advised him to go to the Corporation, which, in effect, he did by approaching one of the Fellows, William Prescott. Deeply impressed by Ticknor's arguments, Prescott asked to have them in writing.[17]

The statement prepared in response to this request clearly demonstrated that the enthusiasm of the young, wandering student had given way to the chastened judgment of the teaching scholar. "I most sincerely wish that it [Harvard] were now in a condition to be raised above the highest wants felt among us, and to prevent so many of our young men from seeking in solitary, unaided exertion, & in foreign countries, the degree of Instruction, which we cannot offer them.—But this does not seem to be possible. If we can ever have an University at Cambridge, which shall lead the intellectual character of the country, it can be I apprehend only when the present college shall have been settled into a thorough & well disciplined high school, where the young men of the country shall be carefully prepared to begin their professional studies; and where in Medicine, Law, & Theology, sufficient inducements shall have been collected arround [sic] & within the college, aided by regular courses of instruction in the higher branches of general learning and science, to keep Graduates there two years at least, & probably three. As, however, we are not arrived at this desireable [sic] condition, & cannot very soon hope to arrive there, the first thing to be done, in order to satisfy the reasonable demands of the community, is, to take measures to make the college *a well disciplined high school,* in which the knowledge preparatory to a professional education, shall be taught *thoroughly,* & the habits & character of the young men fitted for the further intellectual exertions to which they are destined."[18]

As a result of this letter, the Corporation circularized the faculty in regard to the state of the College and established a committee to digest the findings. When a large majority of the professors were found to oppose any real innovations, the Corporation was unwilling to act. Nothing substantial was done until 1823, when a student rebellion, followed by mass dismissals, shocked the College into self-examination. The Corporation gave way to the Overseers, representing a more widely influential group of men, for whom the opening of the College and its transformation into a university became the objects of reform.[19]

The effort of the Overseers began with an excited discussion at a religious club to which Ticknor, Norton, and Ware belonged.[20] (Ware was one of the two College officers to whom the results of the 1821 faculty investigation had been given.)[21] After several evenings of talk, it was agreed to call a meeting of selected persons to consider the problem of the College. On July 23, 1823, Justice Joseph Story, General William Sullivan, George B. Emerson, the Hon. Richard Sullivan, Charles Lowell, John Gorham Palfrey, and Dr. James Jackson gathered at Ticknor's house in Boston. Four of these men were Overseers and a fifth had formerly been one. Jackson and Ticknor were professors, but neither was closely associated with the ordinary life of the College. Indeed, Ware and Norton, both of whom had originally requested a meeting following the disturbances at the College, had advised against resident instructors attending.[22] William Prescott and Harrison Gray Otis, members of the Corporation, would also have been present but for a meeting of the Fellows on that day.[23]

Ticknor struck the keynote of the discussion, which began at nine in the morning and continued without interruption through dinner until six at night.[24] In his general conclusion he echoed the Prescott letter. *"Changes,"* he exclaimed, *"must take place in the present constitution and organization of college."*[25] Without reform, it would lose the support and confidence of the society upon which it depended and would find itself not the leader but the first victim when the period for universities arrived. In other words, he said, "we must accomodate [*sic*] ourselves more to the spirit & wants of the times and country in which we live."[26] Specifically, he recommended that the College be broken up into departments, that classes be divided on the basis of proficiency, that a limited choice of studies be allowed, and that unmatriculated students be admitted.[27]

Ticknor's purpose in 1823 was not just to make Harvard a good high school; it was also to find "a beneficial compromise" between the old system and "the most liberal conception that would be demanded by one of the really free and philosophical Universities of Europe."[28] The College should be considered "as a place where all the Branches of human Knowledge will, at last, be taught; and where, of course, there shall no longer be an attempt to compel every Student to learn something under every Instructer [sic]."[29] Prescribed study in all subjects would be wrong, "now the branches are become so numerous."[30] Departmentalization could be indefinitely increased "without a change of system, & thus the whole institution be made to keep even pace with the increasing demands of the Community, without any further alteration in its essential plan."[31] The result obviously was to be the "open University"[32] of which Ticknor wrote to his friend Jefferson.

The almost biological development of Harvard College as department grew from, or appeared beside, department would produce facilities calculated to encourage graduate study. Ticknor's position makes little sense if one does not suppose that he meant that instruction at Harvard should ultimately be more advanced than that of the old college. As departments increased in number, courses in erudition, and electives in variety, any given young man might well spend additional time at his studies. What was left untouched in four years could be examined later. This was one germ of graduate education. From Ticknor's time, this idea was never to atrophy altogether at Harvard.

Responding favorably to Ticknor's remarks, his guests agreed that a committee of Overseers should be appointed to examine the College thoroughly. This group was elected on the following day, and within another twenty-four hours, the Corporation, acting on a request from the other board, constituted President Kirkland, Prescott, and Otis a committee to confer with the Overseers.[33] The enthusiasm for reform which had shown itself in Ticknor's Boston house was not so evident in the Yard. In fact, the President did not seem very zealous for change and took the reformers' difficulties as a good joke.[34] Moreover, the Overseers' committee chairman, Joseph Story, did not perhaps have quite the influence which a Boston man might have possessed.[35] Nevertheless, the investigation went forward; and in May, 1824, a report was ready: "In a society, like ours, which is continually expanding and embracing more elevated objects of research [said the Story committee], the nature and extent of an University education, and the methods of instruction, must be, in some degree, liable to change, so as to be adapted to the spirit of the age. A course of studies, fully adequate, at one period, to all the wants and wishes of the community, may be ill fitted for another of higher cultivation. A moderate knowledge of classical literature, of philosophy, and the sciences, may satisfy all that the ordinary business of life requires, at an early period of national existence; and yet it may fall far short of the demands, even of humble education, in a more aspiring age. . . . The great question must always be, what modes of instruction are best adapted to the present exigencies of our society, so as to give the most finished education in the shortest period that our pursuits require."[36]

In discussing the best teaching methods, the committee recommended, among other things, that the College be divided into separate departments, each with its own head, and that a distinction be made between subjects indispensable for a degree and those in which the student might exercise a limited choice.[37] Such changes would not remake Harvard into either a simple gymnasium or a pure university. The committee had taken seriously Ticknor's suggestion of a compromise, retaining an undergraduate program but rearranging it in such a way that the curriculum as a whole could expand beyond the needs of any single student.

The new departure was soon challenged. A second committee headed by John Lowell inquired into the affairs of the College and presented a report. In the end, however, the Story findings were accepted by a large majority[38] and submitted to the Corporation as the basis for new College laws. These regulations, effective in 1825, divided the College into departments; authorized the faculty to make such changes and substitutions in the course of study as were required or justified by diversities of intellectual powers, habits, and progress in the various divisions; and ordered that in the foregoing arrangements the wishes of the students be consulted as far as was consistent with the nature and objects of liberal education. As in the past, resident graduates were mentioned in a provision setting dues for them.[39]

The revised laws did not transform Harvard into a university overnight. In particular, they failed to establish an earned M.A. degree. Still, the innovations of 1825 contained the seed of an elective system and set up the machinery for expansion.

As the work of the Overseers and the Corporation moved forward, the attitude of the faculty became crucial. Unfortunately for the new program, it was hostile. Professor Andrews Norton objected sharply to the committee's failure to consult the faculty directly, constantly, and freely. Although, in his eyes, this was a fundamental mistake,[40] he did not attempt to block all reform. For him, the ultimate purposes of religious and moral education remained constant; but he recognized that in the cultivation of the intellect change was inevitable. "The most important objects of study vary with the general progress of learning, which is every day extending its limits, with the circumstances of different countries, and with the destination of different individuals."[41] The faculty, he said, thought the College was not the sort of institution the country demanded or would support, nor the sort it had ample means to become. They believed it capable of assuming "a much higher character, and of being much more extensively useful";[42] but they had seen "the work of improvement undertaken by gentlemen from without, and plans proposed, which, as it seemed to them, were wholly inadequate to effect the purposes intended."[43] The Story plan, "taken as a whole, does not seem to afford any settled and distinct conception of the character which it is proposed to give the College. Is it to be a University? One would think that this should be gradually aimed at."[44] From the evidence, however, Norton doubted that that could be the mark. How was degradation of the College to the rank of a high school to be reconciled with the stated purpose of reform?[45]

Here Norton was confronting a compromise without recognizing it, or perhaps without wishing to recognize it, as such. Ironically, the point of his criticism was that same Germanic distinction which underlay Ticknor's original thought. Although Norton had not himself observed the differences between high school and university abroad, he had friends who could instruct him. George Bancroft had corresponded with him from Germany, and Edward Everett was on his side at Harvard. That Everett was an ally, if not a leader, of the opposition symbolizes one of the primary difficulties in the early reformation of Harvard. Out of the faculty conviction that its experience had been slighted came a proposal for representation of the teaching staff in the Corporation. The term "Fellow" was to be restored to something of its early meaning. When the governing boards denied, in effect, that the English precedent still held in Massachusetts, Ticknor concurred, and thereby seems to have lost whatever support for his reforms he might have expected from professors such as Everett.[46]

Even if some concert had been possible between Ticknor, Everett, and Norton, they might yet have failed to carry the whole faculty with them. On the one hand, Everett's discontent with things as they were took the form not so much of reforming zeal as of a desire to remove himself to grander theaters of action; and Norton's attitude was cautious: "No error [he said] is more likely to be prejudicial than a rash adoption of modes of education which have been found to succeed elsewhere, without regard to the peculiar circumstances of the institution in which they are copied. No reasoning will probably be more deceptive and mischievous, than reasoning from imperfect analogies, in which essential circumstances affecting the character of different institutions, or in which the habits, manners, state of society, and literary wants of different countries are not sufficiently considered."[47]

On the other hand, other members of the faculty felt too little ardor for general reform to propose it to the Overseers when an inquiry was made into the condition of the College in 1824.[48] By the time the laws of 1825 had become effective, the instructors' dissatisfaction with the old order, to which Norton had testified, had been transformed into decided opposition to the new system. As a result, the faculty so successfully pared it down that a university could hardly have developed even if the need for financial retrenchment had not at that moment intervened.[49]

In 1824 the College expenses amounted to $33,404.79, or $758.41 less than income;[50] in 1825 they appear to have been $33,749. In 1826 they had risen to $34,564.48. In 1826, moreover, student fees brought in $2,450.25 less than they had in 1825. Consequently, the 1826 expenditure from permanent funds exceeded by $3,265.73 the 1825 outlay from this source. In view of this considerable item and of others, a committee appointed to look into the financial state of the College recommended a retrenchment of $4,000 or more. Lowering of the tuition charge from $55 to $30 per annum called for an additional cut of $5,000. This meant a total reduction of $9,000, or approximately one-quarter of the budget.[51] The implications of the situation were great; and the committee, Charles Jackson, Nathaniel Bowditch, and Francis C. Gray, did not flinch at pointing them out: "We are not insensible how great a benefit it would be to the public and how great an honor to the College, if we had Professors, who might confine their instruction in each department, to such as had mastered its rudiments, and who might immediately make known here, the discoveries of other learned men in all countries, and extend the boundaries of science by their own. But when it is found that the income of the College is so reduced that this object cannot be attained but by refusing elementary instruction, or by offering it at so high a price that few can receive it & that the number is constantly diminishing, so as to increase the burden on each individual, we have only to regret that the patronage bestowed on the College, and the state of Society among us, do not permit us to enjoy the privilege any longer."[52]

In this crisis Ticknor acknowledged that the plight of the College demanded sacrifice, but he insisted that something more must be done or "the College can never regain its former rank and consideration."[53] The speedy introduction of an effectual system of instruction, he hoped, would restore to it the respect it had formerly enjoyed. In other words, he apparently believed that debt might be avoided by raising the prestige and presumably the income of the College; but the Harvard authorities acted upon the more cautious policy of limiting operations in order to keep expenses down.

Just a few years after this decision was reached, a British traveler remarked that there was an abundant desire to learn in America but that this was not accompanied by an adequate reward for learning.[54] If this was true, even those men who did not question the importance of advanced education to the individual or to civilization could quite reasonably insist that the meager demand for learning did not warrant the building of universities. The need for them had to be widely, as well as intensely, felt. In slighting this point, educational reformers were sometimes impractical; in refusing to be paralyzed forever by temporary stringency, they showed their courage.

II

During the 1820's knowledge of German higher education served primarily to emphasize the inadequacy of the college. No serious effort was made to create an American replica of Göttingen or Berlin. Direct borrowing did not begin until the 1830's, when Harvard attempted to establish a seminar after the German pattern. This pedagogical device was in use when Ticknor was abroad, but it apparently made no great impression upon him. It had, however, struck Philip Lindsley, lately come to Nashville from Princeton. In 1825 he called attention to Heyne's philological seminar at Göttingen and to its role as a supplier of classical professors and teachers to the Continent of Europe: "We have our Theological Seminaries [said Lindsley]—our Medical and our Law schools—which receive the graduates of our colleges, and fit them for their respective professions. And whenever the *profession* of teaching shall be duly honoured and appreciated, it is not doubted but that it will receive similar attention, and be favoured with equal advantages."[55] Three years later the *North American Review* praised the German philological seminars, or "seminaries," as they were then called,[56] in an article which described their operation, the demand for their members as teachers in gymnasia and universities, and the inestimable benefit to the public resulting from them: "They [the philological seminaries] impart to the student a scientific knowledge of the profession he is going to practise as teacher, form his character and habits as such, by causing him to study the art of communicating his ideas in the simplest and most engaging manner, to shape and to finish the thoughts of his pupil according to his own model, and to instil into his tender mind those delicate and elevated feelings of honor, which are the best safeguard against illiberality of opinion, and against the abuse of confidence."[57]

Not long after this was written, a German classicist with a Tübingen doctorate began teaching Latin at Harvard. Charles Beck[58] had come to America in 1824 and had taught for some time in secondary schools. With this experience behind him when he came to the Yard in 1831, he began immediately to plan a philological seminary, designed in part to train teachers.

President Josiah Quincy was friendly toward the experiment, although he refused to surrender to the clamor against existing schools for not advancing as fast as the spirit of the age. Educational authorities, he maintained, should yield "nothing to any temporary excitement,—nothing to the desire of popularity,—nothing to the hope of increasing their numbers: nothing to those morbid cravings for farther supply, which the cheapness and abundance of exhilirating [*sic*] literary elements and their evaporating qualities have a tendency to create."[59] Yet he did not oppose all reform. He believed that at different stages of society the means adopted for arousing and directing the "intellectual principle" had varied according to prevailing opinions and influences.[60] He would bring Harvard into conformity with the influences he felt to be dominant. "The duty to consider science & learning, as an independent interest of the community [he said], begins to be very generally felt and acknowledged.—Both in Europe & America attempts are making to rescue the general mind from the vassalage in which it has been held, by sects in the church, and by parties in the state;—by giving to those interests as far as possible, a vitality of their own."[61] In an effort to promote this vitality, Quincy later experimented with a general system of voluntary study; but first he listened to a Beck variation on the theme.

The earliest formal recommendation of a seminary appears to have been laid before the Corporation on June 23, 1831.[62] Pointing out the need for special instruction for teachers, Beck said: "We should carefully distinguish between that degree of information which may be sufficient for an individual whose object is to develope [*sic*] & cultivate the powers of his mind, & that comprehensive knowledge necessary for instructing, embracing the whole branch in which instruction is to be given; these two kinds of knowledge differ materially in their object, extent & the manner of their acquisition."[63] The regular college, he went on, did not and should supply the learning necessary for the instructor, whose need for special knowledge had been accentuated by the development of classical learning in the preceding fifty years. America should not always be dependent upon Europe for knowledge of this sort. Although progress would have to be slow, circumstances favored improvement. In particular, Beck stated: "A classical Seminary . . . should be formed by degrees but still the final object should be fixed & well understood. Such a Seminary should give 1) a complete instruction in classical philology, comprising a thorough acquaintance with the language, literature & history, in the widest sense of the word of the Greeks & Romans. 2) a complete course in history & 3) in mathematics. This wd [*sic*] constitute a philosophical school as I shall call it, corresponding to the philosophical faculty of European universities, & in common with the theological[,] law & medical schools complete the structure of our university."[64] The teacher in a classical school should command the knowledge communicated in the three departments of the philosophical school.

Beck next described in detail the operation of the first, or strictly philological, department. Instead of terminating study of the ancient languages at the end of the junior year, as was customary, the student would continue for two or, if possible, three years. Instruction should be by lectures characterized by independent thought and continual recourse to the sources. This practice would foster habits of independence and thoroughness in the students and insure them against the baneful effects of dogmatizing. To these lectures would be added some practical exercises, probably by the students. They would write dissertations and would submit to examination before receiving certificates. To enable men, especially the impecunious, to remain in Cambridge for a fifth or sixth year, funds must be made available. By these means, Beck concluded, a class of professional teachers would be created, of whom the most distinguished might be chosen to fill chairs of classical literature in the colleges. Unfitness for any other calling would no longer be, as it had frequently been in the past, the sole qualification for the profession of teaching.[65]

With this or presumably a similar plan before it, the Corporation voted, on August 25, 1831, to establish a department to teach the theory and practice of instruction, with Charles Beck as the principal instructor and Cornelius C. Felton as his assistant. The President and these teachers were constituted a committee to prepare rules and regulations governing the venture.[66] After a number of weeks the committee submitted an outline of laws, which was referred to the President and Francis C. Gray of the Fellows.[67]

The seminary was to be made up of prospective teachers and others desiring to pursue a course of classical study for general purposes. The instruction, to be advanced and critical, would embrace two years, beginning with the senior year. It would be of three types: lectures by the instructors, interpretation by them, and interpretation and other practical exercises by the students. Student participation would be frequent. Certification would be qualitative as well as quantitative. After two years, those wishing to become instructors must pass a rigid examination consisting of a dissertation displaying all the student's literary skill as applied to a previously prescribed subject, a general oral examination, and an interpretation of an author not included in the regular program.[68]

On December 13, 1831, the President and Gray approved the plan with the significant reservation that no preference should be shown to students who were preparing to teach.[69] Obviously, advanced study was not to be overtly professional, whatever the motives of the students and the aim of the professors might be.

Following this action, the department completed its arrangements; and Beck recommended that a notice of classical studies be inserted in a catalogue of lectures and voluntary exercises. Specifically he suggested this schedule of studies:

FIRST TERM

1. Lectures on Greek literature by Felton, once a week.
2. The *Philoctetes* of Sophocles, explained by Felton, once a week.
3. *Captives* by Plautus, explained by Beck, once a week.
4. Cicero's *De Officiis*, explained by students under Beck's direction, once a week.

SECOND TERM

1. Lectures on Roman literature by Beck, once a week.
2. Cicero's *De Officiis*, as in first term.
3. The *Philoctetes* of Sophocles, as in first term.
4. Demosthenes *De Corona*, explained by students under Felton's direction, once a week.

THIRD TERM

1. Demosthenes *De Corona*, explained by Felton and students alternately.
2. Cicero's *De Officiis*, explained by Beck and students alternately.[70]

These offerings were obviously limited to one field; but the course was to be elastic. From a philological beginning, the seminary was expected to grow into something broader.[71] Almost at the outset both Beck and Quincy contemplated the eventual addition of mathematics to the department.[72] That the President regarded the school as an experiment[73] may have indicated some uncertainty on his part. He was, however, willing to give Beck a chance; and we know that Beck had a faculty of philosophy as the ultimate goal.

Only in one quarter was the future dark. The proposal for funds to provide aid to students had not been accepted. Only operation of the school, which opened for the academic year 1831–32, could reveal the tragedy of this departure from the original recommendation. At the end of one term Beck believed that experience had proved the practicability of the undertaking.[74] Nevertheless, he was uneasy, fearing that novelty might have accounted for part of the success. Clearly, something was needed to take its place. It could scarcely be expected, Beck said, "that any graduate will be found to continue his residence in C. one more year and devote himself principally to these studies. And yet it is of great importance to the continuance of the establishment that there should be from next commencement some graduates however few who will pursue these studies as their principal occupation who might serve as a nucleus for the second branch of the Seminary which may be said to exist, as yet, merely nominally."[75] Financial assistance for needy and worthy students was imperative, because the seminary was not yet sufficiently famous to attract those who wished to become professional classicists and who might later look to the prestige of the seminary for help in placement. Because it was unable to offer stipends to students, Beck questioned the seminary's ultimate success.[76]

Some members of the Corporation apparently shared his misgivings; for in June, 1832, that body accepted a committee report suggesting that appointment of graduates to the office of proctor would offer desirable encouragement and that proficiency in the philological department might be considered as one recommendation for the post.[77] This was the seed of graduate student aid, but it did not blossom into a general program. Lacking it, the seminary withered and was forgotten.[78]

IV

"The Spirit of the Age"

Harvard's experience was but one symptom of a general uneasiness over higher education in the United States. The colleges were being accused of failing to keep pace with a pervasive desire for reform.[1] They were warned that they would soon be deserted if they did not better accommodate themselves to the business character of the nation, and it was strongly urged that they be remodeled to adapt them to the spirit and the wants of the age.[2] In practice this meant the addition of courses parallel to the old curriculum and, by implication, the abandonment of a unitary undergraduate program. More slow-moving educators naturally questioned the advisability of change with the result that a serious controversy was well on its way by 1830.

I

In taking its stand Yale College touched in a backhanded but significant way on a policy for the development of universities. In 1827 its President and Fellows appointed a committee to consider eliminating compulsory Latin and Greek. Before publishing an opinion, the committee sought the advice of the faculty, which responded with two statements. One, presumably written by President Jeremiah Day, was concerned with matters of general theory; the other, the work of Professor James L. Kingsley, dealt with the particular questions posed by the Corporation.[3] Both statements argued against change. After hearing them, the committee presented a concurring report of its own to the Corporation, which accepted the findings before it and ordered their publication, together with as much of the faculty statements as was expedient.[4] Once in print this conglomerate document became famous as the Yale report of 1828. In it are imbedded the arguments of the conservative academic policy of the period.[5] The report as a whole embodies the classic American defense of the single prescribed course as it had developed up to that time. In many respects, it epitomized the Yale described contemporaneously by Captain Basil Hall: "It was extremely agreeable to see so many good old usages and orthodox

29

notions kept up as vigorously, all things considered, as possible. How long the able and zealous professors of this celebrated establishment will be able to stem effectually that deluge of innovation and would-be improvements in doctrine, discipline, and pursuits, which is sweeping over the rest of the Country, and obliterating so many of the land-marks of experience, I cannot pretend to say. Meanwhile, every thing that came under my notice, seemed judiciously regulated."[6]

However deserving of this Tory applause, Yale was not entirely blind to the German example which inspired men like Ticknor. The official committee report and the second faculty statement do not dwell at all on foreign institutions; but the first faculty statement explicitly discussed the role of Yale compared to that of a German university. The argument began by considering the proper object of collegiate education and proceeded to a defense of the compulsory course and to the proposition that undergraduate work was not professional. Here Day's opinion might have ended, had he been ignorant of European education. He was not, however, and devoted three substantial paragraphs to it. Yale, he said, was not patterned exactly after European universities; nor should it make a ludicrous attempt to imitate them. The German institution most nearly equivalent to the College was the gymnasium. If to the theological, medical, and law schools attached to Yale there was added "a School of Philosophy for the higher researches of literature and science,"[7] the four departments together would constitute a university in the Continental sense of the term; but the collegiate department would still have its distinct and appropriate purpose. Under existing circumstances it would be idle to remake the College along university lines.

Thus baldly stated, Day's view appears to have been a veto; but it was qualified. When he said that Yale should not make a ludicrous attempt at imitation, he added the clause, "while it [the College] is unprovided with the resources necessary to execute the purpose."[8] Moreover, he contrasted German university students and Yale men on the basis of their attainments and went on to say that the first and great improvement needed in New Haven was higher admission requirements. Finally, though doubting that a college without formal discipline would be popular, he said: "When the student has passed beyond the rugged and cheerless region of elementary learning, into the open and enchanting field where the great masters of science are moving onward with enthusiastic emulation; when, instead of plodding over a page of Latin or Greek, with his grammars, and dictionaries, and commentaries, he reads those languages with facility and delight; when, after taking a general survey of the extensive and diversified territories of literature, he has selected those spots for cultivation which are best adapted to his talents and taste; he may then be safely left to pursue his course, without the impulse of authoritative injunctions, or the regulation of statutes and penalties."[9]

Connecting these remarks with the report's central thesis, one finds the fragmentary but unmistakable outline of a concept which was later to have wide currency. A college should remain a college in the old-fashioned American sense until it had the material means to offer something more than ordinary undergraduate teaching. Even when this came about, it should maintain a unified, general course at the undergraduate level; but it might add facilities for specialized study to graduates. Then it would be in fact comparable to a German gymnasium and university combined. College admission requirements should be raised; but collegiate and university work should be kept separate. In this respect the principle followed at Yale differed from that at Harvard. In New Haven the undergraduate department was to remain distinct, whereas in Cambridge undergraduate and graduate classes might be identical. One system emphasized the unity of the arts course, the other the diversity of individual talents. From this difference two distinct types of graduate work could develop— one the product of supplementing the traditional college, the second of transforming it.

The Yale policy required no such break with the past as did Ticknor's. In fact, when Yale produced a comparable young reformer, Daniel C. Gilman, he accomplished his greatest work outside of New Haven. Nevertheless, the Yale of the twenties was not without its young blood, inflamed with the German doctrine. When the author of the first faculty statement wrote that the universities of Germany had lately gained the notice and respect of informed Americans, he might have specified Henry E. Dwight, who while not an officer of the College, was the son of its late president, Timothy Dwight.

It is unlikely that the younger Dwight's letters from Germany in 1825 and 1826 were unknown in New Haven. These revealed a great enthusiasm for the German universities and a sharply critical attitude toward American higher education. They also contained several comments about Göttingen which resemble the remarks on German education in the report of 1828. The German universities, said Dwight, had four faculties—theological, legal, medical, and philosophical; the universities corresponded only to the professional departments of American colleges; and the German students, before entering the universities, had had a classical education in the gymnasia superior to that available in the American colleges.[10] Parts of the faculty statement sound almost like a commentary on these opinions. Old Yale is apparently saying to young Yale: yes, we may ultimately become a university but we must not compromise the College, either financially or academically.[11]

Was the implication that increased resources might sometime allow expansion the vague, if not positively insincere, concession of the conservative who intends to oppose change but does not wish to appear arbitrary? Or did the Yale authorities actually contemplate graduate study at some future time? No conclusive answer is possible. Yet the fact was that, while the report of 1828 was being written, funds for graduate fellowships were accumulating in the College treasury. During the academic year 1811–12, when Henry E. Dwight's father was still alive, a florid, well-dressed Connecticut farmer in his middle thirties passed the autumn, winter, and part of the spring term at New Haven as a special student in the classes of the President and in Professor Benjamin Silliman's lectures in the department of natural philosophy and chemistry. Sheldon Clark was possessed of intelligence and independence of mind, but he had been prevented from entering Yale at the customary age by his parsimonious grandfather upon whom he was then dependent. The grandfather's death brought both moderate wealth and liberty to Clark, who took advantage of them to fulfil in part his old ambition. Although he did not often reappear after leaving New Haven in the spring of 1812, presumably to plant his crops, he retained a devotion to learning. For years, he plowed his stony farm, fattened cattle, taught school in the winter, loaned money, and, in general, increased his productive capital. Moreover, he did not marry, so that he was presently a man of wealth with no family of his own. In 1822 he came to Silliman asking for a private interview. Out of it came a deposit with the College of $5,000 for the endowment of a professorship. After this generosity, Clark was entertained by the President and professors in what was apparently a most gratifying manner; for his first gift was followed by a second.[12] Under its terms the College received $1,000, which was to be permitted to accumulate interest for twenty-four years. At the end of that period the Corporation was to appropriate $4,000 for the founding of a scholarship or scholarships. The annual income from the $4,000 should be divided into two parts, one to be granted for two years to a student from the class to be graduated in 1848 and thereafter to a scholar selected from each even-year class. The second portion was to be awarded for two years at a time to a member of the odd-year class, beginning in 1849. Students receiving the grants must stand highest in a special examination covering all branches of literature and science included in the college course. Scholarship-holders must reside in New Haven for nine months of each of the two years immediately following graduation and must devote themselves to a course of study prescribed by the President and "academical" professors and adapted to their particular genius and prospects of usefulness but not including the studies of any of the three professions.[13]

Clark's philosophical bent combined with respect for formal education may have interested him in advanced, nonprofessional study. But would an American farmer of 1824, even with an unusual taste for academic life, have thought of endowing a fellowship without some prompting from educators? One can imagine an occasion on which the President of Yale or perhaps Professor Silliman, who was on very good terms with Clark, spoke to him of a need to keep studious young men at their books after graduation from college. Possibly the snares of infidelity associated with study abroad were mentioned. At any rate the gift was accepted by the Yale authorities, who could hardly have forgotten it when the possibility of advanced study was discussed.

When the stipulated twenty-four years had elapsed, the Clark Scholarships were announced. In 1849 the younger Timothy Dwight, grandson of the president under whom Clark had studied, received one of the grants as a member of a Department of Philosophy and the Arts,[14] which was in part created because the Clark fund made some support of graduate study a reality. This department was the link between the Yale of the 1828 report and the Yale of the modern Graduate School.

II

Early in 1830 the *New York American* printed a letter attacking the spirit of the age and citing the Yale report of 1828 as a warning against the actual injury which would result from the establishment of a university. The admonition was directed in particular at the friends of an institution which was then being projected.[15] Originally called the University of the City of New York, it ultimately became known as New York University. The first open meeting in its behalf had been held on January 6, 1830.[16]

Much thought and money were spent on elementary education, ran the chief argument presented at the meeting, but had not the higher branches been neglected? Something was needed for young persons who were staying at home while training for the learned professions; for youths in danger of dissipation; for all young men preparing for agricultural, commercial, or higher mechanical pursuits; for those already so engaged, who desired further information; for persons of advanced age and of leisure, who might study for pleasure; and for persons from all parts of the country seeking the advantages of concentrated talent, information, and activity. A great metropolis was the proper location for a university; and the one projected was to be situated in the heart of the city. The institution would be supplied with a well-selected and extensive library covering all branches of knowledge, with specimens illustrating natural history, and with apparatus for experimentation. It would have professors to teach all these subjects, and it would be open to everyone of good moral character and of sufficient preparation to avail himself of its privileges. Students would be allowed to attend one or more courses, according to their capacity or intended occupation or profession. The cost of the university would be moderate, its physical plant simple.[17]

Neither this statement nor the minutes of the early organization meetings contain evidence that a graduate school, pure and simple, was anticipated. When on January 14, 1830, a standing committee adopted an outline plan for the project, it stated that the principal aim of the proposed institution should be "to extend the benefits of education in greater abundance and variety, and at a cheaper rate, than at present they are enjoyed."[18] A committee reporting in March, on a program of instruction, struck a similar note. "The object of the University is to extend the means and opportunities for acquiring knowledge, and by no means to degrade the standards of literature by an indiscriminating distribution of its honours."[19]

Nothing was said of raising the standards of literature. Yet the founders of the University thought of providing for advanced study,[20] possibly under the inspiration of a current newspaper controversy over higher education. On December 24, 1829, Joseph Leo Wolf, a German living in the United States, began the discussion by recommending adoption of a university plan similar to that in his homeland. He stated that a university should be a *Universitas Literarum* [sic], a place like the University of Berlin, where all knowledge was taught. Only those should be admitted who could give evidence by testimonial or examination that their education was sufficient to prepare them for professional studies. A knowledge of classical languages and a considerable familiarity with their authors should be one of the first requirements for matriculation, because of the beneficial effects of such study on the minds and the principles of youth. Ferdinand R. Hassler, a Göttingen man of thirty-five years' standing and superintendent of the United States Coastal Survey, took sharp exception to the establishment of admission requirements. They were wrong in principle as well as contrary to German usage. In reply to Hassler, Wolf insisted that at Berlin, Halle, Bonn, Marburg, Leipzig, and Munich no one was permitted to matriculate as a student except by legal testimony of a classical education in a gymnasium, or by examination. He did not recommend equally strict requirements for Americans but argued that admission regulations should be made more rigid as soon as openings for liberal education were increased. "There is no science, no matter what, into which a man can enter, profoundly without a thorough school-education."[21]

Graduate study was discussed again in October, 1830, at a Convention of Literary and Scientific Gentlemen called together by friends of the University. This "Congress of Philosophers"[22] included Edward Livingston, Albert Gallatin, Churchill C. Cambreleng, Theodore Woolsey, Henry E. Dwight, Thomas H. Gallaudet, Francis Lieber, Jared Sparks, William C. Woodbridge, and John Trumbull, as well as Hassler and Wolf. Four college presidents and a number of professors attended;[23] and although two other academic men of considerable distinction, Moses Stuart of Andover Theological Seminary and Henry Vethake of Princeton, could not be present, they sent letters of advice.

If the organizers of the convention had hoped for agreement on academic policy, they must have been disappointed. An attempt was made to focus debate on specific points of discussion or inquiry; but the attention of the meeting wandered. Every discussion, said one reporter, was arrested without one's being able to discover at what conclusion the convention had arrived.[24] The gathering did, however, serve as a sounding board for a few individuals who insisted upon the distinction between the American college and the German gymnasium on the one hand and a university on the other. Woodbridge pointed out: "In Europe, the line is distinctly drawn between the students of different ages, and in different periods of advancement. In our institutions, those of all ages are mingled. There, there are schools adapted to every age. The Latin schools and the gymnasia take the place of our colleges, and young men do not appear in the university, until the age of eighteen."[25]

Francis Lieber referred to the correspondence of American colleges with German gymnasia,[26] and when William H. Keating, a chemistry professor with European training, stated that the American colleges were probably, on the average, equal to similar European institutions, he had German gymnasia, French lyceums, and the English schools of Eton, Harrow, or Westminster in mind. He added that the United States had nothing of a higher grade. "Yet the condition of our country is such, as amply to call for it. Our colleges afford no facilities to those young men who, either from the affluence of their circumstances, or from their thirst after knowledge, are disposed to devote a few additional years to the acquisition of a thorough knowledge of any one department of science or literature. The number of these young men is already great; it is daily increasing, and it is certainly desirable that they should find, at home, those facilities which they are now obliged to seek abroad."[27]

Henry E. Dwight implied that the colleges of this country were inferior schools when he spoke of the very general feeling in America "that we need a University like those of Germany."[28] "Graduates after leaving the colleges of the United States [he said], usually abandon their classical studies, because there are no Universities to which they can resort, and attend lectures on the higher branches of classical literature. If this University should in this respect equal the ardent hopes, and may I not add the expectations of its friends, many of the graduates of our colleges will visit it for the purpose of pursuing criticism, and we shall ere long see some of that enthusiasm, for classical literature, which is now so visible in Germany."[29]

The difference between the college and the university was most elaborately discussed in a paper prepared by Joseph Leo Wolf: "The principal point to be kept in view, is, in my opinion, the distinct line, which should be drawn between a college and a University, as has justly been observed by several gentlemen of the Convention. Both may exist under the same head, but separately from each other. But the question is: what is called for? is it a university, or a college? and what are the objects of each?

"A college has to privide [*sic*] for the *eruditio* of young men, if I may style it so; to fit them for the common vocations of life. Of this kind, the same as are called *Gymnasia* in Germany, we have a sufficient number, and among them many, which may rival with the most famous of Europe.

"A University, however, is to satisfy the higher demands of science; *Universitas literarum* [*sic*] is its object. . . . The students who are to be received in the University, must be expected to have passed previously through a regular college education."[30]

General distinctions were not enough, however, to guide the new enterprise. There remained the need for a specific policy adjusting ideals to circumstances. What exactly could the University wisely attempt to do? Albert Gallatin dealt with this question in an address revealing his appreciation of learning on the one hand and his concern for practical affairs on the other.[31] Two objects were known to be contemplated, he began: "One is, to elevate the standard of learning, to complete the studies commenced in the colleges, to embrace in the plan of education those branches which may not be included in that of the existing seminaries of learning; in a word, to assimilate the University to the most celebrated establishments abroad, which are designated by that name. The other is, to diffuse knowledge, and to render it more accessible to the community at large."[32]

No insurmountable obstacles stood in the way of attaining the first object in due time; for the University should supply unsatisfied wants. Consequently it did not need to teach divinity, medicine, or law, which were available elsewhere. "Our attention in this upper department, may at first be confined to general science and literature, to what are called abroad the philosophical faculty, or the faculties of science and letters,"[33] in which the students would be college graduates or men of similar age. The diffusion of knowledge would be more difficult to provide for. Moreover, it would not be easy, Gallatin wrote privately, to connect "the study of sciences and letters carried to a higher extent than is usual in the colleges of this part of the country, with popular and general education fitted for men not designed for the liberal professions."[34] Perhaps an "English college," by which Gallatin meant a nonclassical institution, was the solution. The dead languages might be included in the University's offering, but they should not be treated as "the primary, fundamental, and absolute requisite of a learned education."[35] So considered they blocked the greater part of mankind from every branch of knowledge; but an English college would open a new road to the highest learning. In other words Gallatin proposed to meet the clamor of the times for useful information; but, while introducing a specific alternative to the Greek-Latin bottleneck, he did not advocate a general scheme for educating practically everybody.

When this and many other speeches had been delivered, the Literary Convention adjourned; and the Council of the University, its governing body, went to work. A committee, of which Gallatin was a member, was appointed to prepare a plan of organization. It was also instructed to correspond with other colleges and universities and to take steps toward securing a charter. Before the end of the year the committee began reporting statutes for consideration by the Council, which in late January, 1831, adopted the Constitution and Statutes, as amended.[36]

Chapter iv, which determined the structure of the University, showed traces of Gallatin's thinking. The new institution would have two general departments. The first comprised professorships and faculties for instruction in the higher branches of literature and science.[37] The second included a complete course of English literature, mathematics, and science.

Moreover, just as Gallatin had spoken of "the prodigious progress of science,"[38] the statute provided for expansion of the first department with "the progress of discovery."[39] There was, however, to be a classical course, as well as the English component in the second department. That the Council went beyond Gallatin's suggestions here may mean that he did not influence the organization of the University of the City of New York as strongly as his old political leader, Jefferson, did the University of Virginia although he left his mark on the new experiment.[40]

Once the Council had given shape to the University, it petitioned the state legislature for a charter.[41] By asserting that one of the two aims of the institution was to present "some of the advantages for a finished education which are enjoyed in the great universities of Europe,"[42] the Council seems to have committed itself formally to some form of graduate instruction.[43] Its most important action, however, was to establish a planning committee for the two undergraduate courses only. Perhaps because this group was empowered to consider a blending of the two courses, which Gallatin did not approve, possibly because the upper department was not mentioned—one does not know—the resolutions on this matter were first tabled; but they were ultimately passed. Soon afterward the charter was granted, and the Council set up another committee to report on organization of the University. In October, 1831, still another committee was appointed to consider revision of the statutes. Finally on March 13, 1832, the Council set up a committee to investigate the possibility of opening the University in the fall.[44]

This group enumerated the indispensable needs of the University: seven professorships, devoted to intellectual philosophy, English literature and belles-lettres; Latin and Greek language and literature; mathematics and civil engineering; natural philosophy, astronomy, and mechanics; moral philosophy and evidences of revealed religion; chemistry; history, geography, and statistics. With these, it was said, the University facilities would equal those available elsewhere in the country. The committee also recommended fee-supported professorships in Oriental languages and literatures; German language and literature; French language and literature; Spanish language and literature; Italian language and literature; and the philosophy of education.[45] No mention was made of a faculty for instruction at a level higher than the customary one.

Yet the advanced department was not entirely forgotten. In September, 1832, a Council committee advertised the department of learned languages as combining ordinary classical studies "with that higher exegetical instruction in Classical Literature, which is given in many of the Universities of Europe."[46] Moreover, at the formal inauguration of professors in the autumn, James Milnor, the presiding officer of the Council, stated that the founders thought it practical to furnish "such whose inclinations, talents, and expectations might lead to desires more extensive [than the nonclassical ones], not only with the portion of learning usually dispensed in colleges; but, if desired, with that more exalted measure of attainment, especially in classical studies afforded by the most eminent Seats of Learning in the transatlantic world."[47] Whether or not the University fulfilled this expectation was the responsibility of James M. Mathews, its first Chancellor. With his friends, he controlled the Council and the University for more than six formative years.[48]

Mathews was a handsome and ambitious clergyman. Both his admirers and his enemies would have vouched for his enterprise;[49] but they disagreed violently over his character and his policy. The anti-Mathews forces believed that his real objective did not jibe with the University's ostensible purposes. In 1833, for example, three disaffected professors claimed that, despite the Literary Convention, the Chancellor did not dream of an institution more elevated than a college.[50] Mathews had been a member of the committee which designated the professorships without specific regard for a higher department. Yet on at least one occasion which cannot be explained away as a disingenuous bid for public favor, he asserted: "The Institution . . . was never designed for a mere College. It is a University; & while it includes the course of instruction usual in our Colleges, it has avowed its . . . design to be such an enlargement of the means of Education as may not only carry students so disposed, beyond the limits of the usual College course but also provide ev[er]y facility for instruction to those who may desire it in particular branches of Letters or Science. . . . [This instituiton is pledged that its work] be so fitted as to invite to it not only undergraduates but also gentlemen who may have already take[n] their degrees at other Institutions or our own; and who may feel inclined to carry their studies forward to higher proportions [?], & more maturity."[51]

Whatever his views, Mathews was not a wise leader. An effort to rule rather than to persuade cost him the co-operation of almost every professor[52] to pass through the University during his incumbency. To this fault he added financial irresponsibility and extravagance, and he spent heavily for physical plant rather than for men and books. Reversing the original plan to house the University plainly, Mathews sought grandeur, arguing from an allegedly general feeling that to attract gifts the University needed a building corresponding to "the prevailing taste in architecture."[53] This called for a costly medieval monument even though Mathews had once spoken disparagingly of "the rude Goth" and his fatal influence on the arts.[54]

Faculty dissension and a dubious use of funds did not, however, immediately paralyze the University. In 1835 a department for instruction in the higher branches of literature and science and in professional studies was announced. Matriculated members would be admitted on Baccalaureate diploma or on examination. Holders of a Bachelor's degree could receive a Master's degree after a three-year course in any of the Faculties, followed by the proper examinations. The department of higher studies was to offer instruction in:

FACULTY OF LETTERS AND FINE ARTS

Sacred literature
  1. Lectures on the style, imagery, civil polity, ethics, and antiquities of the Bible.
  2. Lectures on the sources of biblical illustration.

Hebrew and oriental languages
  Lectures on the languages and literature of the Hebrews and other oriental nations.

Greek
  1. Lectures on the Greek language and literature.
  2. Lectures on particular authors.

Latin
  1. Lectures on Roman history, antiquities, and literature.
  2. Lectures on particular authors.

Intellectual and moral philosophy
  1. Lectures on the history of philosophy.
  2. Lectures on intellectual and moral philosophy.
  3. Lectures on the philosophy of education.

English literature and belles-lettres
  1. Lectures on the history of English language and literature.
  2. Lectures on English literature.

History
  Lectures on the philosophy of history.

French
  Lectures on French literature, accompanied with biographical sketches of French writers.

Spanish
  Lectures on Spanish literature.

Italian
  Lectures on Italian literature.

German
  Lectures on German literature.

Literature of the arts of design
  1. Lectures on the principles of the arts of design.
  2. Painting as a profession.

FACULTY OF SCIENCE AND THE ARTS

Mathematics
1. Lectures on the higher mathematics requisite for a study of mécanique céleste.
2. Lectures on the application of mathematics to the arts.
3. Lectures on the history of mathematics, the present state of the mathematical sciences, and the modes of prosecuting discovery.

Natural philosophy
1. Lectures on the higher mechanics and on the application of the principles of mechanics to the arts.
2. Lectures on practical and physical astronomy.
3. Lectures on the history and present state of the physical sciences.

Chemistry and botany
1. Lectures on the application of chemistry to the arts and on the chemistry of nature.
2. Lectures on botany.

Geology and mineralogy
1. Lectures on the principles of mineralogy as applied to geology and the arts.
2. Lectures on Scripture geology or the consistency of the Mosaic history with the present appearances of the different formations and strata.

Architecture and civil engineering
    Nature and use of materials; elements of construction; principles of design in architecture, and of the plan, location, and construction of public works.[55]

Here, obviously, was the higher department of the statute; but the University, keeping close to tradition in one respect, agreed to award the M.A. degree not only to matriculated graduate students but also to others who did not necessarily have any formal education beyond college.[56]

This practice and a regulation permitting "attending" students make it impossible to assume that all holders of an M.A. degree or all students registered in the higher department were graduate students in our present sense. In 1837 Mathews stated that many of the students in the higher department of science and letters were graduates of institutions in various parts of the country;[57] but he seems to have exaggerated. In the academic year 1836–37, fifty-three students paid full tuition.[58] The majority of these must have been undergraduates, however, as the usual graduating classes numbered twelve or more from 1836 through 1838.[59] The residue would have been small. If advanced students did enrol, they did not remain sufficiently long or work seriously enough to receive recognition on commencement day, for the Master's degrees awarded between 1836 and 1840 were apparently in course or honorary.[60]

After 1837 there was little probability that graduate students would be attracted to the University. In November of that year the Finance Committee of the Council reported that unparalleled pecuniary distress was delaying payment of subscriptions[61] and joined another committee in recommending that the chairs of Latin and Greek, and those of mathematics, chemistry, and natural philosophy be combined "so far as may be done without lowering the standard of undergraduate education below what is usually found in the most respectable Colleges around us."[62] The maintaining of extraordinarily high standards was not mentioned. The depression of 1837 was obviously making itself felt in a university built in part on the pledges of prosperous times.

Even so, in March, 1838, a committee was appointed to devise and execute plans for enlarging and improving the departments;[63] and soon afterward the University received a subsidy from the state. In announcing this aid to the Council, the Chancellor took pains to point out that the institution's distinctive character as a university had been of crucial importance in winning public support: "Had we been merely a College, and our instruction been limited chiefly to undergraduate branches of Education, our prospect of patronage from the State, would have been comparatively small. . . . But when the enlarged plan of the University was unfolded, showing that it comprises instruction in the entire range of the arts and sciences, as well as Education for the Professions of Law and Medicine, its claims to a liberal share of the patronage of the state were at once recognized."[64] This, as Mathews recognized, referred to the potentiality of the University, not the actuality. Yet he also reported that assurances of a balanced budget had been given the legislature; and he therefore expressed the hope that the Council would "without delay, proceed to place all the departments of the Institution on a footing that will answer the reasonable desires of our friends in this matter."[65]

That this meant retrenchment rather than expansion is revealed by the action which followed the Chancellor's recommendation. Committees on the several faculties were requested to suggest departmental arrangements which would be most economical and best adapted to bringing the expenditures of the University within its income.[66] These groups postponed submitting a plan until the Finance Committee had issued its report,[67] which proved on June 5, 1838, to be full of cheerless findings. Deficits ranging from approximately $5,000 to $10,000 had existed each year since the opening of the University. Construction and furnishing had cost more than $200,000, whereas paid-in subscriptions totaled only $83,130, plus an endowment toward one professorship. The University debt stood at almost exactly twice this latter sum—$170,583.48.[68]

Conceivably the University might have met this crisis without sacrificing its original aims. Unfortunately, however, its affairs were not to be straightened out in an atmosphere of calm. For months an academic storm had been brewing; now it broke about the head of the Chancellor. On August 30, the governing board, nearly all of the original members of which had resigned in the course of time, approved a joint recommendation of the committees on the faculties that the Faculty of Science and Letters for instruction of undergraduates consist of one professor of languages; one of natural philosophy and mathematics; one of intellectual and moral philosophy and logic, who should also teach history; one of evidences of revealed religion and belles-lettres; one of chemistry, geology, mineralogy, and botany; and one assistant professor of languages, who should aid in other studies of the freshman year as occasion demanded.[69] This reorganization left seven of the eight faculty members without duties or salaries.[70] The next step, on September 28, was to discharge these seven men,[71] one of whom, Henry P. Tappan, later tried to undo the tragedy of 1838 by founding another great university in New York. When, early in 1839, Mathews resigned, the process of disintegration finally came to an end.

After the troubles of 1838 the statutes continued to provide for a higher department, but they were not fully carried out. When the 1839–40 catalogue announced no higher department, it must have been clear that the University no longer represented an active experiment in graduate education. Instead this aspect of the enterprise proved to be the *"half made, half furnished, . . . ephemeral affair"* against which Moses Stuart had warned at the outset.

III

While the University of the City of New York was seeking a practicable way to increase and diffuse knowledge, a bequest to the United States from James Smithson, an amateur British scientist, made this aim a public concern. Smithson's will called for the establishment of a learned institution in the city of Washington, but was silent on practically all matters of detail. Consequently, beginning in 1835, the President and Congress—or, as it turned out, a series of Presidents and Congresses—faced the nagging problem of determining what the Smithsonian Institution should be. At first sentiment strongly favored the founding of a national university, one Senator remarking that it seemed to be taken for granted that the bequest was meant for creating a university, although the word was not used in the text of the will.[72]

Before Congress finally decided against this line of argument, the question of graduate studies was raised. In 1838 President Van Buren instructed Secretary of State John Forsyth to seek advice from scientific and educational experts in connection with the Smithson gift. The aging and astringent Dr. Thomas Cooper, who earlier had given Jefferson valued educational counsel, recommended the founding of a university open only to college graduates. Examination should be strict. Among other subjects, the curriculum might include higher algebraical calculus, the application of mathematics to astronomy, elementary electricity, and galvanism, and the principles of botany. But said Cooper: "No Latin or Greek; no mere literature. Things, not words." He rejected all belles-lettres and philosophical literature "as calculated only to make men pleasant talkers." (He also objected to medicine and law.) Ethics and politics were unsettled; and the status of physiology and political economy required more consideration than Cooper could give at the moment. In general, those studies should be cultivated which saved labor and increased and multiplied comforts for the mass of mankind. "Public education should be useful, not ornamental." In conclusion, he said that the course must cover not less than three academic years of ten months each; instruction should be free, and examination for admission rigid.[73]

Another of Forsyth's correspondents, President Francis Wayland, who had yet to undertake the greatest of his reforms at Brown University, answered somewhat differently. The country, he argued, did not lack instruction at the college level; and professional schools of divinity, law, and medicine were properly the concern of the sects or of the states or districts. Therefore, the Smithsonian, which he assumed would be national and educational, should occupy the gap between college and professional school in order to carry classical and philosophical education beyond the one and to supply a foundation for the other. "The demand for such instruction now exists very extensively. A very considerable portion of our best schools [scholars?] now graduate as early as their nineteenth, twentieth, or twenty-first year. If they are sufficiently wealthy, they prefer to wait a year before studying their profession. Some travel, some read, some remain as resident graduates, and many more teach school for a year or two, for the purpose of reviewing their studies. These would gladly resort to an institution in which their time might be profitably employed. The rapidly increasing wealth of our country will very greatly increase the number of such students."[74] An institution of this sort would furnish teachers, professors, and officers of every rank to other schools and would send a new grade of scholars into the professions, thereby adding to the intellectual power of the country. "As the standard of education was thus raised in the colleges, students would enter the national university better prepared. This would require greater effort on the part of its professors, and thus both would reciprocally stimulate each other."[75]

The subjects offered in the Institution should, with law and medicine, be those of the college, "only far more generously taught—that is, taught to men, and not to boys—":[76] Latin, Greek, Hebrew, the oriental languages; modern languages and their literatures; mathematics; astronomy, engineering; the art of war, beginning where it was left at West Point; chemistry; geology; mining; rhetoric and poetry; political economy; intellectual philosophy; physiology; anatomy; history, law of nations, and the general principles of the law, the Constitution, and so forth.[77] Degrees should never be conferred in course or *causa honoris* unless by the recommendation of the faculty. Once a man had graduated, he should be allowed to teach classes in any subject of the regular course and to receive payment for tickets. This practice would stimulate the regular professors, who were also to be paid in part by the sale of tickets; and it would train men to be teachers. These plans, however, came to nothing when Congress decided against using the Smithson funds to found a national university. Higher educational policy was not to be formulated in Washington.

V

The Expansion of Learning

THE expansion of learning will not create problems of fundamental policy either for those custodians of higher education who remain unconvinced of the importance of new studies or for those who believe that students should have a free choice of courses. The one group will categorically refuse to alter the curriculum, and the other will simply concern itself with finding means of teaching new subjects. The academic man who believes both in the encouragement of learning and in a prescribed curriculum will, however, find himself in a predicament. He will wish to welcome new studies; but where will he find a place for them? By the decade after 1840, the established course for undergraduates was already so crowded that some colleges could no longer follow the precedent of adding new chairs from time to time and of allowing their incumbents to teach undergraduates. To accept more studies into the four-year course would mean that no subject would be adequately accommodated, but to deny the claim of new studies might lead to their neglect or to the founding of new institutions beyond the control and influence of the old. By the mid-Forties, Harvard and Yale thought they saw a way out in the creation of departments of arts and sciences independent of the undergraduate course but answerable to the college authorities. These departments did not immediately prosper and were eventually overshadowed by the scientific schools which developed from them; but they marked a step in the direction of the Johns Hopkins University, where the labors of Daniel C. Gilman, formerly of Yale, received the blessing of Charles W. Eliot of Harvard. Both men had served their apprenticeships as educators in the departments which the decade of the Forties produced.

I

Both Harvard and Yale inaugurated new presidents in 1846. Edward Everett, who came to Cambridge from the Court of St. James, did so

46

believing that he was making "an experiment of a most perilous nature to my reputation & happiness";[1] but he said that he was content to adorn his Sparta.[2] Originally he had hoped to lecture at the law school on the law of nations, but he found that his duties as President did not leave him time for preparing a course. The opportunity for a brilliant personal performance was sacrificed to the minute and far-reaching demands of administration. Contrary to his expectations, Everett was obliged to undertake reform in almost every existing department;[3] and he presided over the creation of a new one as well. Even so, he liked to move slowly—"to let things go on in their accustomed train, till I become well acquainted with the precise state of the institution; & I can then judge what changes are desirable & practicable."[4] There can be little doubt as to his own preference when he said:

"There are two kinds of changes:—the gradual which being made little by little are not felt & leave great interests unaffected:—the revolutionary which come at long intervals,—with a crash,—& subvert relations & interests of men & things—Institutions must choose between them."[5]

On coming to the presidency of the University at Cambridge, the name on which he insisted, Everett was no novice in educational matters. As a young man he had taught at Harvard during the period of the Ticknor reforms. Previously, as one of the first Americans to study in Germany, he acquired sufficient familiarity with German academic practices to write about them. Significantly, he had considered the German universities purely professional schools.[6] The implications for Harvard of his experience and thought were apparent in his inaugural address. Had the time not arrived, he asked, when the Harvard system might be expanded in two directions, "by establishing a philosophical faculty, in which the various branches of science and literature should be cultivated, beyond the limits of an academical course, with a view to a complete liberal education" and by organizing a school of theoretical and practical science?[7]

Later events were to show that these suggestions were not idle rhetoric concocted for the occasion. Both his vanity and his scholarly interests moved Everett to support the transformation of Harvard into a university. At the same time, his thinking centered primarily on the religious and moral aspects of education: "I place all my hopes for the reform & elevation of the University on the influence of Christian Principle as one of vital power & reality."[8] He wanted *"Christo et Ecclesia"* rather than *"Veritas"* to appear on the college seal; and, although he desired to make available to young Americans an education equivalent to that of Europe, he wished still more to raise the tone of manners, morals, and religious principle.[9] Since graduate education was principally an intellectual matter in which truth figured more prominently than religion, Everett's preoccupation with the latter represented a bias toward collegiate reform. Nevertheless, his reference to the possibility of expanding the University identifies him as a friend of efforts to establish a graduate department and a scientific school. Widespread approval of his address suggests, moreover, that the supporters of the College were ready to follow the new President.[10]

The faculty, in particular, shared his mild expansionism. When he solicited professorial opinion on the possibility of introducing an examination for the second degree, on setting up a new department of arts and sciences, or on prolonging the regular academic term for an additional year or two, the response was decidedly favorable. Within the area of general agreement ideas varied widely, however. Henry W. Torrey, instructor in elocution, had some misgivings about the popularity with students of a fifth year of college, "especially when we are unable to tempt them by endowed scholarships or fellowships"; but he did not oppose advanced study in principle. Tutor Francis J. Child remarked that in the classics the philological schools of Germany might be imitated to great advantage. Beck and Felton, as one would expect, approved of expansion, as did the Hollis Professor of Mathematics and Natural Philosophy, Joseph Lovering, although for very different reasons. Lovering supported the addition of a fifth year as an alternative to the elective system, which he criticized, while Beck and Felton welcomed both election and the extension of the course. Edward T. Channing, Boylston Professor of Rhetoric and Oratory, wrote of furnishing "a suitable apparatus for those who, ambitious of high scholarship, are now compelled to seek it abroad, & also for those who wish to prepare themselves for professions not commonly included among the 'Learned.' " This faint echo of the twofold proposal in Everett's inaugural address was heard more loudly in the response of Benjamin Peirce, Perkins Professor of Astronomy and Mathematics, who recommended revision and expansion of scientific instruction. But, he said: "Judging . . . from a conversation which I had a few years ago with one of our oldest graduates, I fear that they will meet with the opposition of an uncompromising conservatism, which is disposed to claim for every blockhead, who is a graduate of three years standing, a vested right to the title of master of arts [.] It will, therefore, be worthy of consideration whether it may not be a better plan to establish a new and independent school for instruction in the higher departments of learning."[11]

For several years Peirce had been calling the attention of the Corporation to the subject of a scientific school.[12] Even before Everett's inauguration, the President and Fellows had appointed a committee to consider changes in the scientific department.[13] Consequently, it was natural for Everett to ask Peirce to draw up a detailed plan. On July 27, 1846, the two men conversed for two hours on the matter.[14] Peirce contemplated a distinct school of practical and theoretical science, to serve, among others, college graduates who wished to study science generally or to perfect themselves in any of its branches. French, German, history, geography, and rhetoric were also to be offered.[15] In other words, Peirce linked reform of the scientific department with the idea of an independent university department of a partially graduate character.

On November 28, 1846, the Corporation appointed a committee consisting of the President, James Walker, and John A. Lowell to report a plan for a school of science and literature,[16] thereby officially opening the way for the fulfilment of Everett's reform program. With Peirce's scheme before him,[17] the President drafted the committee's report,[18] which the Corporation and the Overseers adopted in February, 1847.[19] This paper maintained that the time had come to undertake the experiment of a school of science and literature but recommended that the Rumford Professor of Chemistry ought first to be elected. The Scientific School should offer advanced instruction in theoretical and practical science and the other usual academic branches, to graduates of Harvard or other colleges and to other qualified persons. Its students were to receive a suitable diploma following a stated period of residence and attendance at a certain number of courses, these to be determined by the faculty.[20]

Following the appointment of the Rumford professor, the Corporation selected a Board of Faculty for Direction of the Scientific School, consisting of the President; John W. Webster, professor of chemistry and mineralogy; Benjamin Peirce; Asa Gray, professor of natural history; Joseph Lovering; Eben W. Horsford, Rumford professor; William C. Bond, director of the observatory; and George P. Bond, assistant observer.[21] Although the new department was clearly weighted in favor of physical science, it was not designed to be exclusively scientific, being regarded as an experiment without a set character.[22] Furthermore, the authorities, notably the President, did not intend "to exclude a higher training in philological and classical learning, especially with a view to the formation of accomplished teachers for classical schools and colleges."[23] Everett's plans, in fact, went even beyond this resuscitation of Charles Beck's ideas on philological education. With Jared Sparks, he discussed including history in the new school: "Although we call it 'Scientific' [he explained], we have made provisions for Students of Classical learning and should be glad to increase the attractions for young men desirous of spending a year in finishing their education. Three members of the present Senior class enquired of me yesterday, whether arrangements would be made for an extended course of History."[24]

Sparks did not join the enterprise; but the classicists, Beck and Felton, were added to the staff. Actually Everett went to the point of interpreting his own wish for a department of philological studies as a desire "to render the school as far as the very different circumstances of the country demand & admit, a kind of German University."[25] He also thought of the scientific school "as a means of throwing off from the College proper, some of the branches of study now nominally pursued by the under-graduates, but so superficially as to be of no utility on their own account; while they fretter [sic] away the time, which might be much better employed on the standard academical studies."[26]

In effect a kind of graduate school of arts and sciences was shaping up in Cambridge by the summer of 1847. Everett wrote to England of fair prospects of success for the department[27] although he was himself depressed, feeling personally slighted and powerless in the affairs of the College. To George Ticknor he wrote, "I shall before long have the programme of our projected scientific school to shew [sic] you. It will look well on Paper; how it will work remains to be seen[.]"[28] Specifically, the Treasurer, Samuel A. Eliot, seemed to be blocking his attempts to administer the plans.[29] In addition the regular funds of the College were not available to the new school.[30] On June 1, Everett was obliged to veto a suggestion that Sparks teach in the school if he could be relieved of instructing the juniors; for in that case the Corporation would in practice be appropriating college money to the school.[31]

Then, on June 7, 1847, Abbott Lawrence notified the President and Fellows that he was prepared to give $50,000 for the support of scientific education in the University. Both Everett and Lawrence were members of a club for informal discussion of scientific matters, and conceivably the President broached the subject of patronage there. At any rate, he was vitally interested in the Lawrence benefaction and felt slighted when its fame was not identified with his effort. "After having taken all the responsibility of organizing the Scientific School;—of procuring the appointment of Mr [.] Horsford, whom not a member of the Corporation knew;—encouraging him to propose the erection of a laboratory which no one had thought of,—suggested to Mr [.] Eliot the probability that Mr. Lawrence would endow it, which had not entered into his head & called Mr [.] Lawrence's attention to the subject when after having had Mr [.] Eliot's letter some days in his hands he had not (as he told me) read it, I find the endowment of Mr [.] Lawrence,—in which seemingly the entire Organization of the School will for the present merge,— brought out to the public in a manner to connect with it every name but mine."[32]

The gift did result in a merging of the two aspects of the school or, perhaps one should say, the submerging of the literary side. On July 12, 1847, the Corporation referred the subject of the Lawrence donation and the organization of the scientific school to a committee made up of the President, the Treasurer, and Benjamin R. Curtis. Upon submitting its report one month later, this group was instructed to confer with Lawrence. Having done so, the committee decided that it would be inexpedient to offer anything but chemistry until the professors of geology and engineering should be appointed. Four days later the school was named the Lawrence Scientific School, no mention of literature being made in the title.[33]

Nevertheless, literature was not eliminated from the curriculum without misunderstanding and opposition. Charles Beck said flatly: "It is to be regretted that the name of *Scientific School* has been given to the newly established department of the University. The subjects of this department so clearly described in the inaugural address of President Everett, are but partially indicated by the present name. Yale College, which has lately established a similar department, has been more fortunate in the selection of its name, calling it Department of Philosophy and the Arts."[34]

Yet according to James Walker, sometime Acting President, a Fellow and a professor, the Corporation thought that the school should be exclusively scientific at the outset, "that the ancient languages & history should not be proposed to be taught in our first essays."[35] Looking on the new department as the germ of a university, Everett had a different impression of the decision to confine the scientific school to science, properly so called, for the present.[36] In his view, the Corporation still intended in principle to make a start on the original plan in so far as was possible.[37] The Treasurer conceded that the advertisement of the school should include philology but added: "I cannot convince myself that it is a study which should be considered as scientific, in the usual acceptation of the term; & I should be disposed to make it as little prominent in the notice of the school as would be respectful to the professors. I am persuaded, too, that so few persons will be found to avail themselves of the opportunity for instruction, that any detailed promise of courses of lectures &c. will be not only unavailing, but in some danger of ridicule."[38]

In this situation, it is not surprising that Everett met with Walker early in 1848. After a full conference, the President gave way; so the two men could agree that it would be better, for the present, wholly to suspend the philological department.[39]

The Corporation acquiesced in the elimination of the nonscientific side of the new school, and Everett communicated the decision to interested members of the faculty. To Child he wrote that a course in Anglo-Saxon would not be practicable. This, he explained, was contrary to his individual preference, "to which I adhered as long as I saw any prospect of carrying my views."[40] A similar letter to Professors Beck and Felton stated that the Corporation had dropped the philological department because they have been "much influenced ... by understanding this to be the judgment & wish of Mr[.] Lawrence." In a consoling vein he continued, "I trust that it will be soon found expedient to attempt the fulfilment of the original plan in its full extent when we shall hope for the great benefit of your co-operation."[41] Although officially treated as a temporary arrangement, the liquidation of nonscientific courses was permanent.

At the same time advanced study suffered defeat in another quarter. In the fall of 1847, Everett and the Corporation undertook a revision of the College laws. A draft, apparently written by the President, contains this paragraph: "The degree of Master of Arts shall be conferred by anticipation on every graduate of this University or any other respectable collegiate institution, who shall have resided for a year and a half in Cambridge, and pursued his studies as a member of either of the Professional Colleges or of the Scientific School, and who shall, before Commencement day, produce the certificate of the Steward that he has paid all College dues, including the usual fee for the degree, and a certificate from the Librarian that he is not a delinquent at the Library."[42] This or at least its substance was approved by the Corporation on June 18, 1848, and sent to the Overseers, together with the other titles of the new code.

A small meeting of the Board concurred in everything except the awarding of the M.A. degree in anticipation of the usual period. At the moment of defeat, Everett called this law one of no importance.[43] Yet in the draft the title had been starred to indicate that it represented a significant change.[44] Once more, apparently, the President had swayed from his own original position.

Everett reiterated his old opinions, however, when he had given up the trials of the presidency and had taken a relatively tranquil place among the Overseers. Speaking for their visiting committee in 1849, he reviewed the history and prospects of the new department. "The original project [he stated] ... included all the branches of academic learning, and of course comprehended the literary and philosophical branches, as well as the scientific. It was thought that most of the arguments in favor of the general plan of an extended system of education, applied with equal force to both the great branches of human culture; and especially as the business of instruction is daily becoming more important, that it was particularly desirable in this respect, that philological education should be carried farther than is practicable in the four college years. Accordingly, in the first organization of the Scientific Faculty, it comprised the Professors of Greek and Latin, as well as the Professors in the various branches of science."[45] So organized, the scientific school, plus the schools of medicine, theology, and law, might be considered to form, "upon the basis of the ancient and venerable collegiate foundation, an institution closely resembling the universities of Europe, especially those of Germany."[46] This would justify the foresight of the founders of Harvard, who had bestowed upon the infant college the name "University."[47]

With this Everett approached the end of his report and of his unsuccessful campaign for a broad program of graduate studies. He added only the suggestion that full activity in the scientific courses would demonstrate whether or not the community demanded an institution for advanced education.[48] Harvard's next serious effort to explore the need for such education had just begun under the direction of President Thomas Hill when Everett died, a scholar and educator of unfulfilled promise.

II

Compared with Harvard, Yale was placid; but it was not inert. The Corporation left practically everything it could to the faculty; and New Haven was too small to possess a public opinion independent of the professors,[49] who thought alike on academic matters. "We are all of the same college politics," said President Theodore D. Woolsey at his inauguration in 1846. On the same occasion he characterized himself and his associates as "progressive conservatives";[50] and both Woolsey and Jeremiah Day, the retiring president, reasserted the precedence of mental discipline over knowledge. More specifically, Day pointed out that while a college was not an academy or high school, neither was it a university. If a "philosophy" class of students in advanced learning were added to the facilities for theological, legal, and medical studies, a university would exist even if there were no college. Such a development did not appear likely in Day's opinion, but he insisted that the college should move forward. Subjects formerly unknown were claiming a rank among traditional courses.[51] Woolsey, who had been educated in Germany as well as at Yale,[52] spoke in a vein reminiscent of his cousin, Henry E. Dwight. He approved expansion in the natural sciences and expressed his hope of seeing "the time when a school in all these branches of knowledge shall induce many to reside here after finishing their college course."[53]

Apparently the College authorities had long wished to make arrangements to teach resident graduates and others in fields not included in the existing departments.[54] In July, 1846, the Corporation received an outline of a school of science, the chief author of which was Benjamin Silliman, Professor of Chemistry, Pharmacy, Mineralogy, and Geology. At the suggestion of Woolsey, then still a professor, the scheme was broadened to proved advanced instruction in nonscientific subjects.[55] Day; Silliman; Woolsey; James L. Kingsley, Professor of Latin Language and Literature; Denison Olmsted, Munson Professor of Natural Philosophy and Astronomy; and Edward E. Salisbury, Professor of the Arabic and Sanskrit Languages and Literatures, were appointed a committee[56] to report "their opinion of arranging under distinct departments of the University the courses of instruction which are and ought to be given to others than members of the undergraduate classes, and which are not in the departments of Theology, Law and Medicine," and to plan the organization of the new department if it seemed expedient to open one.[57]

A year later the committee recommended the establishment of the Department of Philosophy and the Arts embracing philosophy, literature, history, the moral sciences other than law and theology, the natural sciences other than medicine, and their applications to the arts. Instruction might be given by professors not already members of the departments of theology, medicine, and law, by professors of the college proper, and by such others as the President and Fellows approved. Second courses of lectures in the same branches would not be given, however, without the consent of the previous lecturer. Graduates of Yale and other colleges and all other young men of fair moral character were eligible to pursue the studies of the department as they desired. Dismissed students and undergraduates might not enrol without express permission. Instructors were to make their own arrangements in regard to remuneration. The faculty of the department was to consist of the president and professors actually teaching in the department.[58]

Where the Yale of 1827 had balked, the Yale of 1847 felt both able and obligated to act. In explaining its stand, the committee explicitly recognized mental training as an object of instruction; but instead of using this idea to obstruct expansion, Woolsey and the others turned it to the advantage of their plan. From time to time new branches of study were called for by the public. If put into the undergraduate course, the report said, they would crowd it and interfere with its purpose as a training ground. If new subjects were offered in a distinct department, the committee clearly implied, this would not happen. Moreover, "there is a demand on the part of our graduates and others, for instruction in particular lines beyond what is wanted, or can be given in the college course";[59] and Yale did have the elements necessary for a new department. It also possessed several endowed scholarships, presumably those established by Bishop Berkeley and Sheldon Clark, and was likely to have more. The opportunities arising from these would be greatly enhanced by providing the scholars with formal instruction instead of leaving them to themselves.[60] In anticipating more endowed scholarships for graduates, the committee may possibly have had something specific in mind. In 1848, Charles Astor Bristed, a Yale graduate who had lately studied at Cambridge University, established a scholarship, to be held by its recipient until he would regularly take his Master's degree. Bristed's intention may have been known in 1847.

Following Corporation approval of the committee's plan, the catalogue for 1847–48 announced the new department. With a warning that all students in philology and mathematics must be well grounded, these courses were offered:

1. School of applied chemistry.
2. President Woolsey, twice a week, on Thucydides or Pindar.
3. Benjamin Silliman [Sr.], lectures on chemistry, mineralogy, and geology. [This was apparently a regular college course, open to students of the new department.]

4. James L. Kingsley, twice a week, instruction on a Latin author agreed upon with the student.
5. Josiah W. Gibbs, lectures on points of general philology.
6. Denison Olmsted, lectures on natural philosophy and astronomy; if desired, private instruction in experimental philosophy and astronomical calculations.
7. Anthony D. Stanley, instruction in calculus or analytical mechanics.
8. Noah Porter, instruction in psychology, logic, and history of philosophy.
9. Edward E. Salisbury, instruction in Arabic grammar and points on relations of Arabic to other Shemitish dialects.
10. Benjamin Silliman, Jr., instruction in elementary and analytical chemistry, mineralogy, and metallurgy.
11. John P. Norton, instruction in applications of science to agriculture and analytical chemistry.[61]

This ambitious program was perhaps substantially fulfilled only in laboratory science.[62] Nonetheless, its literary side was not held in abeyance as it was at Harvard. When Timothy Dwight, the younger, studied in the Department of Philosophy and the Arts during 1849–51, approximately twenty men were enrolled. Some five or six were apparently graduate students, most of whom met with Woolsey twice a week during the academic year 1849–50 to read Thucydides and in the following year to read Pindar. These exercises were stimulating and helpful beyond anything Dwight had known in his undergraduate career, partly because President Woolsey was dealing with graduates and partly because Dwight himself was more free than he had been before. Those years, he said, were "the most valuable of the educational period of my earlier life."[63] Not only was the work itself significant, but it was also more highly organized than the studies of former resident graduates with the result that advanced students acquired a position of their own in the University.[64]

The new department was not large, but it did have students. The ascertainable numbers of Bachelors or Masters of Arts pursuing courses other than applied chemistry or engineering in the early years are given in the accompanying tabulation.

1852–53 3	1857–58 3
1853–54 3	1858–59 2
1854–55 9	1859–60 10
1855–56 8	1860–61 . . . . . 9 [65]
1856–57 7	

At the same time that it established the Department of Philosophy and the Arts, the Corporation appointed a professor of modern languages;[66] and as the years passed such men as William D. Whitney and Daniel C. Gilman became associated with the school of science and arts.[67] In 1851 the authorities also introduced an earned degree, the Bachelor of Philosophy, for noncollegiate students;[68] but this could not be called an advanced degree. The Ph.D. had still to come.

In 1856 the Silliman Professor of Natural History, James D. Dana, put aside the reserve of the older generation to ask the Yale alumni: "why not have here, THE AMERICAN UNIVERSITY!" The potentiality of the Department of Philosophy and the Arts was exciting: "Only a little wider expansion of the scheme,—such as is contemplated, in fact,— and it will cover the highest branches of literary as well as scientific education, adapted to carry forward the graduate of the College, through a full university system of classical or other studies. Let there be a one or two years [*sic*] course of lectures and instruction arranged, which shall include general history, philology, ethnology, belles lettres, the history of philosophy, and other intellectual studies, and the number of resident graduates would greatly increase, and a new era dawn upon American learning. Not till this is accomplished, will the department of philosophy and the arts projected, become a realized fact. Not till then, can we hope to prevent our youth from seeking in the atmosphere of Germany the knowledge for which they yearn."[69]

The Corporation did not immediately accept this challenge; but in four years' time it was ready to grant the Ph.D., which was proposed by the faculty for high attainment in mathematics, philology, or such other branches as might be taught in the Department of Philosophy and the Arts. In urging this degree on the governors of the College, the professors echoed Dana's argument for an American university: the conferring of a Ph.D. would keep Americans at home.[70] The student who did remain in this country could, after 1860, receive his doctorate at Yale; but he had to work for it. Two years would be devoted to study of two distinct departments of learning in the Department of Philosophy and the Arts. Persons not holding a degree as evidence of a command of Greek and Latin would have to pass an examination in those languages or in subjects not included in the advanced course which the faculty was willing to accept as an equivalent. Candidates for the degree would also be required to pass a final examination and to present a thesis proving high attainment in their studies.[71]

Up to this point, the Yale Department of Philosophy and the Arts had borne some resemblance to the Lawrence Scientific School. From the time when the Harvard department had dropped its nonscientific courses the early parallelism of the two schools had actually been imperfect. Yet the similarity between them impressed Charles W. Eliot.[72] The action taken by Yale in 1860 meant a parting of the ways. By instituting the Ph.D. Yale systematized graduate study,[73] thus realizing the original promise of the department opened in 1847. When Harvard later became deeply concerned again with graduate education, it had to begin afresh; and perhaps for that reason its plan followed a pattern quite different from the innovations of the Forties.

The initial success of the Yale policy of 1860 was not spectacular, but it was enduring. The holders of B.A., M.A., or Ph.D. degrees in the Department of Philosophy and the Arts numbered nine in 1861–62, nine in 1862–63, seven in 1863–64, and 15 in 1864–65.[74] The new doctorate was actually awarded in 1861 and was sought after many times in the years which followed. In reviewing the record of the Department up to 1869, Eliot found evidence of legitimate success "on a really high level, if also on a modest scale."[75] The existence of this program, "unpretentious but genuine, and perseveringly offered to a few real students" helped to prove to his satisfaction that there was "a small but steady demand in the older American communities for instruction higher than that of the ordinary college course, and yet different from that of the law, medical, and theological schools."[76] Yale's success pointed the way "to improvements which ought soon to be made at all the more important American 'universities,' which will then better deserve their ambitious title."[77]

III

In the late winter of 1847, while Yale was considering the establishment of the Department of Philosophy and the Arts, the faculty of Western Reserve College appointed a committee to report on a course of instruction for resident graduates.[78] On April 14, the committee recommended a program embracing the ancient and modern languages and the natural and exact sciences, including higher mathematics.[79] The authorities must have approved the project without delay; for the catalogue of 1847–48 announced systematic instruction of graduates by lecture or recitation in the Hebrew, Aramean, Greek, Latin, and modern languages and literature; logic, ethics, and aesthetics; select branches of mathematics and physics, particularly civil engineering and celestial mechanics; analytical and agricultural chemistry; and animal and vegetable physiology.[80] The use of the word "systematic" to characterize the new course suggests that the College thought of it as an improvement upon the usual American practice of leaving resident graduates more or less to their own devices; but no great increase in staff could have been anticipated as instruction was to be gratuitous, except in modern languages.

Certainly the enrolment in the graduate courses did not justify much expansion. Eleven holders of Bachelor's or Master's degrees appeared in 1847–48; the following year only six such students were reported.[81] After that the new course attracted no students although the announcement of the graduate courses continued to appear in the catalogue until 1851–52. By 1852 the project had collapsed. The explanation for its failure is presumably unpopularity with students; but this unpopularity cannot be charged to the program alone. Beginning in 1850, Western Reserve College was convulsed by one of those academic rows to which colleges are susceptible. The issues were partly personal but they also involved a proposal of financial retrenchment. Although this did not carry, a situation in which the suggestion was able to gain some support could hardly have been one in which the new program would flourish. By 1853 the struggle within the College had grown so intense that no students remained in the senior class to graduate.[82] Without graduates, obviously, a graduate program was a mockery.

That Western Reserve College failed in its attempt to provide systematic graduate studies is probably less notable than that a program for graduates was tried at all in a struggling Western college. What moved such an institution to enter a field which many older and better-established colleges had yet to explore? Too much can be made of the fact that Western Reserve College has been called "the Yale of the West." Although the Yale contingent in the faculty was very strong, one can hardly assume that the leaders of the young college felt bound to do everything that the older college did and even to anticipate it. The recommendations of the Western Reserve faculty committee on April 14, 1847, antedate the report of the Yale committee charged with the consideration of what became the Department of Philosophy and the Arts. Yet it is perfectly possible that the president of Western Reserve College, George E. Pierce, and the faculty committee, Professors Henry N. Day, Nathan P. Seymour, and Samuel St. John, knew what the Yale faculty was thinking before an official report was made in New Haven. All these men were graduates of Yale, and one, Henry N. Day, was a nephew of ex-President Jeremiah Day of Yale. Perhaps, too, some of the influences at work moved east rather than west. Suffice it to say that a number of Yale men, some in New Haven and some in the Western Reserve, were thinking along similar lines in 1847 and that like ideas produced like actions.

VI

Diagnosis and Prescription

THE future of graduate studies seemed brighter after 1850 than ever before. The discrepancy between the college course and the sum total of learning, especially in physical science, was steadily growing as research progressed. A clear need existed for something to fill the void. European university life continued to stand as an inspiration and a norm, if not a model, for American reform, while patriotism showed itself in a recurrent demand for a Great American University. Even the heartbreaking problem of finance appeared near solution when, in the middle of the decade, William Astor and Peter Cooper showed some willingness to listen to the champions of higher education.

Just at mid-century one of the older Titans of reform, President Francis Wayland, produced a summary and a critique of the contemporary academic scene. His *Report to the Corporation of Brown University* called public attention to the impossible position of the American college. Originally it had taught a few subjects and taught them well, but with the nineteenth century a new era had dawned. On the one hand, a host of new sciences had arisen; and, on the other, the demand for education had broadened. In this situation two alternatives had presented themselves; the time devoted to education could be extended, or every new branch could be introduced into the traditional four years by curtailing subjects already treated. The latter policy had been adopted to a greater or lesser extent and with extremely unfortunate results. If a student did his work thoroughly, he could get no farther than the rudiments of a subject; if he surveyed the entire field, he could acquire only general and abstract principles by a process of rote learning. Furthermore, Wayland continued, such methods deadened the minds of instructor and student alike. If this was true, a crisis certainly existed and had to be met if higher education in the United States was to be rehabilitated.[1]

Two books, published in 1851 and 1852, foreshadowed typical and significant reactions to the situation. One was Henry P. Tappan's *Uni-*

versity Education,[2] the other Charles Astor Bristed's *Five Years in an English University.* Both writers belonged to New York State families, both were men of cultivation, and both were critical of higher education in the United States. There, however, the resemblance stopped. Tappan was a product of Union College and President Eliphalet Nott's reforming spirit; Bristed was a graduate of Yale where he had once held a Bishop Berkeley scholarship. Tappan, who was one of the professors dismissed from the University of the City of New York, was to become a university president, while Bristed, thanks presumably to his grandfather, John Jacob Astor, could be a gentleman of leisure. One was the humorless crusader, the other the wealthy man of letters interested in many things but personally involved in few. Tappan's "oracular"[3] mode of expression contrasted with Bristed's informal essay style, which struck one critic as being intolerably flippant and slangy.[4] Finally, Tappan was Germanic in the tendency of his thought, Bristed thoroughly English in his academic loyalties.

Tappan's book began with a discussion of the four divisions of education—the primitive or practical, the artistic and aesthetic, the professional, and the "ideal or philosophical."[5] It was with the last category that he was primarily concerned: "Here the capacities of the mind are considered, and the system of education is shaped simply for *educating* —leading forth—unfolding these capacities. We now leave out of view the mere utilities of life, the demands of particular arts, the preparations for a particular profession. We ask, what man is—what he is capable of becoming? We find him endowed with high powers of thought, observation and reasoning—with imagination and taste—with conscience and moral determination. And in all these he is capable of growing indefinitely —of becoming more and more intellectual, more and more beautiful in his imaginative and tasteful functions,—more wise and good, without an assignable limit."[6] What, then, were the laws and means of promoting this growth? Tappan answered: "We find that all knowledge is adapted to this great end,—that in knowing and reasoning he [Man] comes to know more easily and accurately, and to reason more rapidly and surely; that in forming an acquaintance with the great works of literature and art, and in producing these works, the imagination and taste are continually unfolding and ripening; and that the liberal professions and any employments entering into the life and well-being of society, while in their objective offices they are multiplying benefits on every side, react subjectively and form the discipline by which the soul grows into every form of intellectual power and moral worth, and becomes a partaker of the Divine nature."[7]

This education, he asserted, "does not abstract itself from the pursuits and ends of our human life, or lose sight of any of the great interests of the social state; on the contrary, it embraces them all, and that, too, under the highest points of view. It contemplates every man as having some proper work to perform for the common weal; but that, in order to perform it well, he requires the cultivation of all his faculties, while in the doing of his work, he shall ripen more and more."[8] The perfected man was "a true and cultivated soul dwelling in a sound and active body, prepared for all proper duties."[9]

Tappan, one sees, was an idealist, assuming a Divine nature, which provided a focus for all intellectual, moral, and emotional development. Education had full meaning only so long as it facilitated the growth of an individual soul toward the absolute.[10] This process was manifold and indefinitely prolonged; but it was not without order, a quality which Tappan admired greatly. Formal education had to be fully organized; and because of the nature of things, the result was architectonic. School should rise on school to form a pyramid with its base in mundane affairs and its summit in the clear air of disinterested thought.[11]

The apex of the structure was, of course, the university, where alone the philosophical idea of education could be adequately developed.[12] Because the ideal was a large one, the institution embodying it must be grand in proportions. "By the Universities [said Tappan] we mean . . . *Cyclopaedias* of education: where, in libraries, cabinets, apparatus, and professors, provision is made for studying every branch of knowledge in full, for carrying forward all scientific investigation; where study may be extended without limit, where the mind may be cultivated according to its wants, and where, in the lofty enthusiasm of growing knowledge and ripening scholarship, the bauble of an academic diploma is forgotten."[13] The university was superior to the college. For, Tappan argued, education is either imposed by others on the student or imposed by the student on himself. To provide for the first type, instruction in elementary schools and colleges, appropriate to childhood and youth, had sprung up; for the second, belonging to manhood, only a university would suffice.[14]

If great academic resources and a system designed for mature students characterized the true university, then those of Germany were models. Tappan considered them so, explaining their excellence in two ways. They possessed libraries and all the other materials of learning as well as professors in every field of knowledge, and they were unmixed with collegiate instruction.[15] Without the separate gymnasia, which supplied preparatory work, the university would be of little worth.[16] As it was, the German educational system (that of Prussia in particular) seemed to Tappan a noble one. "We cannot well be extravagant in its praise."[17]

The United States had no universities, no matter what American institutions might call themselves;[18] and reform was moving in the wrong direction. With the vast extension of science the curriculum was enlarged, not by creating universities but by pressing into the four-year course a greater number of studies: "The effect has been disastrous. We have destroyed the charm of study by hurry and unnatural pressure, and we have rendered our scholarship vague and superficial. We have not fed thought by natural supplies of knowledge. We have not disciplined mind by guiding it to a calm and profound activity; but, we have stimulated acquisition to preternatural exertions, and have learned, as it were, from an encyclopaedia the mere names of sciences, without gaining the sciences themselves."[19] Furthermore, in an effort to foster a pure national literature and a proud national character, Americans had multiplied colleges after one pattern. They had made experiments upon "a facile system of education full of pretension and fair promises, but containing no philosophical and manly discipline."[20] In so doing, they had only made matters worse.

In contrast to these remedies, Tappan prescribed the creation of a true university. He acknowledged the difficulties presented by the commercial spirit of the country and by the fact that the avenues to wealth open to enterprise inspired "a distaste for study deeply inimical to education";[21] but he had answers ready. At one point he took the lofty ground that in education, as in religion, the question was not "what men desire, but what they need."[22] Elsewhere he argued that the idea of fitting the colleges to the temper of the multitude did not promise great results. They would answer neither to the commercial and political temper of the country nor to the philosophical or ideal education.[23] Contrariwise, the alternative— universities—did hold promise. "With such institutions in full operation, the public will begin to comprehend what scholarship means, and discern the difference between sciolists and men of learning. . . . Then, too, we shall have no more acute distinctions drawn between scholastic and practical education; for, it will be seen that all true education is practical, and that practice without education is little worth; and then there will be dignity, grace, and a resistless charm about scholarship and the scholar."[24]

Specifically, Tappan asserted, the college should be brought back "to a more limited range of studies, comprising a thorough elementary discipline in languages and mathematics and other kindred studies, conducted with respect to a University course which is to follow."[25] In the university itself there should be at the very begining "a choice, varied, and ample library, second to none in the world in books to aid students in attaining ripe scholarship, and in promoting investigation in every department of knowledge."[26] This library should specialize in valuable and directly available resources for scholarship rather than in curious and antiquarian items; it should be esteemed rather for quality than for the number of its volumes. All the necessary apparatus for physics and chemistry should be collected, an observatory provided, a cabinet of natural history founded, and a gallery of fine arts opened. Four faculties should be constituted: philosophy and science, letters and arts, law, and medicine. The first would embrace systematic philosophy, history of philosophy, the philosophy of history, logic, ethics and evidences of Christianity, the higher mathematics, astronomy, physics, chemistry, and natural history. The second would cover philology, Greek language and literature, Latin language and literature, Oriental languages, rhetoric and English literature, modern literature, the history of the fine arts, and the arts of design.[27] In the beginning these subjects might be divided among ten or twelve professors aided by lecturers. The professors might deliver courses of lectures without accepting formal appointments, but regular chairs should be endowed to make the incumbents independent of tuition fees. Professors would be obliged to give popular courses to the public as well as to lecture to members of the university, who would be admitted by examination or on the basis of a Bachelor's degree from any college and who should enrol as candidates for degrees.

Tappan proposed two grades of degrees. The lower was to consist of Master of Arts, Doctor of Philosophy, Doctor of Medicine, and Bachelor of Law; the higher was to include Doctor of Laws, Doctor of Theology, and others signifying a high and honorable attainment in medicine, and in philosophy, science, letters, and art. The first class of degrees would be awarded upon examination at the end of three or four years of study. The second category would be honorary. For these not only distinguished men might qualify but also individuals who studied at the university longer than was required for degrees of the first class.[28] For taking a degree would not preclude further study. In saying that students might indefinitely pursue favorite branches of science or learning in general,[29] Tappan simply stated a corollary of his contention that the second or manhood phase of education never closed.[30]

Although Tappan was guided by the University of Paris, the early form of the English universities, and most especially the universities of

Germany, his plan was not a complete or exact replica of any of these institutions. His admission that at the outset an American university could not be so elaborate as foreign universities was a practical modification; and his elimination of the faculty of theology altogether represented a break with theory abroad. Moreover, his view of the relation between college and university had its American as well as its German analogue. In 1828, more than twenty years before the publication of *University Education,* Yale had published its interpretation of university reform. In this plan, it will be recalled, emphasis fell on the college as a disciplinary institution devoted primarly to the classics and mathematics. Specialization was reserved for the university as a graduate school.

On at least one point, however, Tappan and the Yale of 1828 differed sharply. The New Haven group wrote in terms of an unspecified time when a university might be financially possible; Tappan pled for immediate action: "We have delayed this great work of founding Universities too long."[31] He argued that New York City was the proper site for a beginning and anticipated that it would be easy to collect $450,000,[32] saying that donors would raise to themselves "a grander and more imperishable monument than the obelisks and pyramids of Egypt."[33] With this proposal, *University Education* ends.

Bristed's *Five Years in an English University* was chiefly an account of Cambridge and of the author's personal experience as a student there.[34] To this he added strictures on American education. Of the book as a whole, however, no more need be said than that it was something of a popular success.[35] The passages of special significance are those on the English system of inducements to study. Bristed describes the competition for fellowships and its effects on young English scholars. When, as young Bachelors of Arts, they were competing for fellowships, they developed markedly. This was a period during which new traits of character, mental and moral, appeared; new capabilities and veins of thought were displayed, and different kinds of knowledge from all quarters were sucked up as if for mere amusement.[36] Bristed obviously approved heartily of this process and applauded the contribution of financial incentives.

Toward American education his reaction was very different. He found the greatest failing to be the colleges' lack "of specific endowments, foundations to support as well as encourage learning."[37] "Very promising young men are often compelled to quit college in the middle of their course, or to be temporarily absent teaching school or raising money in some similar way, to the great detriment of their immediate studies. As for resident Graduates wishing to pursue some literary or philosophical faculty beyond the college course, there is no provision for them whatever, nor any opening beyond the comparatively small number of Professorships and Tutorships. It is the want of funds, and those funds specifically appropriated to these purposes, that prevents, more than anything else, our Colleges and Universities from having such teachers (both in number and quality), giving such systematic instruction, and diffusing about themselves such a classical atmosphere as will in a considerable measure correct the effects of bad previous instruction."[38] This was the point to which all friends of American colleges and universities should turn their attention. In short, said Bristed, *"We want endowments."*[39] Clearly, the grandson of John Jacob Astor appreciated the power of the dollar.[40]

Bristed's prescription was repeated in the *North American Review*. This periodical was sharply critical, even unpleasant, in its reception of *Five Years in an English University* but agreed that the "great want of American Colleges at the present day is the endowment of a moderate number of Scholarships and Fellowships, for the encouragement of liberal studies."[41] Admittedly, the time and country were not friendly to such studies; and they might die out if they were not more carefully fostered. The ambitions of undergraduates were too much directed to their careers, and the cares of manhood were projected forward into the period of preparation. "To limit this forecast, and contract the horizon of boyish ambition [wrote the reviewer], the College itself must be able to offer something to contend for,—some prizes within the walls, to be won by what is, after all, a nobler contest than any of those which await us in the crowded thoroughfares of the world without,—prizes of intellectual distinction. . . . Additional incitements are needed, especially for the prosecution of those studies which are peculiarly academic in character, and which, though they are the basis of all thorough intellectual training, have but an indirect connection with the business of the active world and the student's future success in life."[42] As ideas of this sort became commonplace in the Fifties, a demand for fellowships appeared regularly as a part of university policy.[43]

VII

Reform in New York State and Pennsylvania

I

NEW YORK City did not respond immediately to Tappan's call for an American university worthy of the name; but in 1851 Albany did try to create one. By that time many natural scientists had become acutely dissatisfied with the academic treatment of their subjects. The sciences seemed to warrant more attention than could be afforded them in courses set up within the framework of the traditional college, or in so-called scientific schools growing slowly in isolation or perhaps on sufferance beside the old arts establishments. Separate but equal facilities did not suffice, particularly when their equality was questionable.

Furthermore, organization was becoming increasingly common and important in scientific affairs. The United States Coastal Survey and the state geographical surveys encouraged co-operative work; and the recently founded American Association for the Advancement of Science provided a national forum for scientific discussion. It was only natural for its members and others to think of joining forces to teach the most advanced branches of science. The logic of this ideal led to increased concern for graduate study, which the University of Albany sought to provide.

This institution gained the support of a group of scientists who were united by common interests, by institutional connections, and by personal acquaintance. Two of them, Benjamin Peirce and Louis Agassiz, were professors at Harvard. Benjamin A. Gould, Jr., an astronomer, and Josiah D. Whitney, a mineralogist, were also associated with Harvard. All were known in Albany, where another member of the group, James Hall, was carrying on research in paleontology. These contacts extended to New York City, where Oliver Wolcott Gibbs worked in chemistry. In addition, Alexander D. Bache, superintendent of the Coastal Survey, belonged to the circle, as did Samuel B. Ruggles of New York, a layman but a strong supporter of science. Most of these men were members of a club, first called the Florentine Academy and later the Scientific Lazzaroni. They devoted some effort to the science of eating oysters[1] and climbing mountains, but their more serious purposes were to beg financial support for scientific instruction and to destroy their abominations, "old fogeyism" and indifference to higher education. Their attitude is illuminated by a comment on one of them. In writing of the United States, Captain Basil Hall had wondered what answer could be given to the American boy who was able to prosper without elaborate academic training. At the foot of the page on which this remark appears, some reader of a Harvard College Library copy has scribbled: "Ask Benny Pierce."[2]

The Lazzaroni discussed a polytechnical institute as early as 1850, when Gibbs talked to Ruggles of such a scheme.[3] Because of utter disgust with the way things were done in Cambridge, Whitney and others proposed a polytechnic school for New York City, to be staffed by William Chauvenet, the astronomer and mathematician; Gibbs; Gould; Hall; Whitney himself; and someone in engineering. The virtues of New York were the city itself, possessed of a central location, communications, and a mercantile population needing scientific instruction; the Astor Library; openings for making a living; and the opportunity of founding an academy of sciences.[4] Before these plans had materialized, however, they were drastically changed by the incorporation of the University of Albany in the spring of 1851. Whitney no longer talked of an institute. As he cruised with Gibbs among the instrument-makers in the Latin quarter of Paris during the summer, his thought turned to Hall and "his University."[5]

The Lazzaroni had very definite ideas concerning the need for a university and the form it should take. "There is [wrote Bache] a great and growing demand in our country for something higher than college instruction; and one great University, if fairly set in motion, would thrive. To make it, the Professors must leave positions in which they are now comfortably established. For the sake of being together, I know that the leading scientific men of the country, with few exceptions, who are bound to carry out plans which they have in hand, would leave their present homes. They could not do this for an uncertainty. There are men enough to make one very brilliant institution by their high qualities and learning."[6]

Bache's view was substantially correct. Whitney, Gould, Peirce, and Agassiz all expressed their readiness in principle to teach at the University of Albany; Hall, a resident of Albany, was attracted to the idea from the beginning.[7] To their statements of professional interest, however, the scientists added important reservations. Whitney, Gould, Peirce, and

Agassiz all wanted to be sure that the university would not be a financial uncertainty. Peirce even went so far as to specify that it should not be dependent upon private wealth; and Eben Horsford bluntly asked Hall, "where is your *money*[?]"[8] Whitney, Gould, and Peirce also recommended or demanded faculty independence; and Agassiz urged non-sectarianism.[9] In short, the scientists sought security and academic freedom. In exchange for these they were prepared to form a university faculty.

The cost of the first requirement was suggested by Peirce's estimate that the university would need $20,000 per annum if it was to support Agassiz in zoölogy, James D. Dana in mineralogy, Hall in geology, Joseph Lovering in physics, Ormsby Mitchell in astronomy, John P. Norton in chemistry, Peirce in mathematics, Horatio G. Wright in engineering, and Jeffries Wyman in comparative anatomy. The sum would have been greater had Peirce not assumed that the professors would teach daily classes during only three months of the year.[10] This was his favorite plan for building a distinguished teaching staff. Given easy transportation by the new railroads, part-time lecturers could congregate periodically to constitute an inexpensive faculty. If this principle were followed, universities could be founded on a shoe-string.

The attractions of Albany were far from negligible. The city was a center of scientific activity, in particular of the New York geological survey, through which James Hall was making famous the riches of the state in materials for stratigraphic and paleontological study. Local support had become completely enthusiastic by the last months of 1851,[11] and the State Legislature, a possible source of funds, was conveniently located in the city.

To the advantages of situation the University added those of plan. The Trustees did not intend to duplicate the facilities of other institutions, but rather "to take the pupils at the point where they are now left, and furnish such means of professional and profound research, in all the departments of human knowledge, as do not at present exist in the new world, and must be sought in the Universities of Europe."[12] This distinction made a real difference to at least one influential New Yorker, Dr. T. Romeyn Beck, secretary of the State Board of Regents. He had been doubtful of the success of the University, thinking at first that it would add another to the already too numerous colleges; but he became convinced that those engaged in it had a higher objective and believed that the plan would be carried out—"that we might have in Albany a university equal to European universities and become in time equal to the celebrated

University of Berlin."[13] Following his conversion to the cause, Beck became chairman of a commission established to promote the project.

When the American Association for the Advancement of Science met in Albany in 1851, the new University was not discussed in its official sessions; but it was apparently a serious topic of private conversation.[14] Perhaps heartened by this interest, the friends of the University organized a series of meetings in its behalf.[15] During the spring of 1852 a number of famous scientists and men of affairs were invited to speak in Albany. Among them were Benjamin Silliman, James D. Dana, John P. Norton, Louis Agassiz, Benjamin Peirce, Ormsby Mitchell, Wolcott Gibbs, Alexander D. Bache, Joseph Henry, T. Romeyn Beck, James Hall, and Samuel B. Ruggles. Not all are on record as having made formal addresses; but enough expressed themselves favorably, in public or in private, to constitute with the University commission what amounted to a pressure group. Its immediate object was to influence the Legislature, then in session, to pass a bill for defraying the tuition of a number of students at the University. As reported to the Senate, the measure provided free education for young men to be selected from each of one hundred and sixty Senate and Assembly districts.[16]

Samuel B. Ruggles keynoted the appeal for state support. By profession a lawyer rather than a scientist, he was by avocation a champion of the public welfare. Earlier he had been active in canal affairs in New York State and later he became concerned with international monetary policy. In the Fifties his object was to improve higher education, particularly in the physical sciences.[17] He began a speech, "In Behalf of a National University," by referring to his earlier championship of internal improvements. Struggle over this issue, he intimated, had ended with general support of the physical and intellectual betterment of the state. These two aspects of progress were interrelated—if one was good, then the other was good. As for education, its true aim was to lessen the inequalities in the intellectual culture and in the condition of the people; and the secret of its success was the concentration of strength. This was to be the governing principle of the new university whose friends proposed "to unite and combine in one mass, a body of learned men, far exceeding in number and strength anything that has yet been presented to the American world."[18] The established colleges had a place; but the varied demands of the age required something "broader and more diversified—something more capable of assisting the student to pursue special departments of knowledge to their extremest limits, and perfect himself in the practical applications of science."[19] The colleges could not meet this need because they were obliged to provide one course of broad fundamental culture and because they were limited in the subjects they could offer by the three or four years devoted to undergraduate study.

Other promoters of the project voiced similar thoughts. Duncan Kennedy, secretary of the University commission, did not deprecate the college; but he insisted that a place existed for a different kind of institution above the college: "When a young man graduates at one of our colleges—from the very best of them—he is not distinguished for his acquaintance with any one department of science whatever. He can not be. Indeed he is not expected to be. When he enters college[,] he is compelled to engage in a great variety of studies. He is to engage in the study of languages—dead and living—while the whole circle of science is to occupy a share of his attention. How is it possible, that in the space of three or four years, he should become proficient in the various departments which thus engage his energies? The truth is, that when he graduates, he has received only the rudiments of a perfect education; he has a smattering of everything, but is master of nothing; and this without any fault on his part, and without any reproach to his Alma Mater. Everything connected with his educational course has, by necessity, been so arranged, that the result cannot be otherwise. Hence, when he leaves the institution, he is not fitted to engage, with intelligence, in many of the most ordinary pursuits of life."[20] Kennedy further pointed out that, while provision was made for prospective lawyers, medical men, and theologians, there was none for a student choosing a branch of natural science: "he must either abandon the object of his aspirations, or seek its ultimate accomplishment by resorting to a foreign country. Sir, this ought not so to be. During the earlier periods of our history, there was an apology for this deficiency. We were poor, and all our efforts had to be directed to the development of our physical resources. But we are poor no longer, and we should now begin to regard our mental improvements."[21]

Ray Palmer, an Albany clergyman, followed somewhat the same line. Referring to the scientific schools at Yale and Harvard, he said that these experiments were generally considered to promise, at most, but partial success. "The truth is, the present allowance of time, for college residence, forbids the attempt to accomplish much more than a mere commencement of such an education, in many of the sciences, as is needed to qualify for professional eminence, or even for the emergencies of practical life, in the present condition of our country. It is plain, therefore, that the time has come when, not another college for ordinary academic education, but a genuine school of science, far more elevated in its aims and means, should be established. The want has been distinctly recognised; it has not yet been met; it is becoming every day more urgent."[22]

Finally, a memorial, presented to the Legislature by Beck and Kennedy on behalf of the University commission, also spoke of the restricted sphere of a college and of the all-inclusive nature of a university. If the co-operation of the State was obtained, the memorial suggested, the Trustees of the University of Albany were ready to offer immediate instruction not only in technological subjects but also in general chemistry, mineralogy, geology and paleontology, pure mathematics, geometry and celestial mechanics, physical geography and meteorology, astronomy, comparative anatomy, zoölogy, physics, descriptive astronomy, botany, and political learning. Invoking patriotism to buttress their case, the memorialists asked why American boys should be forced to seek in European monarchies the advantages that a free homeland should afford them.[23]

Sentiments such as these were apparently shared by some men outside the immediate University circle.[24] Its pleas, however, were not heard as a lone voice, for many educational institutions were clamoring for state aid. Although the friends of the project maintained that the University was no ordinary institution, all that they could reasonably hope for was a general decision in favor of appropriations for academic purposes— a practical pork-barrel settlement, containing a chunk for the University —unless they could come out the victors in a knock-down and drag-out fight with the supporters of other institutions. Either of these possibilities might have been realized, had not the Senate contained a faction which was both obstinate and skilful. The motives of this group as a whole are not on record; but perhaps significantly one of its members talked of the tendency of academic appropriations to sway the government from its moorings and to seduce it into a career of fancy operations, speculation, and extravagance.[25] A man with these views might not disapprove of the University of Albany itself, but he would fight the practice of legislative hand-outs.

Both sides apparently believed that the measure was popular; for the supporters of aid pushed for immediate action while the opposition strove to hold off a final vote as long as possible. To accomplish this end, opponents of state aid used the whole apparatus of obstruction by parliamentary rule. Their tactical offensive consisted of a barrage of motions to recommit, to adjourn, and to table the matter. Victory came to them when a tabling motion was passed after more than six weeks of debate, and just two days before the end of the session.

In the session of 1853, Senator Azor Taber, leading the movement for the University and the colleges, secured a resolution that the papers relating to a national university be withdrawn from the files of the Senate and referred to the committee on literature. There the project rested.[26]

As if failure to obtain funds were not enough to kill the undertaking, some of the scientists, among them potential faculty members, became disgruntled. The belief was expressed that several of the nonscientific men backing the project did not have the true interests of science or of the University at heart. As early as January 28, 1852, Josiah D. Whitney had written to James Hall: "As to the University, it seems as if it had fallen altogether into the hands of the *Old Fogies*—a pretty piece of business such men as [Francis?] Wayland, Bishop [Alonzo] Potter & T. Romeyn Beck will make of an organization—What a scientific spirit was shown by the Right Reverend Bishop in his lectures in Boston when [or where] he laid it down that there were physical & physiological phenomena which it was a sin to investigate &c &c!"[27] Benjamin Peirce wrote: "I think I see indications of breakers ahead and have no kind of belief that the university is going to succeed without a struggle—It seems to me indeed that the chairman of our committee is not very openly with us, and may be against us. At any rate while the form of his words is fair, they seem to me to be arranged with diplomatic accuracy and a careful determination not to commit himself."[28] Gould, on his part, was disgusted that intrigue, including personal charges against Whitney, should enter the negotiations.[29] In other words, the University at Albany could offer the scientists neither financial security nor complete academic freedom.

Nevertheless, the collapse of the project was gradual. In June, 1852, Gould advised Hall to "leave Beck & his crew in the lurch,"[30] but Hall did not take the advice. In the early part of 1853 meetings were again held on behalf of a university. Out of them grew the National University Association, the executive committee of which included not only Hall but also Ruggles, Bache, Peirce, and Mitchell.[31] The Lazzaroni were evidently still interested in the movement, but neither the Association's president nor its secretary belonged to the inner circle. Peirce suggested that the Association undertake simply to collect facts and opinions on such questions as what were the existing universities of the world, why they differed so from country to country, and what specifically an American university must be in order to succeed.[32] In August Ruggles happily reported that the finances of New York's canal policy had been triumphantly and finally settled, leaving the State free to foster scientific and literary institutions. A recent full mill tax levy, which would yield an annual $1,200,000, eliminated the possibility of a deficit. "Rely on it, the next session of the legislature, will be *the golden moment*—."[33]

Yet despite an imposing name, the distinction of its officers, and the wealth of New York State, the National University Association dropped out of history. By December, 1853, Whitney could write, with only slight distortion of the truth: "The University at Albany seems to have completely fizzled out."[34] Two years later plans for the annual meeting of the Association did not call for an address to the Legislature, the secretary informing Peirce that the policy of pressing the University had been abandoned for the present.[35] Peirce reacted by writing to Bache: "Our arrangements for meeting . . . must be disconnected from Albany";[36] and when in the following year he circulated a widely read plan for an American university, he made no mention of Albany as its site although he had originally drafted the plan with Albany in mind.[37]

II

A few miles from Albany, Union College also tried to provide instruction for college graduates. Its catalogue for the third term of 1852 listed seven advanced departments: agricultural chemistry and chemistry as applied to the arts; mining and metallurgy; higher mathematics and astronomy—theoretical and practical; the higher calculus of engineering; language and the philosophy of language; history and the philosophy of history; and comprehensive metaphysics. With literary, scientific, and "University" programs, these departments were intended by the Trustees to give the student freedom of choice between courses.[38]

The catalogue for 1853 proved that the College authorities were thinking in terms of competition with European universities: "The Graduate's Department will consist of at least five Professors, giving more comprehensive instruction than the College course anywhere permits, in Natural Science, Mathematics and Astronomy, Ancient Philology and Literature, History and Metaphysics; and designed for a three years' course, to secure as thorough and complete scholarship in General Literature and Science as may be attained at any European University."[39] The purpose of the department was to prepare men for professional life or for exclusive devotion to "Literary and Philosophical pursuits."[40] The Trustees also intended to furnish opportunity "for that advanced study and attainment which the growth of our Nation begins loudly to demand."[41] Science could not be diffused before it had being and could benefit the public only "when provision has been made for a greater accumulation in our own country."[42]

These statements show some development in the thinking of Union men between 1852 and 1853. The claims of the latter year were more grand, and the future tense was more apparent than in 1852. Professorships in technological subjects were dropped, while the five chairs proposed were to be assigned to studies proper in a philosophical faculty. Moreover, the 1853 catalogue emphasized the advancement rather than the diffusion of knowledge. It also announced the College's intention of subsidizing needy students. In short, Union proposed a higher faculty and a fellowship system.

The subsidy scheme began well. On January 28, 1854, President Nott and his wife made out to the College a trust deed, one article of which stipulated that securities valued at $45,000 should always be devoted to the establishment and maintenance of nine prize scholarships for graduates or fellows of the College, each of which would carry an annual stipend of $300. Only net income was to be so used.[43] The prizes would be awarded to outstanding scholars in their respective classes or to "young men of eminent attainments (not graduates)." Candidates must sign a pledge against drinking or smoking and must be unmarried and resident in the College. In addition to hearing occasional recitations, the stipendiaries would be subject to call by the President. Men selected as resident graduates were also eligible for two or more auxiliary or prize scholarships, to be awarded at the discretion of the President. The deed further provided for supplementary compensation and for the granting of more than one prize to a man.[44]

It was understood that the beneficiaries of the fund would study under active and regular supervision;[45] but a program of graduate studies failed to mature. On July 25, 1854, the Trustees did appoint President Nott; his son-in-law, Bishop Alonzo Potter; and those Trustees who lived in Schenectady to a committee charged with working out a course for resident graduates of the College and for other interested students.[46] In 1853 the catalogue had stated that instruction by three professors would begin in 1854. The catalogue for 1854 could, however, only promise this instruction "with the coming year."[47] When 1855 arrived, the announcement contained the same qualifying phrase, which was repeated the following year. The catalogue for 1857 noted that a three year graduate course was being arranged but specified no opening date. Tomorrow, and tomorrow, and tomorrow! Finally in 1863 the catalogue was silent on the subject of an advanced course.

III

Reform of the University of Pennsylvania was proposed in 1852 by one of its trustees, Bishop Alonzo Potter. By that time Potter had had an active academic career as Professor of Mathematics and Natural Theology and of Moral Philosophy and Political Economy at Union College; and he was seriously disturbed by the state of education. He was aware of the crisis through which the universities of England were passing; and, while he saw by no means the same situation in America, he felt that "the waning influence of our Colleges, and the various attempts at reconstruction which we see around us, afford significant intimation that some material changes are needed."[48] A few colleges, Potter knew, were attempting to introduce some degree of choice into the undergraduate curriculum; Albany was prepared to steal from Philadelphia the glory and satisfaction of founding a true university; and Union was making provision for graduate students. The University of Pennsylvania was small and inefficient in comparison to what it might and should be. It was, Potter thought, competing in a narrowing field, not only with other colleges but with high schools and academies as well, for the demand for collegiate education was declining just as facilities for it were expanding. In the face of this, he advocated a type of instruction which other institutions could not easily supply.

His views on the nature of education pointed in the direction of a university. The educator must counteract the tendency toward material and practical objectives rather than high scholarship. Like the Yale faculty of 1828, Potter believed that the primary aim of liberal education at the lower level was "to develope [*sic*] mental power and activity, and to inspire a generous taste for goodness[,] truth and beauty."[49] To permit students a choice of subjects would simply render education more flimsy and superficial than it already was. Potter resembled Henry P. Tappan in contending that while there was one stage in which the student required direction, there was another in which he could safely be left to himself. In this distinction lay the salvation of the college and the justification for a graduate course.

The demands upon education were, "*first*, that our *elementary training* for boys up to *eighteen* or *twenty* be much more *thorough* than it now is—inducing more accuracy—more power of thought—more taste—more love of learning, and more capacity for earnest and vigorous search after truth. *And secondly*, That our seminaries of learning *furnish to young men* from twenty to twenty-five, who have previously been well *disciplined,* or who exhibit a strong bent towards *specific* studies, *an opportunity to pursue those studies much further than any college now takes them,* and with more or less reference to active professional pursuits."[50] More specifically, the second requirement amounted to a need for "the *open University,* where young men, *older* and *better trained* than our ordinary collegians, with *more active desire for improvement,* can resort—where graduates of our colleges and other young men bent on gaining knowledge can resort and have the teaching of the best masters. Where, too, no individuals should have, as in our colleges, an *entire monopoly of the business of teaching* in any department; and where, as in the European Universities, such inducements should be held out in the form of *prizes, scholarships, fellowships,* as would secure the highest attainable excellence in all departments; these distinctions to be awarded only after the most rigid scrutiny by written examinations."[51]

Potter's proposal was printed in 1852 together with a by-law which threw additional light on the plan of reorganization. Section 2 made it clear that the fellows were not to be simply subinstructors; for it definitely stipulated that "all fellowships shall be established with a view to the pursuit and communication of learning, in connection with the University."[52] Section 5 enjoined the professors to set up their courses with an eye to advanced instruction in each department as well as with reference to industrial or professional considerations. Clearly higher learning was to have an acknowledged place in the University.

The proposal and by-law provoked violent reaction. Several members of the faculty prepared sharp and, in some cases, rude statements of opposition; and Potter replied with a formidable rebuttal. The Trustees made appointment after appointment to hear a report on the matter, but none seems ever to have been submitted.[53] Finally Potter dropped his plan; so that the only significance of the controversy was its revelation of academic feeling and thought.[54] Although the debate wandered into such tangential matters as the character of the German universities, it touched with some frequency on the question of the practicality of graduate institutions in America. What kind of a demand for graduate study really existed? What support could be expected from the public, from students, and from professors?

From the outset Potter had believed the reorganization scheme to be workable. His faith in the willingness of the community to back the University and the interest of such men as Tappan, Bache, Peirce, Dana, and Agassiz supported him in this position. Did not Bache write that there was nothing Utopian or impracticable in the plan? "It wants *resolution* and *money* only to become a fact."[55]

That *only* must have disturbed Professor John F. Frazer, one of Alexander D. Bache's close friends.[56] Frazer considered a large endowment an absolute necessity on the grounds that an expanded university could not hope to be self-sustaining.[57] "I do not think [he wrote] that there exists at present, in our country, any extensive demand for more thorough training in fundamental studies, nor for opportunities of further acquirement of knowledge, than at present exist. There is certainly among our people no general belief in the value of a thorough education, nor in our present condition is any thing [sic] of the kind necessary, either for success in the pursuits of life, (even, although such pursuits should be strictly professional,) nor for the attainment of the most eminent positions in society; on the contrary, it appears to me, that the public opinion in this country is every day expressing itself more and more decidedly against any mental discipline or education whatever, and in favor of as little instruction as is compatible with success in the pursuit of ordinary business."[58] Despite this skepticism, Frazer readily conceded that it was vitally important to improve the state of opinion as soon as possible and that nothing seemed more likely to produce this change than a great seat of learning.[59]

So nice a balance of sympathy and misgiving was too mild for Professor Henry Vethake. More than a decade earlier he had been one of the professors to revolt against the Mathews regime at the University of the City of New York. In 1852 the independence of spirit remained, but not the reforming zeal. Like Frazer, Vethake took a dim view of the demand for graduate education; but unlike his colleague he expressed himself with scant respect for Potter and with little concern for the alleged faults of American education.

Vethake thought it a mistake to suppose that in the United States *men*, as distinct from youths, wanted instruction in literature, science, and the arts or at least that more than an exceedingly small number of *men* wished for such learning. Almost every youth in the United States, said Vethake, "expects, at twenty-one, to be engaged as a principal, and not merely as a subordinate or assistant, in the occupation which he has chosen; and at twenty-five, an age when, according to the letter on the new plan presented to the trustees, students might be supposed to be in attendance on a seminary of learning, which would furnish an opportunity to them to pursue *specific* studies 'much further than any college now takes them,' there are few who have not an expectation of being the heads of families, living in comfort, and even luxury. The anxiety that has been described to make one's way in the world, at a comparatively early period of life, may be pronounced to be a very undue one, but this cannot hinder it from being a fact; and it is with the fact, only, that I am at present concerned."[60]

With this Vethake carried the fight onto what was usually the home-ground of university reformers, boldly asserting that even in Germany very few students attended the faculty of philosophy and that those who did were chiefly persons preparing for careers in teaching, civil service, and diplomacy—that is, persons for whom there were no equivalents in this country. In the United States scarcely anyone deliberately chose to teach unless under financial pressure and then only as a temporary expedient. Nor was a political office, held either by appointment or election, a thing for which an American "in his sane mind, would ... set about systematically to make a special preparation for filling ... with advantage to the public."[61] Appointments were not made on the basis of fitness; and victory of the opposing party or the operation of rotation in one's own party might mean loss of a job.

Sharp as were these criticisms, those of Professor George Allen surpassed them. Allen made no effort to temper his disapproval and annoyance. In his eyes the plan was completely uncalled for. "The Letter [he wrote] proposes for actual adoption—what many a scholar had already often dwelt upon as a pleasing day-dream—the transfer of a European University (according to the author's conception of it) to our own country. It is not too much to say, however, that there is always an antecedent presumption against every attempt to transplant institutions from their native, to a foreign, soil. . . . And it is not unreasonable to presume, that if we are ever to have an American *University*, it must be the development and modification of the American *College*—it must be a *supply* naturally shaping itself to meet a real (and not factitious) *demand*.

"Were the plan of the Letter even less foreign in its aspect than it is, there would still be the strongest presumption against its success, from the absence of all satisfactory evidence of demand for an institution of the kind. We have, on the one hand, the obvious phenomenon of American life—the universal hurry of every man to be engaged in business for himself at the earliest possible age."[62]

Allen admitted that on the other side of the argument there were Tappan's book, the Albany project of Agassiz and his colleagues, and some professorships recently established at Pennsylvania; but he summarily dismissed this evidence of demand. "Of Professor Tappan's work

I know nothing; M. Agassiz is a foreigner; and the attempt of even a hundred of our distinguished Naturalists and scientific men to start an institution, in which they could lecture on their favorite subjects, may prove conclusively, that they have a generous zeal for imparting knowledge, or that they are in want of employment, or both, (as the case may be,) but it does *not* prove, that there is now an existing and growing number of graduates, and other young men of from twenty to twenty-five, who have become aware of so great a need, or so strong a desire, of *hearing* those naturalists and scientific men lecture, as to have become willing to put off the study of their professions three years to do it . . . let it be shown in *any* way, that those who wish *to be taught*, and not merely those who wish *to teach*, suggest and call for courses of non-professional studies to be superadded to our actual college-courses, and *then* it may be allowed, that the testimony is to the purpose—that a *demand* for the University of the Letter really exists."[63]

If it was not safe to rely on mere love of learning, argued Allen, it would be necessary to offer courses of study required for complete education and demanding the assistance of teachers; distinction and degrees of real interest to the student; and prizes, scholarships, and fellowships furnishing considerable pecuniary emolument or conferring valuable privileges. Even these inducements might not be compelling. New courses of study by themselves would have only a feeble power of attraction; degrees could not appeal as strongly as they did in Germany or England, where professional careers required a university degree; and financial inducements would have to be substantial and must actually exist. "A By-Law . . . which offers large pecuniary inducements in the shape of Prizes, Scholarship-emoluments, and Fellowship-salaries, as soon *as the money can be got,* would not seem to be precisely the kind of legislation to produce a rush of graduates from ancient Harvard and Yale, from the Colleges of Ohio and Tennessee, from Texas and California. The *Yankee* graduates, at any rate, will inquire before they start, whether the cash has been paid in."[64] It would be still more important to show that the endowment for the new chairs, to be filled by celebrated men, had been secured.[65]

Potter answered that these arguments were beside the point. The great question pertained, he argued, "not to what young men, as they are now educated, may *desire* or be *seeking,*—though on that point I differ widely from some of the views presented. The question is not whether 'an increasing class of young men, after graduation,' '*suggest* and *call* for courses of non-professional studies to be superadded to our actual College-courses.' . . . The true question, as I conceive,—and it is one which cannot be disregarded with wisdom or safety, is this:—Do not the interests of higher education, and as dependent upon it, the interests in this country of science, of erudition, and of true culture generally, *require* that young men should have at one stage of their training, more of that thorough, accomplished and enthusiastic drill, which induces accuracy, taste, power of thought and desire for knowledge, and at a later stage, more advanced teaching, with more range of choice between different teachers and studies, and more powerful stimulants in the way of prises [*sic*] and distinctions?"[66]

Here Potter seemed to be shifting his ground; but in so doing, he arrived at a position of great significance for the history of graduate education. One portion of the academic world, of which Henry P. Tappan was perhaps the most notable spokesman, was inclined to ignore the question of actual demand for advanced study or to take a rather lofty view of it. Other men, such as George Allen, were so impressed by an alleged lack of demand from those who were to be taught or by other practical difficulties that from the outset they opposed the creation of a university as impracticable. Neither the "philosophical" nor the "common-sense" position was entirely tenable. The first was too visionary, the second too unimaginative. Had not Potter and others taken a third stand, reform might have been permanently blocked. Granting both a cultural need for higher learning and an actual lack of demand for university instruction, they asked, in effect, can we not meet the need by stimulating the demand artificially? This tendency of thought foreshadowed the time when the fulfilment of America's material promise, which had once made extended education appear unnecessary, would make the most advanced instruction financially possible.

VIII

A Great University for New York City

THE failure of the University of the City of New York to live up to its name did not entirely dissipate all hope for a great metropolitan center of learning. Henry P. Tappan had advocated one in 1851. Yet, aside from reform activity at Columbia, little or nothing was done until 1855. In the spring of that year Tappan sounded an academic reveille before the New York Geographical Society. America, he said, was awakening to the fact that New York was a metropolis, important to the culture of the land. Cities, he continued, were the proper seats of learning; for they possessed wealth and facilitated "the fellowship of congenial spirits" necessary to scholars.[1] In a large city there was no substitute for a university, particularly as a humanizing influence. Therefore, the local colleges should abolish the four-year course and absorb the grammar school, to become something like the German gymnasia. A university should then be created on a scale commensurate with the requirements and the magnificence of the city.[2]

When in the late summer Tappan again elaborated his ideas on the true character of a university, he no longer acted as the knight errant he had previously been. For he found sympathetic spirits in the American Association for the Advancement of Education which met in New York and considered the problem of a national university. The President of the Association, Alexander D. Bache, introduced the question by stating with characteristic Lazzaroni emphasis that a great university was *"the want of our country, in this our time."*[3] By a university he meant complete faculties of science and letters with, perhaps, faculties of law, medicine, and theology as well. Various efforts, said Bache, had been made in this direction within the past thirty years. Recently, at Albany, a university had seemed about to materialize; but young Americans still lacked adequate preparation for active life. Many went abroad to seek opportunities not offered them at home, doing so at the possible expense of "some things worth quite as much as knowledge."[4] The

82

need was admitted by the advocates of general culture, who had supposedly been most suspicious of a university. While they believed that the foundation should be "the well cemented granite of classics and mathematics," they recognized "that other materials may enter into the superstructure according to the design of the edifice;—that the engineer, the miner, the chemist, the metallurgist, the mechanician, the teacher, the farmer, should have special modes of training;—that history, English literature, moral and mental science, political economy, education, should all receive a higher treatment than is possible in our colleges, the courses of which are too short, and the pupils of which are too young to permit the necessary development."[5] The university must not, however, merely diffuse knowledge and stay in proper relation to general education; "it must lead in the advancement of science through the researches of its professors. . . . Pupils should not only resort to it to learn what had passed into the books of the day, but what had been discovered by its teachers themselves. The living account of active research would thus inspire the pupils, and the professors would have not only hearers but followers."[6]

On the practical side, Bache warned that a university required "a large endowment, not to be expended in costly buildings, but in museums, laboratories, collections of nature and art, and in sustaining liberally a corps of professors worthy of the institution and of the country."[7] At the same time he claimed that the material for such a faculty already existed in America. This was an essential part of the Lazzaroni argument. For them the problem was not to train qualified professors but rather to find some means of bringing together learned men who were scattered over the land. The Lazzaroni unquestionably thought of themselves in this light. A university would have given them opportunity to meet, teach, and exchange ideas with regularity and effect.[8]

Tappan followed Bache in this full-dress discussion of a national university. Speaking, ironically enough, in the chapel of the University of the City of New York from which he had once been dismissed, he surveyed with a sweeping eye the progress of educational development in Europe. It was based, he argued, upon the liberation of philosophy from scholasticism, of thought and investigation from ecclesiastical prescription, and of scientific method from the dicta of authority. With the university spirit, the ordinary colleges had nothing in common. In England where they had all but absorbed the functions of the universities, the latter had remained static while university study in Germany was free, independent, and unlimited in horizon, disciplinary work being relegated to the gymnasium. The gymnasium offered all the intellectual matter that English and American colleges could pretend to and led to proper development of the university. Here the "good of the past is preserved, the evils are eliminated, the imperfections are supplied, and the unity of all true progress is demonstrated."[9]

Tappan's eloquent remarks received immediate praise from Benjamin Peirce, who attached to them the greatest importance for the understanding of what the university and the relations of the colleges to education should be. "I confess that for the first time, have I had a perfectly clear understanding of this whole subject. I have known that our views in many respects were quite erroneous. I was aware that the name of American System, as applied to our colleges, was altogether erroneous. It is in its very basis such a system as would not have originated in a free people from their own action. It has no element of freedom in it. Its rigid restriction to a period of four years; its conferring of degrees without examination, merely as such, merely as honorary titles, are altogether opposed to our system of free education and the free principles of our country."[10]

This enthusiastic response gave promise of a fruitful alliance between Tappan and the Lazzaroni; for they complemented each other. Tappan would expatiate on the inadequacy of American education in broad philosophical and comparative terms; the scientists would insist on the need for the most advanced instruction in new branches of knowledge. The one approach was charged with Germanic associations and the other possessed practical appeal to an increasingly scientific age. The Lazzaroni might check Tappan's oracular tendency, and he could give systematic structure to their aspirations.

A coalition actually did materialize early in 1856, with Tappan as "General."[11] The founding of a great university in New York City had apparently become the ruling passion of his professional life. Although he had accepted the presidency of the University of Michigan, he did so only as a temporary measure. His heart remained in the East.[12] Indeed the Michigan post was a source of vexation; for it forced him to carry on his New York business by the exasperatingly slow means of correspondence. The bitterness of ultimate failure in New York was to last for years.[13]

In the winter of 1855–56, however, Tappan's faith appeared to be unconquerable; and for a time events seemed to favor his cause. A great mass of thought on university matters seemed to him to be moving over the country from the greatest minds.[14] Financially the future was brightening, too, for Peter Cooper was planning to give heavily to education.[15] Moreover, the Astor Library was becoming a great learned institution under the direction of Joseph G. Cogswell, a scholar trained in Germany.[16] Even some members of the Council of the University of the City of New York approved the idea of a new university.[17]

Quite logically, Tappan's first move was to forward to Cooper a plan prepared by Tappan's son-in-law, Francis Brünnow, the astronomer.[18] The proposal called for a combined University and Academy of Sciences and Arts of the City of New York. This "union" was to be composed of university professors empowered to associate others with themselves. Tappan believed this to be a new idea, an improvement on Berlin and Paris, as the Academy in the former city and the Institute in the latter were distinct from the universities. The title, University and Academy, would prevent confusion between the new institution and the old University of the City of New York in the event that its Council refused to adopt the name of University College. The Free Academy (now the City College) was to become Free College, and Columbia would continue to be known as a college. In brief, higher education in New York was to be a pyramid with existing institutions at the base and the proposed University and Academy at the top.[19]

Tappan also wrote to William Astor, with whom he had previously discussed university matters personally. Now he elaborated on his ideas, first insisting on the inevitable success of a university, once founded, and then considering the possibility of setting one up in New York. In conversation Astor had revealed strong doubts on both points, saying that he feared Tappan was wasting his time. Tappan, in his letter, replied with two general arguments. A university was required to complete the American system of education. Being necessary, it would vindicate itself once it had been introduced, as the Croton water system had done. The failure of men to appreciate the full extent of the need before the fact was immaterial. Moreover, young men generally responded with enthusiasm to the idea of a university; for approximately one hundred and fifty of them were then enrolled in such institutions abroad. That Columbia College and the University of the City of New York were small proved nothing; they were not universities. "A small affair, an abortion, a sham, a great name upon a small body, would fail, and ought to fail. A University worthy of having 2000 students, would have them in New York as well as any other part of the world."[20] Secondly, the university would succeed because there never once had been a true university which did not. Nothing was more successful, nothing more permanent, than a true university. Universities had survived the changes of time and the shocks of revolution because it was to the common interest of mankind to protect and preserve them. By success Tappan meant, among other things, that the universities had attracted students in direct proportion to the advantages they offered. If the people of the country were so low that the rule did not hold, then a university should be created to leaven the lump.[21]

In regard to his second favorite subject, that of a possible university in New York, Tappan became quite specific. Noting that individuals had perhaps done more for higher education than governments and apologizing for his boldness, he outlined three ways of accomplishing the end he had in view. The first called for action by William Astor, whose father, Tappan reminded him, had founded the Library and had stated in his will that any surplus funds of the Library might be used for lectures. This suggested a university. The Library could not attain its full utility and power until it gathered around itself scholars competent to put it to its highest use. "Now amid all my thinking on this subject—do you deem it possible that I should not have said to myself—'What a noble destiny is possible to this family! Here is one munificent benefaction in the library. Now if with this an immortal University be connected, how this name goes down to posterity—never to die—honoured and blessed by all men! A large sum will indeed be required to do this; but a sum that can give no shock to this vast estate: and then around it will be thrown a protection stronger than the force of law in the grateful remembrance and admiration of human hearts.[']"[22]

Subscription was a second resort. If a proper plan was adopted and if Astor or someone else would head the list with a half-million dollars, the total might be brought up to the necessary minimum of $2,000,000. Tappan added that he spoke advisedly, for he had donors and assurances in view. Yet there had to be a beginning, so that people would be convinced that an important effort had been undertaken. The third possibility was for a university to be financed, like any other great public work, by the city. Mentioning Cooper's gift of $500,000 for scientific purposes, Tappan suggested that "the city invite him to unite his benefaction with a public appropriation."[23] If Cooper and the city co-operated, the elements of the university would be the Astor Library; the Cooper building, serving as the physical center of the institution; an annual appropriation from the city to sustain the faculty; and the gifts of private citizens for establishing a museum, an observatory, and the like.[24]

The tactics of the General, one sees, called for movement in several directions at once. The approach to Cooper and Astor was simple and direct; the appeal to the city required careful handling. Tappan believed that Mayor Fernando Wood might be pleased to appear the prime-mover in the project. A public appeal by the scientific men was, therefore, to be avoided. Later they might seem to rally around the Mayor.[25] Still, Tappan could communicate privately with Wood, which he seems to have done. He also encouraged the circulation of two pamphlets, which he had written, with the hope that short notices of them might be printed in the leading newspapers. Notice in the press would furnish the occasion for some pertinent remarks on a university in New York and help pave its way politically. Tappan thought, too, of support from subscribers. "All we want," he wrote, "is the adoption of a true plan, and a beginning that shall ensure confidence."[26]

The immediate problem was to obtain a commitment from Cooper or Astor, either of whom seemed capable of undertaking the entire project. If they did not prove sufficiently strong, others could be found;[27] but perhaps a further search would not be necessary. Tappan looked favorably on Cooper's plan to establish a "Union" with professorships supported by rents from the institution's building, a portion of which would be let to the city. Cooper was disposed to carry out his own part single-handed but held himself open to suggestion. Tappan wanted him to embrace a plan for a university and an academy of sciences and to announce it publicly. He could then complete it as far as he was able to alone, and afterward others could come in.[28] In March Cooper still insisted on the name "Union," but Tappan was not worried by terms: "We want to get the *thing.*"[29]

Later in the same month Tappan feared that the authorities of the Free Academy would try to win Cooper over, but this did not happen.[30] By April Tappan was once more sanguine. When Samuel B. Ruggles reported that Cooper had offered $100,000 for additional professorships,[31] Tappan showed no surprise. This was only a beginning, he wrote in his enthusiasm. "Let the Institution be founded on a right plan, and give the unquestionable promise of becoming a genuine University, and money will come showering in upon it. I wish for my part that they [the Legislature] had suffered the name 'Union' to remain. It is a name great enough, and capable of being easily moulded into another great name. The 'Cooper Scientific Institute' individualizes the thing too much, and by giving an impression that it is Mr[.] Coopers [*sic*] private affair may operate against additional endowments. By adopting a right plan, however, we can correct everything. The plan is the great thing.

'Cooper Scientific Institute' too may be changed into 'Cooper University' —I am quite willing to give the name of such a man to a University. I am somewhat of Carlyle's opinion—I go for worshipping Heroes.

.   .   .   .

"There is such an intense earnestness on this subject now on the part of the best men in the country, that we have every thing to hope for. When can we ever have a more auspicious running-together of men and events? This movement of Mr. Cooper comes just in time. It would argue such weakness—detestable weakness to fail now, that I fear we should lose our sense of manhood if we did fail. No, my good friends, we must not fail—we must do it. Shoulder to shoulder we will make it go."[32]

This attitude was echoed in Tappan's correspondence with Benjamin Peirce. "Let us pull together [Peirce had written] in this grand enterprise—Now is the time—the harvest is ripe, and we must be up & doing. The distinction between the University and College must be worked into the comprehension of the men of action."[33] Tappan replied: "I think with you the harvest is ripe. Mr[.] Coopers [*sic*] Institution is now incorporated. A building & eight Professorships are there to begin with . . . [as well as the offer of $100,000]. The Mayor hopes to get an appropriation of some 20 or 30,000 dolls. annually. Here you see the whole thing stands fair before us, if we can only get Mr. Cooper to give the right shape to his institution. . . . I think our great labour will be to bring him around right [as Cooper had some peculiar notions]. If he can be brought to accept a University organization many a 100,000 dollars will come in to aid its full development. You say, 'let us pull together in this grand enterprise—now is the time'—I pray you & Prof[.] Agassiz to consider just now what pull we shall make. Now is the time to make a pull—and we must pull at Mr. Cooper.

.   .   .   .

"Cooper Institute is the foundation—If we can shape that right all is done."[34]

Writing later to Peirce that the Mayor had been promised support from all those interested in the university, Tappan urged that influential scientific and literary men draw up and sign a paper to this effect.[35] Evidently this was done; for Wood did call the attention of the aldermen to the unanimous opinion of these men on the immense importance and the feasibility of the university project. In other ways, too, the Mayor echoed Tappan and his associates. He recommended the establishment of a "University and Academy," and he talked in terms of a graded educational system. He spoke of collecting books and apparatus and of gathering together an eminent faculty in every branch of knowledge. He referred to the Astor Library; to the Cooper gift, which might be supplemented by a city appropriation; and to his hope of other benefactors; he even used Tappan's argument by analogy from the history of the Croton water-works.[36]

Unfortunately the unanimity of opinion, of which Wood spoke, did not produce continued solidarity in action. By the end of the summer, Tappan's correspondence with New York seems to have stopped and the coalition had apparently collapsed. The occasion for a rupture may have been a disagreement over Brünnow's position in the New York project. According to Tappan's recollection, Gould and Peirce formed a cabal against him out of fear that he would bring Brünnow, his son-in-law, to the city.[37] Gould, also an astronomer, may have disliked any friction or competition this promised.[38] Whatever its cause, disappointment in New York led Tappan to accept his post at the University of Michigan as a permanent one and to turn his full energy toward reform in little, far away Ann Arbor. Perhaps the support of the Mayor should have acted as cement for the enterprise. Public aid would certainly have helped, had it been offered; but it did not materialize. Was Wood genuinely interested in the project and was he prepared to back Tappan and the others with more than words? It is easy to doubt the sincerity of a public man of the caliber of Fernando Wood.[39]

Despite the retirement of the General, the university forces did not immediately acknowledge defeat. The movement to centralize professorial talent still had its advocates. One of them, Benjamin Peirce, circulated a printed scheme, *Working Plan for the Foundation of a University*, in 1856.[40] This paper program fitted neatly into the New York university movement. "The best plan for founding a University [Peirce wrote] is that which concentrates the interests of the largest community, and combines the greatest variety of intellect, with the smallest pecuniary outlay and the least provocation of opposition. The most feasible plan is that which is most elastic, and which may be the smallest in its germ, while it is most comprehensive in its full developments. Its professors must be the ablest men in their respective departments; it must be connected with a fine library, a well equipped observatory, and complete collections and laboratories for the elucidation, illustration, and investigation of every species of knowledge. But it is expedient that the library, the observatory, the cabinets, and the laboratories should be under the special control and fostering care of their respective boards of administration, whose local residence and peculiar habits of mind should adapt them to these duties. The general board of overseers should unite all that is necessary to command the universal confidence of the country, and their principal duty should be to secure, by consultation with the professors, the ablest body of officers."[41]

The details of the plan encouraged great flexibility. The departments of knowledge to which professorships should be devoted were to vary from time to time according to the exigencies of the case and the needs of the university; and faculty tenure was to last for only five years. A professor could live wherever he pleased and engage in whatever outside occupation he chose, provided that he did not hold more than three chairs and that he delivered at least twelve lectures a year to a minimum of three students. He could decide on the time of the year for his lectures himself. The resident professors, plus a chancellor, would constitute the faculty and would administer the scientific and literary affairs of the university, but both resident and non-resident professors were to nominate the ablest men worthy to join their ranks. Overseers would elect professors from this list. A man of moderate fortune could found a professorship paying a thousand dollars a year. The university might open as soon as twenty-five chairs had been established, yet its scope could be extended indefinitely.[42]

The core of Peirce's plan was a provision for mobilizing the nation's learned men on a part-time basis. "All the powerful minds of the country [wrote Peirce] can be concentrated upon this institution, not even excepting the presidents of the colleges, the historians and poets, the retired statesmen, the secretary of the Smithsonian Institution, or the superintendent of the coast survey."[43] This suggestion of course raised a fundamental issue: was the American university to be a single establishment gathering together the best and highest in education and research or was it to be simply a generic term covering a group of diverse institutions, all of university rank? Not all of the readers of Peirce's plan were ready to approve his ideas. One critic wrote that he had "of late returned to the conviction that the natural development and gradual elevation of the institutions—already existing would create, instead of one centralized institution, a multitude of centres of light of the first order, something like the German universities, in opposition to the French system of centralization."[44]

In 1856 Peirce's constellation seemed to be in the ascendant. The *Working Plan* had the full support of Alexander D. Bache, who called it "the Lazzaroni Light."[45] Its rays shone through an address Bache delivered before the American Institute of New York City in the fall of that year. This organization sponsored the Crystal Palace fairs; and Bache, in speaking before it, assumed the role of an exposition guide, drawing the attention of his hearers to certain imaginary exhibits—the needs of the time and the institutions which existed, or should be created, to fill them. American schools, academies, colleges, mechanics institutes, government projects, and astronomical observatories, although good in themselves, were not, said Bache, sufficient to the great end of organizing intelligence. "Where," he asked, "is our American University?"[46] Admitting that in earlier days the founding of a university would have been as ridiculous as constructing enormous hotels in the West, he insisted that there had arisen a class of people desirous of entering life fully armed with learning and eager to grow in mind as they advanced in age. The need was not for something to supplant the colleges but rather for an institution to carry young men beyond the undergraduate course and to help those already working to progress. The university, "that great finishing institution for life,"[47] would attract those who were then going abroad to study chemistry, mineralogy, geology, mining, metallurgy, and civil engineering, and to perfect their knowledge of ancient and modern languages. At the university technicians and theorists would meet, the activities of both groups being mutually dependent. Superficial information verged on quackery whereas the deeper the study the more practical it became. Yet Bache could report discovering in a side nook of his imaginary exhibition only "a favorite collection of models and drawings, representing in fragments and in coarse outline, a much needed institution still unreared ... a University of the Arts and Sciences."[48]

The chancellor of Bache's ideal university would deal with all matters of detail in co-operation with the first faculty. Much would, indeed, be left to the discretion of these authorities since a moderately good plan, well administered, was better than an excellent one executed by men of inferior ability. This meant, of course, as Bache stipulated, that the staff must consist of the ablest men available. They should be given time to cultivate science, "for the University should hold this to be one of its cardinal objects."[49] Instruction by first-rate teachers, in creating a living spirit, would penetrate the mind and promote the truth. These aims could be attained without impairing the usefulness of the professors in their regular posts; for the university would supplement, not supersede existing schools.

Some of the elements of a university were now at hand, Bache continued. With enough of the $40,000 income of Cooper Union available to meet contingent expenses and to provide for a chancellor and certain resident professors, sufficient money would be left to furnish courses of lectures in thirty different branches of science. By assigning several subjects to one professor, his whole time might be retained by the Union. Other potential resources were the Astor Library and the Dudley Observatory, to which natural history museums and art galleries should be added. In effect Bache was combining Tappan's program of integrating New York's learned institutions with Peirce's scheme for part-time teaching.[50]

Pleased with the response to his address, Bache wrote to Peirce: "The American Institute is satisfied & I have had a touch at the University of Arts & Sciences. That idea is fermenting & will go."[51] Although the men of wealth remained noncommittal, Bache entertained Cooper at dinner in Washington during January, 1857, and in early February the guest appeared at the Superintendent's office again. Cooper then showed himself to be "very accessible."[52] Peirce and Gould, in the capital at the same time, rode up to New York with him; and Peirce called on Cooper there. The latter was very agreeable but gave the impression that he had no well-developed idea of what he ought to do. He listened attentively but could not be made to fix on anything definite. Peirce also saw Cogswell, who was cordial, and received a call from William Astor, whom he described as "quite pleasant in his form of address upon University matters."[53] Here the project rested, apparently, until June, 1857, when Ruggles announced to the Columbia Trustees the "immense fact"[54] that Cooper was disposed to turn his Union over to the College as the locale for its postgraduate program.[55] On June 15 a committee of five was appointed to confer with Cooper,[56] but it accomplished nothing of importance. Three weeks later, Ruggles' son-in-law remarked: "The Peter Cooper negotiation does not advance,"[57] thereby writing a fit epitaph for the effort to make the Union into a university.

The failure of this project does not seem to have been inevitable. There was money in New York, as Peter Cooper's benefaction demonstrated; and there were talented professors available. Sheer lack of funds and potential faculty did not prevent New York from founding a university. The reasons for failure lie elsewhere. The advocates of a great university for New York had attempted an experiment in the science of association, which Alexis de Tocqueville had called the mother of science in democratic countries.[58] Their task was not to direct or stimulate the growth of a living institution but rather to synthesize an entirely new one, different from anything yet known in the United States. Tappan and his collaborators tried to engineer a union of the efforts and thinking of many men whose settled views were not patently incompatible but certainly lacked a common point of focus. A gifted co-ordinator was needed, but he did not appear. Tappan had ideas and the keenest desire to succeed, but he was not a master of the science—or the art—of making men see and work for a common purpose. Bache might have been successful had he not been, like Tappan, committed to other enterprises. Peirce's genius showed itself in other things than organization. Even if any of these men had possessed the qualities and freedom from other duties which the founding of a university required, he might have failed. The materials available to the creator of a university in New York from 1855 to 1857 were not properly prepared. Philanthropists, great and small, had yet to be conditioned to accept university-building as a worthy and promising cause.

IX

Columbia University

I

WATCHING the Albany project wither, Benjamin A. Gould, Jr., predicted a great effort either at Harvard or at Columbia.[1] The former did not immediately bestir itself, but the latter tried valiantly to become a university. In 1850 George T. Strong, a graduate of Columbia and later one of its trustees, allowed himself to dream of the "erection of Columbia College, with six sister institutions, into a University and its establishment in those princely structures that adorn the upper end of the island, with its richly endowed observatory, its 300 resident Fellows and Professors, and its 1400 free Scholarships."[2] This was merely a flight of fancy. The practical business of reform began on October 4, 1852. On that day the Board of Trustees appointed a Committee of Seven, chaired by President Charles King, to examine, among other things, the expediency of grafting onto the College a scheme of university professorships and lectures in the higher departments of letters and science.[3]

As early as 1829, King, then editor of the *New York American,* had written of the city's need for a university on a liberal scale and had thrown open the press to the cause.[4] During the Fifties, as president of Columbia, he was one of several officers interested in remodeling the College. It was he who presented the motion to create the Committee of Seven. Yet in the movement which followed, he played a role subordinate to that of Samuel B. Ruggles, a trustee.[5] Ruggles' participation in the reforms of the period can be traced back to August, 1852, when he talked with Strong and Benjamin Peirce of putting new life into the College.[6] By September he was deeply enough involved to know of King's intention of asking for the committee to study a university program.[7] With this as a beginning, Ruggles struggled for years to transform Columbia College into Columbia University. He was sometimes obliged to combat militant opposition to change. On other occasions it was his task to prod a lethargic

94

Board into action. His object, however, was not simply to agitate for any sort of change; nor was his leadership significant only because he forced debate over academic policy and finally helped to secure acceptance of a university plan. In time other men, President King or George T. Strong, for example, might conceivably have led a successful reform movement even if Ruggles had not exerted himself; but he combined unique persistence and enthusiasm for improvement with very decided ideas as to its true character. He supported only those innovations which were consistent with a clear-cut academic principle. Not satisfied merely to get reform underway, he strove to pilot it into safe channels.

His opportunity came with his appointment to the Committee of Seven, which went to work at once. By the end of October it was making plans for gathering information both at home and abroad,[8] and in December it had a questionnaire ready for circulation. Had the time come for a university; was there need for one; would students be found? What were the indispensable professorships with which to begin; how, in what order, and in what departments should additional chairs be created? Should professorships be endowed to free the incumbents from dependence on fees; or should fees be exacted in all or some courses? How should a special university degree be granted? Would it not be advisable, if professors were independent of fees, to require each to furnish evidence that he was engaged in investigation?[9]

Rising real estate values in the neighborhood of Columbia presented a question for the Trustees themselves to answer: should the College be moved? Its property would probably yield $20,000 annually.[10] Such an increase in income would bring expansion within the realm of possibility. The Committee of Seven snatched at this source of new wealth, recommending that all or portions of the College property, especially that it then occupied, be sold or let;[11] but the Board as a whole did not share their point of view. Upon the advice of a Standing Committee,[12] the Trustees resolved that immediate sale of the site on which the College stood was inexpedient.[13] Conservatism of this sort was typical of two influential trustees, Gouverneur M. Ogden and William Betts, whose presence on the Standing Committee may explain its position. Be that as it might, in Strong's opinion, the prospects for reform suddenly sank below zero.[14] King was convinced that the university scheme was at an end or brought to a standstill,[15] and Ruggles began to campaign actively on behalf of the university at Albany.

Discussion of a university program was reopened in the fall of 1853. At this time the Committee on the Professorship of Experimental and

Natural Philosophy, of which Ruggles was a member, recommended that instead of taking action on the professorship alone, a committee of the three best qualified trustees be appointed by ballot to inquire into the advisability of moving the College. In the event that removal was decided upon, this body should consider whether or not changes ought to be made in the undergraduate course. They should also study the arguments for and against a system of "University Education," either as a continuation of the undergraduate curriculum or otherwise.[16] These proposals were adopted; and William Betts, Henry J. Anderson, and Hamilton Fish were chosen to serve as the Committee on the College Course.[17]

It is not surprising that Ruggles was not a member of the new committee, since he had dissented from the report of the committee on the science professorship. Why had he dissented? Perhaps he believed that an elected committee, representing a majority of the Board as it was then composed, would be too conservative to contemplate genuine reform. Clearly, it was not committed to a policy of progress as Ruggles conceived of it.

If Ruggles had expected a flat repudiation of expansion, he must have been surprised by the committee's report of November 7, 1853. Although the committee was not prepared to say much about a university program, it did express approval of such a course, in whatever respects it might be proved to be practicable. The committee foresaw difficulties similar to those encountered in England to be overcome, but it did not despair of developing some means of advancing beyond collegiate or "Gymnastic" work. The use of the German word to describe the undergraduate department evinced at least some knowledge of the German system, but no reference was made to a faculty of philosophy.[18] On the immediately practical side, Betts, Anderson, and Fish recommended that the College be moved uptown; and the Trustees voted to act upon their advice.[19]

Before anything could be done, the Board was thrown into a bitter controversy which interrupted its constructive business for some time. The disagreement arose over the nomination of Oliver Wolcott Gibbs to the chair of chemistry. Those who believed that any teacher of science, not an infidel or heretic, should be judged by his ability in his special subject, did not doubt Gibbs' peculiar fitness for the post, while at least one of his friends privately hoped that as a professor he might promote the expansion of Columbia into a university.[20] There were others who objected to Gibbs because of his Unitarian principles.[21] In the end this group constituted a majority.

Failure in this encounter did not halt the Columbia reformers. During the struggle Strong wrote: "Should he [Gibbs] be defeated, we may stand in a better position for the contest as to the strengthening & enlargement of our educational work—the conversion of the second-rate College into a University. And it may be well for us to gain this advantage even by the loss of an individual agent clearly the best in his own department."[22] As a matter of fact the Gibbs controversy did help the cause of progress. By bringing the affairs of the College before the public, it provided Ruggles with an opportunity to challenge the idea that Columbia was a private institution. In a pamphlet, *The Duty of Columbia College to the Community*, he argued that the Trustees were ultimately responsible to the public and that the substance of their trust was to keep the College abreast of the times. That Columbia was not up to date was demonstrated by the contrast between it and Göttingen University, both of which had been founded by George II. After a century, Columbia could claim only six professors and one hundred and fifty students compared with the eighty-nine professors and 1,545 students at Göttingen. In the face of this discrepancy, Ruggles asked why New York with all its wealth should not have "a University and Scientific circle" and expressed his conviction that Columbia College should be developed in order to supply the lack.[23] "A deep, premonitory feeling now pervades the public mind, that a great national University is needed, —not a College, in our narrow sense of the term,—a mere gymnasium, or grammar-school, where some half dozen professors repeat, year after year, the same rudiments,—but a broad, comprehensive seat of learning, science and art, where every student may pursue any path he may select, to its extremest attainable limit, and above all, where original research and discovery by the ablest men the world can furnish, shall add daily to the great sum of human knowledge."[24]

Ruggles' opponents apparently saw the wisdom of sounding, if not the public mind, at least the opinion of the professors. In March, 1854, a plan of university studies was offered to the faculty for comment. Prepared by the Committee on the College Course, the paper called for three departments of advanced study—the schools or faculties of philosophy or philology; jurisprudence and history; and mathematical and physical science. Having entered these schools after three years in the classical course, after two years in the scientific course, or by examination, students might remain in them for three years.[25]

Three members of the faculty, John McVickar, Charles W. Hackley, and Henry Drisler, Jr., accepted a graduate course as desirable in principle but disapproved of some details of the program. McVickar proposed a four-fold division of schools, to include a department of physical science; a department of moral and intellectual subjects; a department of philology; and a department of jurisprudence. He also recommended that an M.A. degree be awarded after two years of postgraduate work.[26]

Charles W. Hackley suggested that jurisprudence be the only subject matter of one school and that history be added to the first school to form a faculty of philology, philosophy, and history. In addition he outlined a faculty of an "administrative" nature, on the German model, to instruct the student in the duties of his political station; and he, too, indorsed an M.A. degree to be granted at the end of a six-year course. The teaching staff was to be organized in three orders—the first, consisting of superintending professors, to teach the three higher undergraduate classes and two postgraduate classes; the second to take catechetical lectures; and the third to address itself to individual pupils. Members of this last group, which was designed to serve as a "nursery" of professors, were to be paid a small salary by the College and were to be permitted to accept private students.[27]

Henry Drisler, Jr., also divided the staff into classes, each department having one or two university or senior professors, two college or junior professors, and two or more college tutors. Prizes of $300 or $400, payable for three years, he thought, might encourage advanced study and help to keep men from being lured away from the college into professional courses. Recipients of these prizes, called Fellows or Tutors, could take the university course to fit themselves for academic life. They might well have prior claim to professorial posts. Where awards were few and vacancies seldom occurred there was no inducement to young men of ability "to keep up that particular Course of study and minute accuracy required in a College Professor."[28]

On April 3, 1854, these communications were submitted the President for his examination. From them he was to make suggestions to the Committee on the College Course,[29] which on July 24 produced a report, together with a draft of a statute. A long and elaborate document, the report contained a proposal for two undergraduate courses—one classical, the other scientific. The first was to cover a period of three years; the second, to be co-ordinate, was to last for only two years. An additional year of study in one of three schools or faculties would be required of candidates for the B.A. or B.S. degree. Having taken the first degree, a student could enter upon two years of postgraduate work. The special schools bore the names suggested in the earlier recommendations—the school of philosophy or philology, the school of jurisprudence and history, and the school of mathematics and physical science. Since university studies were defined as those "which are directly applicable to some definite future calling or profession,"[30] the plan departed in aim from the theory of the German faculty of philosophy and from the ideal of learning as an end in itself. The committee added, however, that as opportunity appeared and means became available, the course might be extended to cover the whole circle of human knowledge. Admission to the advanced schools would not be limited to college graduates; but the M.A. degree would be conferred only after two years of study beyond the first degree. Candidates for the second degree would be required to attend a prescribed number of lectures and to pass an examination.[31]

Superficially the program was an ambitious one, but the committee warned against extravagant expectations arising from a vain comparison of a private college with the great public universities of Europe. One may wonder, therefore, whether or not the eventual creation of a university in the European sense was contemplated. Strong, who was on the spot, characterized the report as: "Long, prosy and feeble; warm water at its tenth dilution."[32] Nevertheless, on September 14, 1854, the committee was authorized to report a statute.[33]

Once more Ruggles found himself in dissent. Early in the winter of 1854 he offered a series of resolutions for deliberation at a future meeting.[34] Once passed, these resolutions would have constituted a reversal of the policy of the committee. The first asserted that moral, mental, and physical science, intermixed, were equally essential to intellectual culture and that they should, therefore, be pursued in a single course to the end of the third or junior year. On this point Ruggles was clearly voicing the old belief of the faculty at Yale, his Alma Mater, that the primary consideration in liberal education was a balance of various disciplines, each of which any given student must acquire. Secondly, he argued that the College should establish supplementary courses in continuation of the curriculum of the first three years, "without reference to professional or artistic pursuits, but solely for higher culture."[35] Degrees should be awarded at the end of the senior year, and unrestricted choice of subjects should be permitted during the two succeeding years.[36]

Obviously Ruggles was raising issues upon the settlement of which the basic nature of reform at Columbia depended. On King's motion his resolutions were ordered printed; but decision on them was postponed in expectation of a statute to be reported by the Committee on the College Course.[37] Within a fortnight, Ruggles and Henry J. Anderson, a member of this group, dined together at the invitation of Strong. The meeting, planned, as it was, deliberately, had all the marks of an effort to reconcile the differences between Ruggles and the committee. If that was the intention, Anderson was an ideal choice as intermediary, for he possessed a flexible and subtle mind, capable of seeing minute bits of good and bad on both sides of an argument. While his guests did some "tall talking" and settled on certain principles of procedure, Strong himself pressed for a show-down within the Board.[38] A crisis might have turned in Ruggles' favor; for action by Anderson at a later time showed his willingness to agree with Ruggles on the virtue of a unitary course.[39] Before the understanding between the two men affected official policy, however, the projected coalition university took the center of the academic stage in New York. Perhaps for this reason, Columbia College had some respite after its first effort at reform.

II

Inactivity during 1855 and most of 1856 was probably salutary; for by December of the latter year, Richard S. McCulloh, the new professor of chemistry, could write that "irritated feeling has yielded to the soothing influence of time. A dominant majority [of the Board] no longer finds its power resisted in every measure by a factious minority. And is, therefore, itself more open to conviction & persuasion."[40] The Trustees seemed ready to listen to some plan for postgraduate courses although their Committee on the College Course shrank from the word "university." "The present [wrote McCulloh to Peirce, perhaps in answer to his *Working Plan*] appears to be a very suitable moment to propose that said 'post-graduate' course be put upon trial by lectureships, such as you recommend. They are to be simply suggested in oral intercourse and their advantages set forth, so that the Committee [on the College Course] may, if they will, adopt the scheme as their own, become its advocates, and even if they wish[,] imagine themselves its authors. You can afford to let them pluck such a leaf from your wreath. Besides, you are too good a mathematician not to know that functions of imaginary quantities need to be made real, if we would not have them absurd."[41] Soon, however, McCulloh lost hope for the immediate future. Commenting that the time was "not *now*" because of the financial condition of the College, he did not doubt that a university scheme would eventually be carried out. "When that day comes," he wrote to Peirce, "there may be lectureships & the brilliant illumination, which perhaps you have foreseen—Would that it had all come to pass!"[42] Strong was also gloomy about the period directly ahead. "It is perfectly clear that my delightful dream indulged in for eighteen years of helping to build up a real seat of learning has vanished and gone."[43]

This despair was premature, but certainly the rate of progress was slow and the way obstructed by disagreement, even among those who were not completely conservative. One can see that a group of trustees, represented by the Committee on the College Course, regretted the necessity of change in the undergraduate program but thought it expedient to establish a scientific course co-ordinate with the classical course. Another faction, led by Ruggles, contended that for three years the college course should remain a unit containing both the classics and science. The ideal of a liberal education must be maintained by altering, not by abolishing a single compulsory curriculum. The two groups agreed on the need for, if not the purpose of, a graduate department; but they were not equally enthusiastic about it.

Perhaps because of these differences of opinion, the Board pursued a confusing course before it finally agreed on a specific university system. Several parties seem to have worked simultaneously on the question of reform without much reference to each other. One of these, a Committee of Inquiry, headed by Gouverneur M. Ogden,[44] was authorized on July 7, 1856,[45] to collect statements and opinions from the President, the faculty, and others on university education.[46] By August, 1857, the investigation was in the main complete. The findings filled a fat volume of information and advice, valuable principally for the light they throw on the type of thinking which must have been current during the period when the Board was slowly moving toward the creation of Columbia University.

In his statement for the Committee of Inquiry, Henry Vethake, characteristically enough, attacked short courses by visiting lecturers as being exceedingly liable to superficiality.[47] Henry P. Tappan also opposed non-resident professors, but he wrote eloquently in defense of the university idea.[48] Mark Hopkins testified to the need for a university, of which he said there was hardly a beginning anywhere in America. In his judgment, it should be entirely separate from any college, so that graduates of all colleges might feel an equal interest and an equal right in it. A university, he continued, needed not only money but also men and the general support of the country.[49] Benjamin Hale, of Hobart College, took a dimmer view of university-building than did the other authorities. A great deal had been written on the subject, he said; but the result, while very good, was also very impracticable. Specifically, no law made degrees a prerequisite for any position.[50] As if in answer to

Hale, Henry Drisler, Jr., who revealed his familiarity with Bristed's *Five Years in an English University*,[51] repeated his earlier recommendation that prizes or fellowships of perhaps $300 per annum be made available to graduate students. The recipients, "continuing, in many cases, the studies in which they excelled, might supply the College with its future professors."[52] Indorsement of a system in which fellows would serve as tutors also came from W. H. N. Stewart of Trinity College, Dublin, who pointed out that provision for a postgraduate course would fall in with this idea as it would give the students who pursued it a position and rank in the college.[53]

More elaborate than any of these statements was the paper presented to the Committee of Inquiry by George T. Strong. "No attempt should be made at the outset [he said] to organize a complete University system, because it is impracticable to do so. A University cannot be organized and set in operation like a bank or an insurance company. Even with unlimited means at hand, a corps of the best teachers assembled, and all the apparatus of instruction provided, the Institution is not created. These are only favorable conditions for its development, or elements out of which it may be formed in time. It must grow and shape itself gradually, and if destined to last, and to become a great intellectual power and centre, it will probably grow up slowly and from a small beginning. If we try to anticipate this natural process, and construct it at once, the structure will fall down again as fast [as] it is finished."[54] In this country, Strong continued, the work of the founders of a complete university, for the first generation at least, must be especially cautious and tentative. They had to create a demand for high education. They had to ascertain by experiment how long and for the sake of what kind of teaching young men would postpone entering on active life, to what rule of discipline they would submit, and whether enough of them could be collected to make reasonable fees for each professor. The founders had also to cope with many other questions which could not be answered in advance.[55] "All that can be done in the first instance is to employ professors of great repute and ability to teach, and to invite (if necessary to *hire*) students to learn; confiding everything, at the outset, to the control of the teachers, finding out, by degrees what we want, and feeling our way towards a code of rules, step by step.

"In other words, we should settle nothing in advance that we can possibly leave open."[56]

Without teachers of the first order and highest reputation there would be no lasting achievement. "They are not merely necessary to the vigor of the Institution, but conditions of its existence. Whether the experiment succeed or fail depends mainly on their presence or absence. With professors of respectable mediocrity or a little above it, a College will languish, but may subsist indefinitely. But a University cannot be planted and long sustained in life without professors of splendid name and ability, especially in a community where such institutions are unknown and where general mediocrity of attainment and aspiration is the obstacle to be removed and the evil to be remedied. If they be obtained, the Academic system we establish for them, even if prematurely and unwisely settled, will do little harm. They must be diligently sought, and, like founders of Universities in all ages, we shall probably be obliged to seek them beyond (as well as within) the limits of our own country and language."[57]

Until the university had been in operation long enough to establish a demand for its teaching, scholarships with stipends should be used to attract students. Probably, said Strong, $10,000 a year could not be more advantageously spent than in hiring thirty young men of moderate means and notable talent to be thoroughly educated in some department of knowledge. There should also be scholarships without stipends. Both types of award should be made on the basis of rigorous examination.[58]

As a first step toward a university system, Strong suggested "that a certain number of young men (alumni having the preference) be forthwith appointed tutors in the College for (say) three years, on condition of their pursuing courses of study to be prescribed to each by the Faculty, and under their direction and control."[59] The second step should be to set up certain postgraduate courses as the nucleus of a university, with the initial offerings in those fields for which there was in practice the greatest demand.[60] This would not result in the ideal university; but with reference to a given set of circumstances, that university was best which best taught what the people of the time wanted or could be persuaded to learn.[61] "Its [the university's] claims and counsels will be always a little above the popular demand, but not too far above it."[62] Should the resources of the institution permit the addition of a higher course of training, which the community had not yet learned to desire, "we should proceed to establish, at once, a third course or school, including professorships of History and Ethics, (already provided for in that of Law,) the Philosophy of Literature, Philology and the Ancient Languages—these last being the central and characteristic subject of this department."[63]

While this advice was being collected but before it had been published, the Board decided to move the College from its old site. The neighborhood had become distractingly busy in general, and, in particular the opening of a new street opposite the College building had destroyed all retirement and privacy.[64] With removal came the probability of increased income; and on January 12, 1857, the Trustees, on a motion by Anderson, directed the Committee on the College Course to bring in a full statute covering the entire program of college and university instruction contemplated in its earlier report. In addition the resolution called for consideration of a single college course as distinct from the two parallel undergraduate courses originally proposed.[65] On February 2, the undivided curriculum was further emphasized when the Board, on Ruggles' motion, referred his fundamental resolutions of November 23, 1854, to the Committee on the College Course.[66] At the same time Ruggles raised the question of spending $5,000 annually to maintain prize scholarships in the postgraduate department.[67]

On March 2, 1857, the committee reported a statute. By way of introduction the authors stated that the familiar structure of the College would be preserved, with the old system augmented not supplanted.[68] The existing curriculum was to be designated the classical course, and by its side a co-ordinate course was to be instituted. Both would be supplemented by a postgraduate program, consisting of schools of letters, science, and jurisprudence, study in which could lead to the M.A. degree. Prizes or scholarships were not mentioned in the statute.[69]

The majority report was followed by a dissenting opinion prepared by Anderson. Not originally an ardent champion of reform, he had, as has already been described, reached an understanding with Ruggles. The statute, Anderson stated, did not sufficiently encourage attendance at the University and only imperfectly united the University with the College. As a substitute for the system outlined by the committee, he advocated a single three-year undergraduate course, followed by a full three-year program of university studies. Bachelors in Honors aspiring to the M.A. degree and willing to pursue the prescribed course should receive honorary stipends to be paid at the conclusion of each academic year. Masters in Honors, who had been Bachelors in Honors, should become Fellows of the University, entitled to honorary emoluments and to privileges to be determined by further statutes.[70]

In this crisis the Board resolved itself into a committee of the whole, presumably in order to engage in unreserved debate.[71] Strong, who usually found the Board phlegmatic, was impressed by its increased life and vigor.[72] The statute remained under consideration for weeks. "I begin," Strong wrote when the committee was still sitting, "to have some hopes of the College. The duncely element is still obstinate and powerful, but the sceptre has departed from it. It has lost its omnipotence of three years ago."[73] When on July 6, 1857, the statute was reported out of committee and enacted by the Board, it was much amended in the direction of the Ruggles and Anderson resolutions.

In its final form the legislation provided for a single course for the first three college years. In the senior year the student would choose between the departments of science, letters, and jurisprudence. Upon graduation three postgraduate schools would be open to him—the school of letters, the school of science, and the school of jurisprudence. In the school of science, pure as well as applied science would be taught; in the school of jurisprudence, history and political economy would have a place beside the technical aspects of law. An earned M.A. degree was authorized for students doing a minimum of two years of advanced work.[74]

III

As the period of general debate came to an end, the task of converting a paper scheme into actuality began. Even before passing the statute, the Trustees requested the President to prepare a table of studies for a postgraduate course to open in September, 1857.[75] With the authorizing of the new system, the matter was again raised and referred back to King.[76] Yet when the Board met in the fall to take final action on the plan of graduate studies, there were not enough members present to constitute a quorum.[77] There can hardly have been much demand for inauguration of the higher departments.

One handicap under which the experiment operated was the lack of student subsidies. On June 1, 1857, Ruggles had successfully put through his motion that a Special Committee of Three draw up a system of prize scholarships. A week later Ruggles, Anderson, and Fish reported that the College could safely apply a sum not larger than $5,000 to a scholarship project. Approximately two-thirds of this money, or $3,150, was to be used to encourage students to undertake the two years of postgraduate work. Individual prizes, ranging from $75 to $200, were to be awarded on the basis of conduct and examination results.[78] This plan was discussed but not approved.[79] The university statute of July 6, 1857, provided for fellowships; but no practical action followed. In 1858 the Committee of Inquiry again raised the question of prizes to induce seniors "to continue their studies in the Institution until the conclusion of the post-graduate course, with such proficiency as to enable the College to derive advantages from their attainments."[80] This suggestion, too, came to nothing.

Despite a setback in this quarter, some progress was made in another when the Trustees appointed several new professors—Charles A. Joy in chemistry, Francis Lieber[81] in history and political economy, Charles Davies in mathematics, and Charles M. Nairne in literature and philosophy. These men delivered their inaugural addresses in February, 1858, following a public statement by William Betts on Columbia's change of location and expansion in curriculum. Each speaker made the point that theoretical knowledge in all its branches was of the utmost practical significance. Charles Joy argued that since abstract science had utilitarian implications, the United States needed "not only the widest diffusion, but also the highest grade of Science. . . . The great want of this country is a University where Science can be taught far beyond the usual College course, where the students may be led into the profounder regions of the interpretation of phenomena, as well as into the practical application of Science to the daily wants of man."[82]

Lieber added: "We stand in need of a national university, the highest apparatus of the highest modern civilization."[83] From this generality, he proceeded to a defense of political economy and philosophy and, in so doing, illustrated the uses of a university: "Need I add that the student, having passed through these fields and having viewed these regions, will be the better prepared for the grave purposes for which this country destines him, and as a partner in the great commonwealth of self-government? If not, then strike these sciences from your catalogue. It is true, indeed, that the scholar is no consecrated priest of knowledge, if he does not love it for the sake of knowledge. And this is even important in a practical point of view; for all knowledge, to be usefully applied, must be far in advance of its application. It is like the sun, which, we are told, causes the plant to grow when he has already sunk below the horizon."[84]

Davies, taking as one of his principal themes the importance of mathematics "as the true basis of the practical," said: "The term 'practical,' in its common acceptation, often denotes shorter methods of obtaining results than are indicated by science. It implies a substitution of natural sagacity and 'mother wit' for the results of hard study and laborious effort. It implies the use of knowledge before it is acquired— the substitution of the results of mere experiment for the deductions of science, and the placing of empiricism above philosophy. But give to 'practical' its true and right signification, and it becomes a word of real import and definite value. In its right sense, it denotes the best means of making the true ideal the actual: that is, of applying the principles of science in all the practical business of life, and of bodying forth in material form the conceptions of taste and genius."[85] Finally, Nairne demonstrated how philosophical investigation might be applied to spiritual questions of "the highest practical moment."[86] As the authorities had intended they should, the addresses taken together constituted an advertisement for Columbia's new departure.[87]

During the early winter of 1858 the faculty attacked the problem of university studies without notable success. Lieber found their plans hopelessly impractical and impracticable;[88] and, as February gave way to March, Strong grew pessimistic, doubting if graduates would come to the University were it to have fifty professors of the first order from Oxford and Berlin. "This people is not ripe for higher education. The ingenuous youth of the Fifth Avenue would not take it as a gift without money and without price. Could we afford to lay out $10,000 per annum in stipends to clever young men and hire a dozen best graduate students every year to stay in college and be pumped into, we might accomplish something. Specimens of higher training thus produced would show people that something was to be gained by devoting an additional year or two to study, but this outlay we cannot afford."[89] Strong's hope still lay in a gradual transition from vocational study to a more liberal pursuit of knowledge. He thought, however, that such a tentative, indirect approach would not find favor with the Board, which wanted to see on paper a complete university system, harmonious in all its parts.

By March, 1858, the Trustees, having tired of talking, of committees of inquiry, and of drafts of statutes, were ready to make a beginning without further delay. They accepted the University in principle and were of one mind concerning the outline and main features of the experiment. Accordingly the whole matter was turned over to a select Committee on the Organization of the Post-graduate Course with instructions to report a plan to be set going immediately or, at all events, by October.[90]

A month later this committee, of which Ruggles was a member, submitted a unanimous report proposing that the university course begin at once at a cost of between $5,000 and $7,000 beyond the College income. The program, with a few exceptions, could be carried out by the existing faculty. Fees were to be collected from all graduate students for instruction in the several departments.[91]

Deferring consideration of the last matter only, the Trustees accepted the report.[92] Then Gouverneur M. Ogden, watchdog of the treasury, introduced a resolution designed to prevent the making of any arrangements, either for staff or accommodations, which would involve expenditures beyond the existing funds of the College.[93] This obviously would have strangled the university scheme at the outset. "It will never do," wrote Strong, "to rescind our action and organize our university at the college exclusively and with our subgraduate teachers alone and thus certify that we don't intend or expect it to succeed—and that our parturient brag and cackle ... meant nothing."[94] Ogden had the support of at least one other trustee; but after a vigorous opposition speech by Ruggles, the subject was laid over to a special meeting.[95] When the Board met again a fortnight later, Ogden stayed away; and the motion was quashed, only one vote being cast for "narcotism" and "paralysis."[96]

On June 21, 1858, the Committee on the Post-graduate Course, speaking through Ruggles, recommended enlargement of the faculty by the appointment of Arnold Guyot, James D. Dana, George P. Marsh, and Theodore W. Dwight, in physical geography, geology and natural history, English literature, and law, respectively. From the annual salary figure, not more than $1,500 for each new man, one can assume that the professors were not expected to devote themselves solely to the University.[97] Yet approval of even this limited program must have encouraged Ruggles, whose friends, Lieber and Peirce, had both advocated a part-time basis for teaching.[98] "Tempora mutantur," exclaimed Strong, "and the temper of the Board has undergone the greatest mutation since 1854, when stagnation and the standing committee reigned and Mr. R.[uggles] was the Catiline of the Senate."[99] At the commencement of 1858, President King could proclaim that the Trustees of Columbia College had created a university.[100]

It was weak, Strong thought, but it would grow into something if it survived three years.[101] It did live until 1861, but the law division alone flourished and only then after modification.[102] This was, however, still in the future for the planners of Columbia's first university program, which was finally organized in November, 1858. In addition to legal studies and civil engineering the offerings were:

School of Science
    Richard S. McCulloh, mechanics of ethereal matter or the present state of heat, light, and electricity.
    Charles A. Joy, chemistry with practical instruction in the laboratory.
    Charles Davies, higher mathematics and the nature and history of mathematical science.

Charles W. Hackley, physical astronomy with the particular use of instruments.
John Torrey, botany.

School of Letters

Francis Lieber, history of commerce and political science.
Charles M. Nairne, ethics and aesthetics.
George P. Marsh, English language.
Arnold Guyot, comparative physical geography in relation to history and modern civilization.[103]

The new course did not receive much encouragement from the public at large;[104] and Ogden called attention to the cost of the experiment—$4,543.28 for the year.[105] But surplus income from College property counterbalanced Ogden's influence.[106]

During the planning of the program for the second year, Lieber characteristically urged the establishment of a comprehensive institution which would surely soon attract students from various parts of the country.[107] A short step in this direction was taken when the professors of the College who lectured in the postgraduate course were empowered to collect fees from students. Those ambitious enough to undertake the work, however, were obliged to pay out of their own pockets for the advertisement of their classes.[108] The neutral attitude of the Trustees, which this indicates, is suggested again by the fact that the organization of the postgraduate program fell upon one man, Samuel B. Ruggles.[109]

Operations during the second year opened no more happy prospects for the development of a great graduate school than had those of the first. The law school grew but only at the expense of Strong's hope that students might be led along from practical, professional subjects into higher learning of a theoretical nature. In December, it was decided that examination in the subjects of Lieber's lectures should not be a requirement for a degree in law.[110] In the future only candidates for prizes were to attend the lectures.[111] Even Strong conceded that compulsory study of these subjects would kill the school as a diet of beef and madeira would stunt or kill a yearling baby.[112]

At about the same time, the Trustees thought of creating a scientific school in co-operation with the College of Physicians and Surgeons; but after a series of conferences between the directors of the two institutions, Ogden revealed that Columbia would operate at a deficit in the following year. Other members of the Board were also disinclined to involve the College in a doubtful experiment. Strong, who usually took Ogden's warnings lightly, could not say they were wrong.[113] Postgraduate study of natural science was apparently no more feasible even for medical students than a profound treatment of the law was for young attorneys-to-be.

In the third year of the postgraduate program, a special committee of five was ordered to draw up measures for reducing the annual expenditure of the College to match its income.[114] The theme of the report, submitted on June 24, 1861, was retrenchment. Although Ruggles approved in general of the recommendation of the committee, of which he was a member, he did not abandon his belief in the value of a university.[115] When the report had been approved, however, the Committee on the Post-graduate Course was disbanded at its own request.[116] Even before this, Strong had prophesied that the day when a "developed Columbia College" would help to make New York "a real center of culture and civilization" would come in twenty years.[117]

Why did the non-legal side of the postgraduate scheme prove feeble? Two explanations of its failure to attract students are suggested by the replies made to a question put by the Committee of Inquiry: "In the absence of civil privileges or political advantages, what motives, beyond interest in the subject, or the way in which it is taught, can you suggest as probably sufficient to induce bachelors to attend and study for higher degrees?"[118] Henry P. Tappan had answered that no true university had failed in the past.[119] Did the Columbia experiment suffer then, because it was false to the university concept? Certainly the postgraduate plan had some of the elements of Tappan's ideal university. It called for an association of productive scholars; and it was supported by several men who believed sincerely in the importance of higher learning. To be sure, it lacked the philosophical unity which Tappan sought; but it seems unlikely that this or any other theoretical imperfection made a material difference. If, presumably, Tappan was thinking not only of form but of content, his answer may bear on the fate of the undertaking. In richness of offerings Columbia was not comparable to the universities abroad and so was barely a university at all as far as competition for students was concerned.

Francis Lieber was convinced that university degrees ought to mean something substantial, something readily understood by the community to possess value "so that they would be sought for on account of their practical use."[120] In Germany the university degree was the gateway to careers in civil service, the ministry, law, teaching, and medicine; but in the United States this was not the case. As the history of Lieber's own course demonstrated, only immediately useful knowledge was acceptable under existing circumstances. Ruggles and Strong were, therefore, probably correct in insisting that, if a university was to flourish, students would have to be hired. In the face of general indifference such a mercenary consideration was the necessary foundation for a program of advanced studies. "The full grown plant we are sticking into the ungenial soil of New York will take no root [wrote Strong]. The utmost I hope is that when it withers and perishes it may leave some nucleus or germ surviving whence there may be natural development and expansion hereafter."[121]

X

Reform in the West and South

I

THE ideal of thoroughgoing academic reform in the direction of graduate education moved West with Henry P. Tappan. A nominal university opened its doors in Ann Arbor, Michigan, in 1841;[1] but it did not begin to flourish until 1852 when Tappan was appointed president following a revision of the organic act. At his inauguration he pointed out the difference between the undergraduate course considered as a gymnasium and a university intended for those who already knew how to study. The structure of the latter, he said, should be determined by the two-fold character of knowledge, part of which was objective to man, part concerned with man himself. The university ought to be divided into two faculties, one of philosophy and science and one of literature and the arts. To these would be added departments of theology, law, and medicine, which were but the applications of philosophy and science to special matters. To make these branches of learning available to students, the university must have complete academic apparatus and a number of men qualified both to teach and to carry on original thought and investigation. Let Michigan follow the Prussian model.[2]

Repeated public statement and exposition of his views were Tappan's most effective tools. In 1853 the University catalogue stressed the necessity of establishing beyond the undergraduate course "those more extended studies in Science, Literature, and the Arts, which alone can lead to profound and finished scholarship."[3] Lectures for graduates and others would form "the proper development of the University, in distinction from the College or Gymnasium now in operation."[4]

The President's report for the same year made it clear that the projected university lectures were designed for students who had completed the undergraduate course. Although the field of science had expanded enormously, wrote Tappan, as did so many of his contemporaries, the four-year course, borrowed from the English colleges, had not been lengthened.

Instead the number of subjects covered in the four-year program had been increased and as a result scholarship had become superficial. If a course of university lectures were adopted, the undergraduate curriculum could once more be devoted to acquiring the elements of knowledge and to learning the art of study while the university student could pursue freely any branch or branches of his own choosing. This would require additions to staff and equipment.[5]

In 1854 Tappan returned to the same theme;[6] and the Board of Regents commented officially that there was more to be learned in the University than could be crowded into four years: "It is our design to offer unlimited advantages in this Institution. Many of the Professors are prepared to give instruction by lectures and otherwise beyond what is required for the primary degrees of the University. So soon as there is a demand for it, lectures will be given in the various Natural Sciences, Mental and Moral Science, and the Languages, Ancient and Modern, on a more extended plan than those now given to undergraduate students; and it is hoped that according to the design of its original founders and of its present Faculty and highest friends the Institution will speedily ripen into a genuine and thorough University."[7]

Tappan's doctrine was also preached to the students, for he personally undertook to reveal the true character of a university to the young men in his charge. (One of them, Charles K. Adams, eventually became president of Cornell University, the first head of which was of course Andrew D. White, sometime professor of history under Tappan at Michigan.) Before traveling East in 1855 to make his New York address on the progress of education, Tappan delivered it in an expanded form before the literary societies of the University. In Ann Arbor he contrasted college and university education even more sharply than he did in New York. The American system, he said, belonged to the scholastic rather than the modern age. Expanding history, literature, and the sciences were crushed into a Procrustean bed. As education became superficial and pretentious, the true idea of it as discipline of the faculties had been lost sight of. German influence was, however, discernible in the new schools at Yale and Harvard and in the university course supported at Union by the Nott fund. Yet attempts to apply modern concepts produced a mixture of opposites.[8]

The students seem to have listened attentively; for Tappan was able to tell a hostile legislature: "The day will come, gentlemen, when my boys will take your places, and then something will be done for the University."[9] The rebuke was sharp; but if ever a university president had justification for forthright speech, Tappan was that man. The publicity given his ideas met with bitter opposition, particularly in the Democratic press.[10] One of his first critics, W. F. Storey, the owner and editor of the *Detroit Free Press,* contended that Michigan did not need a *"high university"* and that it was not the business of the state to provide more than practical education. Universities of the sort advocated by Tappan should be private.[11] These shots were not the only ones directed against the President, but they hit squarely at his philosophical principle of education. His sin on this score was simply compounded in the eyes of his adversaries by his frank admiration of foreign institutions.[12]

In spite of both public and legislative opposition, however, Tappan retained the confidence of the Regents, whose term of office ran until 1858. This enabled him to begin organizing a true university. On September 24, 1855, a committee of the faculty, chaired by the President, was appointed to digest a plan for a university course. Four days later the committee reported an extended curriculum. After careful consideration the faculty accepted the plan with minor amendments.

The new system was based on the traditional four-year time scheme; but it consisted of three departments—classical, scientific, and civil engineering.[13] Not only could students, upon completing one course for the Bachelor's degree, proceed to other courses; but they were also free to choose "particular sciences as subjects of prolonged study, extending through two, three, or more years according to the nature of the science selected, or the degree of perfection at which they aim."[14] This was a first step toward graduate studies; but no distinct graduate school was established nor was an earned degree for advanced work introduced.

Before more could be accomplished, Tappan became the general of the crusade for a university in New York City. By the fall of 1856, however, his attention was again centered on Ann Arbor. His report to the Regents for that year contained another ardent discussion of the university question. Lower schools, Tappan said, would deteriorate if universities did not exist to set standards for education, books, and scholars. "The Universities of Europe are, at this moment, furnishing us with this supply. Many of our young men are educated there. Their scholars are transplanted here. We depend upon the scientific and critical labors of their learned men, who furnish the original works from whence our editions of the Classics and our own scientific works are derived."[15] Scholars studied abroad or studied alone, while colleges without the aid of universities were unable to care for themselves. "The graduate of a College is not prepared to become a College Professor. But the direct object of a University is to prepare men to teach in the University itself, or in any other institution."[16]

No perceptible progress was made in 1857; but in the following year, the President and the Faculty of Literature, Science, and Arts agreed upon a graduate literary and scientific course. They also recommended a change in the M.A. degree and the adoption of an M.S. degree. Influenced by these suggestions, the Regents voted to inaugurate a graduate program, at the same time establishing advanced degrees to be earned by formal study. Previously, the Michigan requirements had been only a small improvement upon custom. Under the new rules, the M.A. could still be taken without postgraduate study; but the M.A. and M.S. were also to be conferred on Bachelors of Arts or of Science who pursued in each semester of at least one year a minimum of two courses, who sustained examination before the faculty in at least three of these studies (the studies to be elected by the candidate), and who presented to the faculty a thesis on one of the subjects chosen for examination.[17]

Candidates for the earned degree had these resources at hand:

FIRST SEMESTER

HENRY P. TAPPAN: History of philosophy; (1) Locke and the development of the Sensational School; (2) the system of Kant and the development of the German Speculative School.

GEORGE P. WILLIAMS: Mathematics; differential and integral calculus.

SILAS H. DOUGLASS: Chemistry and mineralogy; qualitative analysis and determinative mineralogy.

LOUIS FASQUELLE: French literature.

JAMES R. BOISE: Greek literature; the dramatic writers of Greece.

ALEXANDER WINCHELL: Zoölogy; lectures on the vertebrate skeleton, its morphology and homologies.

FRANCIS BRÜNNOW: Astronomy; numerical calculus, theory of interpolations and quadratures, method of least squares.

HENRY S. FRIEZE: Latin literature; Roman satirists.

DATUS C. BROOKS: Rhetoric and English literature, theory of taste, philosophical criticism.

JOHN A. CLARK: Higher algebra.

ANDREW D. WHITE: History; history of England with special reference to the growth of the British constitution.

DEVOLSON WOOD: Physical mechanics of fluids, analytical investigation of the steam engine and locomotive, hydraulic motors.

SECOND SEMESTER

HENRY P. TAPPAN: History of philosophy; (1) Reid, and the Common-Sense School; (2) Hamilton as the expounder of Reid; (3) Cousin and eclecticism.

GEORGE P. WILLIAMS: Mathematics, calculus.

SILAS H. DOUGLASS: Chemistry and mineralogy; qualitative analysis with investigations referring especially to the applications of the science to the arts; manufacture and agriculture.

Louis Fasquelle: German literature.

James R. Boise: Greek literature; the Greek philosophical writers.

Alexander Winchell: Paleontology; lectures on the geological history of the vertebrates.

Francis Brünnow: Astronomy; numerical calculus, theory of interpolations and of quadratures, method of least squares.

Henry S. Frieze: Latin literature; the Roman satirists, with special reference to the *Aetna* of Lucilius Junior and the satires of Juvenal.

Datus C. Brooks: English language and literature, particularly during the Anglo-Norman and Anglo-Saxon periods and the age of Elizabeth.

John A. Clark: Integral calculus; a general view of definite integrals, differential equations, including the theory of singular solutions, partial differential equations.

Andrew D. White: History; history of England with special reference to the growth of the British constitution.

DeVolson Wood: Engineering; mining machines, stability of structures, retaining walls, bridges (wood, stone, and iron).[18]

Students did appear for some of these courses, but the attendance was small. In 1859 there were twenty-nine graduate or special but nontechnical students, counting many in analytical chemistry. As this subject was presumably popular for its connection with agriculture, its full share of the enrolment can hardly be considered graduate in the sense used here, even if some young farmers did hold Bachelor's degrees. Besides natural science, classes were conducted in German, Latin, history, and ancient languages. In 1860 only three students were registered in each of the branches of botany and history, the only nonchemical subjects studied. One nonchemist appeared in courses for the second degree in 1861; and in 1862 three such students were enrolled.[19] The number shrank to two the following year.[20] Clearly Tappan's experiment in "philosophical" education was proving a near-failure.

Lack of student interest did not by itself torpedo the President's hopes. As the new system went into effect, the University was slipping into turmoil with Tappan at the center. Because of his educational policy, his religious views and practices, his want of tact and the common touch, his cultural standards, even his accent and his use of wine, and perhaps his politics, the President inadvertently created many enemies, whose opportunity came with the retirement of the old Board of Regents on January 1, 1858. Under the skilful leadership of Levi Bishop, a Democratic lawyer, an anti-Tappan movement gained momentum within the new Board.[21] Tappan, by inclination a grand strategist in the field of education, was obliged to become a skirmisher amidst the wilderness of academic politics. The first result of this conflict was an atmosphere of bitterness in which a serenely philosophical ideal of higher education could hardly flourish. The climax came with Tappan's dismissal in 1863. This and his expatriation to Europe marked the end of his active promotion of university reform. Enthusiasm no longed led to practical undertakings; even the idealism from which hope had sprung seemed to lose its point. He could on occasion write in the old vein, but his faith in philosophy was disintegrating. "We think and we think on— we think on farther and farther—We get among the Infinites—we pause, and we bow our heads confounded."[22]

With Tappan's withdrawal from Ann Arbor, the University catalogue dropped his theorizing; but the revised requirements for degrees and the program for postgraduate courses remained in print. The Regents and faculty continued to announce their intention "to furnish all the facilities for education belonging to a true University."[23] By his aspiration and his educational campaign, Tappan had succeeded in committing Michigan to that ideal.

II

Without question, as the political anxiety of the Fifties deepened, academic reform took on a new urgency. Although in 1856 James D. Dana saw clouds on the horizon, he urged Yale on toward expansion with the plea that it became the American University.[24] In the South, patriotism also found expression in academic reform as it had in the days of Thomas Jefferson; but the sectional self-consciousness which only tinctured his thought became a dominant theme in the discussion of higher education in the decade before the war. Americans had long felt distaste for education away from home; and for the South of the Fifties, Northern colleges fell into that category. In short, the geographical and cultural base of patriotism had narrowed.[25]

Even men who were not themselves fire-eaters became aware of the regional bearing of university reform. In acknowledging receipt of Benjamin Peirce's *Working Plan for the Foundation of a University*, Lewis H. Steiner, a Baltimorean of notable learned and political interests, wrote: "It is refreshing to meet with enlarged, liberal and unsectional plans at any time, but especially now, when party strife is drawing into its ranks some of our best & worthiest men of all parts of the country. ... Now the closer we bring all parts of the Union together, through the medium of some common bond, the greater will be the difficulties attendant upon any attempt to tear it asunder."[26] After years of teaching in the South, Francis Lieber remarked in his Columbia College inaugural address: "All that has been said of countries, and nations and a national university would retain its full force even if the threatened cleaving of this broad land should come upon us."[27] The most poignant testimony of all came from the pen of a Southerner. In 1857 an Alabamian wrote of the timely and beneficent idea of an American university; but of the success of such an institution, he expressed his doubts. There was a "want of confidence in the permanency of the Federal Union";[28] and any movement in the true interests of the Republic dropped into the hearts of men in the North and the South "like a sadly remembered tune, in which they have neither courage nor voice to join."[29]

This muted note was not echoed in all Southern hearts. More aggressive sectional feeling produced a project which was broached in *DeBow's Review* in 1857. The spirit of the author is revealed in the reasons he gave for believing the University of Virginia to be inadequate for his purposes. It was not "sufficiently Southern, sufficiently central, sufficiently cottonized to become the great educational center of the South."[30] Existing institutions, the argument ran, were poisoning the minds of Americans against the South, teaching that resistance to the Constitution is obedience to God. Professors had gone so far as to give aid and encouragement to robbers and assassins.[31] Since the South possessed no great educational center which would draw together young men from all the slaveholding states, a university to fight Northern doctrine and to promote Southern unity was a political necessity. Moreover, there were too few Southern colleges to meet the needs of Southern youth; and the education they offered was superficial. "Our system . . . is notoriously defective, our standards too low."[32] To raise them, the author recommended the establishment in the South of a central university "in which all the States shall have a direct and immediate interest."[33] It should be organized "upon the most extensive scale, the most thorough and comprehensive basis; let merit and scholarship, not money and time, be the means by which degrees may be obtained; and let the course of study be so complete and thorough, that the various colleges may hold to it the same relation which the preparatory schools all over the country hold to them."[34] The writer estimated the cost of founding and endowing the university at $5,000,000, a sum which he felt certain could be easily raised through taxation of land, other property, and population. Even $10,000,000 would not be a great burden for fourteen sovereign states.[35]

This scheme may be dismissed as a historical curiosity; but a second project, the University of the South, had some early success before it was virtually destroyed by the Civil War. In the summer of 1856, Leonidas Polk, the Episcopal Bishop of Louisiana, addressed a letter to his colleagues, the Bishops of North and South Carolina, Georgia, Florida, Tennessee, Alabama, Mississippi, Arkansas, and Texas. Polk suggested that a university be established under the auspices of the portion of the Episcopal church represented by their dioceses. While abroad in 1831 Polk had first had a distinct idea of a great Southern university. Believing in the need for liberal education for professional men and seeing the unhappy result of isolating technical schools, he had found in the English and Continental universities an approximation to his own ideas. The foreign centers of higher learning had taught him how important universities could be to a nation and how serious was America's lack of them. A university could nourish a Christian, agricultural aristocracy, which the Bishop considered an essential ingredient of a stable society.[36]

By 1856 Polk's sectional loyalty was fully developed. In his opinion a crisis was at hand. Although the dominance of the Northern seminaries and presses was not inevitable, the South was dangerously dependent upon the North for its clergy and for its ideas. Writing privately to a friend, Polk said: "We must either receive or make impressions. We have done our share of receiving! The time has fully come when we should enter upon the work of making aggression as the very essence of our commission. Educational establishments in all departments are the universally recognized arsenals whence available armor is to be drawn for that sort of campaigning, and a sorry plight we shall find ourselves in presently, cut off from those whence we have been accustomed to draw, with no alternative of our own in reserve. . . . I see nothing left us but to unite at once, and hastily, for the common defense."[37] The prospect encouraged Polk to expect success from united action; for the temper of churchmen and the outside public was ripe for such a movement. The Southern mind was being forced back upon itself. Although parents wanted their children to be educated, they were unwilling to send them North; and the Southern colleges were inadequate. The very magnitude of a project seeking to provide everything required for education would be its claim to the confidence and support of the public.[38]

Although Polk's letter to the bishops was less passionate than his private correspondence, it did reveal his uneasiness and his distrust of Northern influence. "In the minds of many, they [institutions in Southern dioceses] are not upon a scale sufficiently extended or full to offer advantages comparable to those to be had abroad, or at the institutions of highest grade in the Northern States of our Union; and, for that reason, are set aside, and our children are expatriated or sent off to an inconvenient distance, beyond the reach of our supervision or parental influence, exposed to the rigors of an unfriendly climate, to say nothing of other influences not calculated, it is to be feared, to promote their happiness or ours."[39]

Following a discussion of Polk's proposal at the General Convention of the Episcopal Church, held in Philadelphia in October, 1856, the Southern bishops present resolved to attempt the founding of a comprehensive university, which would not supplant existing colleges. The bishops believed that since the American experiment in government turned entirely on the intelligence and morality of the masses of the population, the responsibility of originating and sustaining enlightening institutions was clear and imperative:[40] "If there ever was a time in the history of our republic at which good men were called upon more than at another, to unite upon efforts to found such Institutions, the present is that period. At no time in all the past, have we been so threatened with the spread of the wildest opinions in religion and government; and at no period, therefore, has there been so great a call to put into operation and multiply agencies, whose high conservatism shall furnish us with the means of making fast the foundations of the State, securing a sound and healthy feeling in the social condition, and preserving in their integrity the great truths of our holy religion."[41]

Tentative articles of organization drawn up by the bishops were approved by the conventions of the ten dioceses concerned in the project; and a Board of Trustees, consisting of the bishop, one other clergyman, and two laymen from each diocese were chosen.[42] In July, 1857, the Trustees met at Lookout Mountain, Tennessee, and adopted a declaration of principles for the practical management of the enterprise. The University should not be opened until at least $500,000 had actually been secured. Funds subscribed would be regarded as capital, in general not to be touched either for organizing or operating the University.[43]

At a subsequent meeting the Trustees appointed Bishops Polk and Elliott as commissioners to canvass for subscriptions. The two bishops acknowledged the fact that the South already had many colleges but went on to point out that this very situation had prevented any one of them from attaining the highest rank.[44] An institution of this caliber was precisely what they proposed; and in doing so, they sought to lift their proposal above the level of sectarianism. The need of the whole South, not that of the Episcopal church, was their theme. By founding a university, they said, "we shall secure for the South a Literary centre, a point at which mind may meet mind, and learning encounter learning, and the wise, and the good, and the cultivated, may receive strength and polish, and confidence, and whence shall go forth a tone that shall elevate the whole country. We, of all men, should be the most highly cultivated, because we have the most leisure. Labor is performed among us by a caste, and there is, in consequence, a large body of men, who can devote themselves to the elegancies of literature, and to such a culture as shall make their homes the envy of all lands. The world is trying hard to persuade us that a slaveholding people cannot be a people of high moral and intellectual culture. . . . Never was there a grosser error than this."[45] After reviewing the slaveholding character of Hebrew, Greek, and Roman civilizations, the commissioners answered the question: "Upon what has been reared the literary greatness of our fatherland?" "Upon her classification of society, and upon her Collegiate arrangements which have enabled a portion of her people to devote themselves, without interruption, to literary pursuits. This great advantage we possess by means of that very institution which is supposed to check literary progress. And we should now begin to use it. Hitherto the South has been expending herself—enlarging her borders, and working up her resources—'mewing,' as Milton grandly expresses it, 'her mighty youth,'—but now should she find time for nobler things, and enter upon a friendly and glorious rivalry with the rest of the world in letters and culture. There is secured to us by the Constitution of the United States, the most perfect liberty of thought and expression; we have that division of classes which makes one a laboring and the other a dominant class—one a working and the other a thinking and governing class; we possess through our monopoly of some of the greatest agricultural staples of the world, sources of unbounded wealth. What more do we need? nothing but the perception of our own resources—but the determination to assert our rightful place among the learned of the earth—but the will to lay aside petty differences and unite upon a grand foundation for letters and religion."[46]

A university, conceived in this spirit, would not conflict with already established colleges. "The existing institutions will continue to supply and advance the scholarship which they are now giving. They will be the sources whence we shall derive much of our strength and our influence. When their students shall have graduated, if we can offer them a maturer cultivation, they will spend additional years at the University; if they intend to devote themselves to literature and the sciences, they will take up their residence in its neighborhood, and have free access to its libraries, its collections, its lecture rooms."[47]

While cash, securities, or pledges for the necessary $500,000 endowment were being rapidly collected, largely from Louisiana, the practical organization of the University went forward. Polk was put at the head of a committee to draft a constitution and a code of statutes. With the assistance of the United States government and its foreign embassies, a mass of information on higher education in America and abroad was accumulated. Among these papers were books from France and Prussia and from Oxford and Cambridge.[48] Polk's attitude toward this "valuable cargo" was discriminating. "I trust [he wrote to Elliott concerning books received from abroad], . . . that when we come to their examination we shall deal with them neither in the spirit of servile copyists, nor yet with that ridiculous modern conceit which affects superiority to the lessons of experience; but that, with an eye to the peculiarities of our national and local circumstances and necessities, we will give to everything its appropriate value, take what meets our own case, and leave the rest alone."[49] The drafting committee also benefited from personal inspection of American institutions at work.[50]

The admittedly eclectic system[51] embraced in the Constitution and Statutes was financially generous and academically ambitious. The annual salary of the Vice-chancellor, or active head of the institution, was set at $6,000. He was also to be furnished a house. Professors were to receive a fixed sum of $3,000 and a house. In addition to this they were entitled to accept fees from students totaling not more than $2,000. Assistant professors would also receive a salary and lodging.[52]

Structurally the University was divided into schools, their number to be increased as expediency and the progress of letters, science, and art suggested. The schools specified were:

1. Greek language and literature.
2. Latin language and literature.
3. Mathematics.
4. Physics.
5. Metaphysics.
6. History and archaeology.
7. Natural sciences.
8. Geology, mineralogy, and paleontology.
9. Civil engineering, construction, architecture, and drawing.
10. Theoretical and experimental chemistry.
11. Chemistry applied to agriculture and the arts.
12. Theory and practice of agriculture.
13. Moral science and evidences of the Christian religion.
14. English language and literature.
15. French language and literature.
16. German language and literature.
17. Spanish language and literature.

18. Italian language and literature.
19. Oriental language and literature.
20. Philosophy of language.
21. Philosophy of education.
22. Rhetoric, criticism, elocution, and composition.
23. American history and antiquities.
24. Ethnology and universal geography.
25. Astronomy and physical geography.
26. Political science, political economy, statistics, law of nations, spirit of laws, general principles of government, and the Constitution of the United States.
27. Commerce and trade, including the history and laws of banking, exchange, insurance, brokerage and book-keeping.
28. Theology.
29. Law.
30. Medicine.
31. Mines and mining.
32. Fine arts, including sacred music.[53]

To qualify for an M.A. degree, a candidate had to pass an examination in the schools required for the Bachelor's degree—i.e., moral science and evidences of Christianity; Greek language and literature; Latin language and literature; mathematics; physics; and English language and literature. In addition he was obliged to complete successfully examinations in the schools of metaphysics; theoretical and experimental chemistry; political science; rhetoric, criticism, elocution, and composition; French language and literature; and German, Spanish, or Italian language and literature, as the student might elect. An accurate speaking knowledge of French was also mandatory.[54]

Once a man had taken his M.A. degree, he was eligible for a fellowship in one of the schools if he had excelled in any one of the following: Greek language and literature, English language and literature, physics, mathematics, metaphysics, chemistry, or natural sciences. Three resident fellows might be elected annually, for five-year terms. Each was to receive a yearly stipend of $500 and the use of a suite of rooms rent-free. He would also be permitted to offer private instruction to University pupils in return for fees fixed by the authorities.[55]

The site chosen for the University of the South was a high plateau at Sewanee, Tennessee, where the cornerstone of the central building was laid on October 9, 1860, before a crowd of over five thousand people. An oration and many addresses were delivered in honor of the occasion. One of the speakers was the president of the University of Mississippi, Frederick A. P. Barnard, who described the new University as one "in which not merely the rudiments of knowledge shall be taught, but every branch of letters and science might be pursued throughout all its ramifications, and aids may be furnished for the independent research and original investigation by which the boundaries of the field of knowledge may be carried forward into the region of the still unknown."[56]

If the University had been allowed to develop in peace, Barnard would not improbably have become its first head. Polk approved of him, and Bishop Green of Mississippi was an enthusiastic advocate of his early appointment so that he might travel abroad to visit foreign institutions on behalf of the University. "You shall be President . . . if I can make you so,"[57] said Green to Barnard, who actually began to form his staff. Later Barnard came to fear that the new University might turn out to be a dream like " 'Direct Trade with Europe,' 'Norfolk Steam Ferries,' *et id genus omne*";[58] but in the fall of 1860 he was optimistic.

At the time when the University of the South was first projected, Barnard was primarily concerned with undergraduate education. A statement prepared in 1854, while he was professor at the University of Alabama, revealed little interest in graduate studies although it did exhibit his impression that the American colleges, sometimes called universities, were comparable not to the German university, but to the gymnasium.[59] The emphasis of an address, *On Improvements Practicable in American Colleges*, delivered in 1855, was still upon the undergraduate course. Like the faculty of Yale, from which he had been graduated in the memorable year of 1828, Barnard feared that reform along certain lines would endanger the very essence of the college, the proper function of which was to train the mind. He heard practical men, "dazzled by the splendor" of scientific achievement, demanding that the college fit men for occupations.[60] A smaller group, who had pursued the study of letters or science farther than most men, felt a lack "of those aids to higher acquisitions and profounder learning which they see so abundantly to exist in foreign lands."[61] To satisfy both sides, Barnard said, the colleges had arrived at a compromise which pleased no one. Specifically, the curriculum had been greatly extended to include many subjects not of a disciplinary nature. This Barnard could not abide. He saw two possible remedies—to lengthen the period allotted to undergraduate study or to throw much of the work of the first, or perhaps the first and second years, back upon the preparatory schools. Only in the latter case could the colleges approach the foreign universities in plan.[62]

Entertaining such ideas as these, Barnard was ready to be impressed by the advantages of a postgraduate course; and in 1858 he suggested one to the Trustees of the University of Mississippi, of which he had become president in 1856. It was vain, he argued, to remain deaf to the popular demand for knowledge; for it could be obtained nowhere if not in the colleges. At the same time the University curriculum had accumulated so many subjects that the student could spend only five weeks on one of them. Elsewhere various systems had been set up to meet similar situations. Parallel courses had been tried at Brown, Rochester, Union, and to some extent at Harvard. At the University of Virginia, students were allowed to select departments of study. In some cases extra-collegiate departments, devoted chiefly to theoretical and practical science, had been created. Finally the disposition to relieve the undergraduate course had "manifested itself in the establishment, in a college which had previously presented but a single course of study, terminating in the degree of Bachelor of Arts, of a second course intended to commence where the first ends, and leading to the higher degree of Master of Arts."[63] Barnard identified this experiment as that under way at Columbia College, and he pointed out that James H. Thornwell, lately president of the South Carolina College, had written an article advocating exactly the same arrangement. Provision for an advanced degree had been made at Brown and at the University of Virginia. Since this system was clearly in accord with the contemporary spirit of progress and had in effect been tried, the expediency of adopting it could hardly be problematical.

Barnard specifically suggested that the studies then pursued in the University of Mississippi be divided into two distinct and separate courses. "The sub-graduate course may be defined by the very simple process of excluding from the curriculum of study as it stands at present, all those branches of science which are confessedly modern additions, and along with these, the modern languages. This course will, therefore, as reconstructed, embrace the English, Latin, and Greek languages, all the elementary branches of the pure Mathematics, the mechanical branches of Natural Philosophy, Logic, Rhetoric, the principles of Criticism, Moral and Mental Philosophy, Composition, and Elocution. These several branches of study are to be pursued to something like the extent and with something like the thoroughness contemplated in the earlier period of the history of our collegiate instruction."[64] To these courses some chemistry and "the subjects of Natural Philosophy, not strictly mechanical" might be added in the concluding year; but these extra subjects were to be taught in outline only and were not to be tested by examination for the Bachelor's degree.[65] "To the post-graduate department [Barnard continued], may be turned over those branches of science and letters which are excluded from the former [the subgraduate department], and which are confessedly at present, but imperfectly taught; and the number of these may from time to time be increased, by adding new ones as the wants of the public and the growing resources of the University may demand or justify. Thus, it *may* immediately include Astronomy, Geology, Mineralogy, Chemistry, Natural Philosophy, Meteorology, Civil Engineering, the higher branches of the pure Mathematics, Greek and Roman Letters, the Modern Languages and their Literature, Political Economy, International Law, Constitutional Law, and the History of Philosophy; but it probably *will* include at first only such of this list as are most practical in their nature."[66]

Barnard deliberately contrived this duality; for the undergraduate and postgraduate departments represented quite separate phases of education. "If education has really two great and broadly distinguished functions to fulfill—to operate on the mind itself, and to furnish it with material for its own future operations—to draw out or *educe* its faculties, and to supply the same faculties with the aliment which is to maintain their subsequent vigor—and if nature herself points out the order in which these functions should succeed each other, why should we disregard her obvious indications, or neglect to conform our practice, as well to the dictates of common sense as to the principles of a sound philosophy?"[67] In other words, Barnard used a psychological argument to justify the two-story university. Once its character had been recognized, he said: "We shall feel ourselves bound, in short, to rise above the grade of the German gymnasium—which is precisely our grade of to-day—and to assume, by approaches, which the force of circumstances may indeed make gradual, but which must be no less steady and persevering, the character of the German university."[68]

This general line of thought may have resulted in part from Barnard's shift from a professorship to a university presidency.[69] On his own testimony, it was also reinforced by Thornwell's challenging *Southern Quarterly Review* critique of his 1855 address. Thornwell had asserted that the American college was a mixture of gymnasium and university. "From its first establishment in the country, all its arrangements have been made with the evident design of achieving both ends. It is the last stage of a liberal education. It is presumed, not only to have trained the mind, but to have awakened the spirit of liberal inquiry; to have given a taste of the sweets of knowledge, and to have inspired the honourable ambition of seeking it as at once the health and beauty of the soul."[70] This theory, Thornwell continued, was the key to the enormous exactions of the course of study, the secret of the magnificent promises to teach all that can be known. The colleges undertook "to do what in Germany is done by different institutions, and institutions organized upon different principles; and when we are required to state the specific function of an American college we should never overlook this peculiarity of their structure."[71] Barnard had evidently seen and felt this but had not explicitly announced it. He had attributed the gymnastic function to the colleges, and he had also made recommendations which presupposed the other function. "But still, with him [said Thornwell], this other function is something foreign, something that does not enter into the essential idea of the college, and something introduced rather from a concession to the spirit of the age, than from the nature of the thing. Let it, then, be distinctly understood, that this is a part of the work which our colleges propose to do; that they are treasuries of knowledge as well as halls of discipline: let this be explicitly stated and clearly apprehended; and then the question arises as to the arrangements by which both functions can be most successfully performed. Mr. B.'s suggestion, that a longer time is required, is too obvious to admit of doubt; and the other suggestion, that a better preparation, previously [*sic*] to entering, is desirable, is equally undeniable. But shall the college undertake to discharge both offices synchronously? Shall it carry on, side by side, a set of studies which are taught for the purpose of awakening the energy, and another for the purpose of imparting the matter of thought?"[72]

For Thornwell, an affirmative answer was a grievous mistake. The American colleges had "absurdly blended what should be kept asunder" in an unnatural combination.[73] Instead he recommended the introduction of two separate and distinct courses in the college, which might be called the "gymnastic and the liberal."[74] The first would cover three years, while the duration of the second would depend upon the number of studies pursued. They should consist of those which a man of letters or science might desire. The gymnastic course would entitle one to the first arts degree, the liberal course to the second. Only those who had completed the former course should be allowed to enter the latter. "This arrangment would fulfil the conditions involved in the notion of an American college. It would have all the advantages, without the inconveniences of what is usually understood to be the university plan."[75] A voluntary course after a gymnastic curriculum would adapt the college to "the spirit and demands of the age."[76]

With educational thought turning in this direction and with the accumulation of funds at Sewanee, the South of 1860 seemed ready to produce a graduate school. Then the war began; and the original form of the University of the South was all but obliterated. Its buildings and records were burned; its endowment disappeared; Leonidas Polk was killed in action during 1864 while serving as a general in the Confederate army. In the same year Frederick A. P. Barnard became president of Columbia, the nascent university of which he had spoken so favorably in 1858.

XI

The Early Traditions of Graduate Education

THE anxieties of the Civil War did not override all thought for graduate education. It found a strong advocate in Thomas Hill, who became president of Harvard College in the midst of the war; and Hill had the support of the Lazzaroni. Still, like other reform movements not directed at slavery, the cause of graduate education languished for several years after 1861. Even before that date it had displayed some symptoms of anemia, in part attributable to the depression of 1857. Had it been possible to avoid this decline, the work of the prewar champions of university reform might now be more fully appreciated than it is. What followed the war might seem less novel, although no less substantial, than it does.

What did the years before 1861 actually produce? The results of the thought and labor of the period certainly fell far short of the hopes for it. No great American University materialized; and no established college could claim to be a strong competitor of the European universities. No literary classic comparable to John Henry Newman's *The Idea of a University* appeared to persuade Americans that, if they could not found great universities, they could at least write winningly about them. The achievement of the prewar reformers was to establish a tradition of aspiration and experimentation.

When Goldwin Smith arrived in the United States in 1869, he found university affairs in a state of crisis and transition.[1] Although he had been familiar with a similar situation in Great Britain, he, perhaps, did not realize that crisis in academic matters was not new in America. The condition had developed at least as early as the Twenties when the University of Virginia opened its door, George Ticknor agitated Harvard, and Yale formulated the doctrine of slow progress. The criticism of the college which came to full tide at that time ebbed slightly and then rose again. Flood level was reached by 1856.

129

The difficulties in which higher education found itself were very serious. In the face of the expansion of knowledge, Professor James L. Kingsley of Yale argued that the "number of books necessary to exhibit the great facts and principles of human knowledge ... is not great";[2] but Yale itself recognized that natural science, so ably taught by its own Sillimans as well as others, could not be entirely ignored. For every man who believed that the existing curriculum offered too little, there was another who insisted that it had come to include too much. Even when a prescribed course was stretched to the utmost, it simply did not encompass all significant information or teach all the intellectual skills which the times seemed to demand. So long as Americans thought of themselves as colonials this was not an evil. From that point of view it was only common sense to accept as natural and inevitable the fact that American education was fragmentary. In 1816 John H. Smith, president of William and Mary College, could write, "the very few who may wish to study Nat: History, Botany, Comparative Anaty[.] &c had better go abroad where these subjects are better taught than it is *possible* (I speak literally) they can for ages be taught here."[3] Presently, however, reliance upon Europe became hateful as the absolute number of Americans attending foreign institutions increased. Patriotism demanded an American university without denying the undoubted academic preeminence of the European universities. Their excellence was a challenge and inspiration; but the American college could not solve its problem simply by copying the foreign universities, if for no other reason than the insistence of many presidents and professors on some form of prescribed, predominantly classical course as the core of the college.

The urgency of this situation produced the atmosphere in which the first traditions of graduate education evolved. All but the most reactionary educators admitted the need for transforming or augmenting contemporary higher education. To recognize the expansion of learning, the utility of science, and the desirability of keeping American students at home, and to maintain at the same time that a single, prescribed undergraduate course was sufficient was an unmitigated obscurantism which would not be tolerated. If the old-fashioned college could not cope with the new learning, it must surrender its unique position; it must give way to the American university. There was, however, no single, dominant idea of the American university. By 1861 it was apparent that to induce young men to undertake graduate study a practical incentive as well as a love of knowledge was required. Repeatedly, after 1850, educators pointed out the need for financial aid to advanced students, proposing fellowships on the English order but limiting them to a short term. This was one of the few proposals on which agreement was general. No single philosophy of education determined American thinking, nor did a single purpose give form to graduate study. Henry P. Tappan, for instance, had an almost religious faith in the cultivation of intellect for its own sake, whereas Charles Beck saw postgraduate work as professional education for career instructors.

Of the efforts to found universities in the United States, those which provided in some way for graduate work fall into three distinguishable but overlapping classes. Men like Benjamin Peirce thought of the university primarily as a repository of all knowledge, a living encyclopedia. Their chief desire was to assemble in one place the pre-eminent academic talent and some of the material resources which the multiplication of small colleges had scattered up and down the country. A characteristic advocacy of part-time teaching suggests that the promoters of a central university looked to the easy transportation offered by the new railroads as a partial solution to the problem of concentration; but it remained immense. The effort to found a great university in New York demonstrates the magnitude of the difficulties to be overcome; and in fact they were not overcome. This failure may explain Charles W. Eliot's disapproval of building a university *de novo*. When he said that there was "something childish in this uneasy hankering for a big university in America,"[4] his phrasing was perhaps uncharitable to earlier reformers; but history did seem to warrant skepticism.

Another view of the true character of a university was closely associated with Yale although it had its adherents everywhere. In New Haven a university was thought to consist of an undergraduate college to which were added distinct graduate courses or graduate schools, possibly with facilities for unmatriculated students. It resembled a combination of the German gymnasium and the German university but was comparable to neither alone. Such an institution allowed indefinite expansion of the university course-offering without compromising the conventional liberal arts curriculum, and it could come into being whenever one professor was prepared to teach advanced students. A handful of qualified instructors would constitute a university faculty as it did later at the Johns Hopkins under Daniel C. Gilman of Yale. If, however, the graduate school was considered as a mere pigeonhole for courses, the only common feature of which was their undesirability in the arts program, the higher department might lack unity and prestige. Without a

Gilman at its head, it could remain the stepchild of Alma Mater indefinitely.

The third policy is less easily discerned than the other two, but anticipations of it can be found in Ticknor's reforms and in Quincy's voluntary system. Here one can detect a tendency to give the college the intellectual stature and freedom of a university by expanding the subject matter of the liberal arts course and by loosening up the machinery of instruction so that, if Yale appeared to be a rising building in which one distinct unit was constructed upon another, Harvard resembled a plant, growing slowly but surely bigger until its very character seemed to change. As course was added to course and the colleges moved toward the elective system, the time approached when graduate study would be seen as the opportunity to study after commencement day what one had omitted before it. This view conformed to the apparently irresistible tendency of some nineteenth-century colleges to approximate universities with increased course-offerings and in the rising age-level of students.[5] In 1856 one observer noticed that every college "TENDS CONSTANTLY TO BECOME LARGER; more numerous in its teachers, more numerous in its scholars, better equipped with the apparatus of instruction, and more competent to give to larger numbers a more complete training."[6] In the following year, President Benjamin Hale of Hobart College remarked that Harvard was "growing into a true University."[7] Yet while the Harvard system, if such it can be called, established no artificial distinctions between the mental processes of college boy and university man, it ran the risk of slighting subjects or methods which had no conceivable place in a college. For better or for worse, the graduate student was tied to the undergraduate, a circumstance which could retard the progress of graduate education.

If one college or learned group had dominated higher education in the United States or if there had been a national ministry of education, one of these three policies might have been enforced to the exclusion of the other two. In the absence of central control, however, university experiments grew in wild profusion, producing a wealth of inconsistent precedents. The question of prerequisites for graduate study was never settled. According to the Yale doctrine, all advanced students possessed a single cultural background and commanded certain general intellectual disciplines; but graduates under an elective system might have little in common. Another discrepancy appeared when graduate study was sometimes discussed in terms of the higher branches of learning and at other times in terms of elementary knowledge which had no place in the college curriculum. There would of course be a great difference between a department teaching the higher mathematics that interested Benjamin Peirce and one devoted in part to the simpler French classics, which would have been quite consistent with F. A. P. Barnard's proposals. Was university work to be advanced in respect to the content of studies as well as to the status of the student? Was graduate study to be terminated by the taking of an advanced degree, or was it to be continuing education without a formal stopping-point? No final answers were given.

The era before 1861 also left unsolved a problem raised by the concept of the American university as a composite institution with graduate departments superimposed on an undergraduate college with a single, prescribed course. Even if a foreign precedent for discriminating sharply between secondary and higher studies had not existed, the Yale distinction between undergraduate and postgraduate study, between college and university, could have sprung from a desire to teach important new branches of learning, combined with devotion to the single prescribed arts course. When, however, an American was attracted to Göttingen or Berlin by their great learning, he found a two-story academic structure. Associating the scholarly excellence of the Germans with their educational arrangements, he might naturally insist with Professor Münche of Heidelberg that "it is essential, that the preparatory institutions (the *Colleges*,) should be *entirely separated* from the *University*; for they are essentially different in their character; and a union of elements so heterogeneous, would soon lead to the decay of both."[8] Yet the guardians of the college were not agreed that it should play a purely secondary role. Andrews Norton, for instance, opposed the Ticknor reforms in part because he was not sure but that they relegated the college to the level of a high school; and the Yale report of 1828 spoke not only of an analogy between college and gymnasium but also of raising admission requirements. George Ticknor quite frankly admitted that his system was a compromise; and in 1845 Charles Beck wrote: "Our colleges compared to the learned institutions of Germany, occupy a place between the gymnasia and universities, being generally similar to the three highest classes of the gymnasium and comprehending, also, some of the studies of the university."[9] James Thornwell insisted on the mixed character of the American system. If these views were correct, was a sharp distinction between college and university valid? Theoretically, any given institution might be one or the other; but colleges were competitors and tended to rise or to fall to a common level. If one college approximated a university, many probably would. Could the colleges as a class, then, be kept down? If not, was the composite university idea to be scrapped, or could a practical, although perhaps illogical, compromise be reached?

Such were the policies and the problems which the pre–Civil War generations passed down to guide the action and to tax the ingenuity of later times. Much was to happen before highly developed universities came into being. The early reformers had not agreed to make the Ph.D. degree the chief reward for graduate study. The seminar had hardly begun its career. Even research, although frequently mentioned and highly valued, had yet to receive the concentrated attention which later became a distinguishing mark of graduate studies. The prewar reformers left a great deal of unfinished business, but they set the agenda for change. Their experience taught what problems must be solved, their thinking established many of the terms within which others could seek solutions; and their zeal and imagination quickened the will to complete what they had started. "We begin our work . . . ," said Daniel C. Gilman as he took office at the Johns Hopkins University, "after costly ventures of which we reap the lessons, while others bear the loss."[10]

Bibliography

Academic reform was as controversial a subject before 1861 as it is today. Where differences of opinion are glossed over, the value and the interest of the record are relatively meager; but where discussion is frank, the history of theory and practice can have real substance, continuity, and significance. Candor is, of course, encountered most frequently in letters, particularly private ones, and diaries. Trustees and faculty minutes and reports, while sometimes rather bare, can be very revealing, as are many essays and speeches expounding the views of individual persons. Critical reviews of such material constitute another source, small but rich. Academic statutes, college catalogues, course announcements, and other official matter are a mine of information on the settled forms of education and in some cases contain expressions of policy and bits of historical narrative. They often fail, however, to suggest the agitation which may have preceded final decision on a course of action.

The "life and letters" variety of biography and the older histories of colleges and universities occupy a twilight zone between indubitable primary sources and the increasingly numerous works of modern scholars. Books of the former class contain documentary material and bits of information unobtainable elsewhere, but they may be based on reminiscence, hearsay, or other unverifiable evidence. The older accounts are weakened, too, by a rather general indifference to graduate education. More recent research is excellent when at its best. Yet in several cases an understandable but nonetheless uncritical loyalty to particular men or institutions has distorted the truth.[1] Unfortunately, too, modern writing on nineteenth-century education is marred by an inherited contempt for the unreformed college. The distaste of men who suffered from its undoubtedly grave faults has predisposed even later generations against the institution as a whole. The children of reform find it hard to judge fairly of the ancient regime.

Finally, the current literature of higher education occasionally displays an ideological partisanship leading to strained interpretation and error. When academic controversy is reduced largely to a simple conflict between conservatism and progressivism, the subtle actuality of some points at issue is obscured, if not entirely hidden. A false impression of black and white takes the place of such shading of opinion as one must assume was common in the past and as research indeed reveals.

Among secondary sources one must also mention a class of special studies, some on tangential matters like the college curriculum, others on graduate education. Several of the latter are only incidentally historical. What they provide is a catalogue of unrelated cases or a survey of general trends introducing a discussion of current problems or conditions. None deals thoroughly with the period before 1861.

The organization of this bibliography is self-explanatory for the most part. Material on specific institutions is arranged under these general headings: trustees and faculty minutes; reports and related documents; academic laws and regulations; catalogues and announcements; miscellaneous official papers; and unofficial writings bearing principally on the problems of the institutions in question. Reports, laws, and catalogues have been arranged chronologically. Such writings as educational addresses of wide importance are classified by themselves as their significance extends beyond institutional limits. Catalogues and similar publications issued regularly are listed under general series titles although exact titles may vary slightly from year to year. In a few cases, articles and like matter of great interest are listed in an appropriate place by themselves, although the educational periodical or manuscript collections in which they appear are listed as a whole elsewhere; but reports incorporated in official minutes have not usually been singled out unless they have at some time been printed separately.

All of the primary and secondary sources used in this book are recorded here as well as some other materials directly related to the matters discussed. This does not seem the place, however, to present an exhaustive bibliography of American higher education between 1787 and 1861 or of European university education as it affected the United States, although many books which would have a place in these lists have something to do with the subject of this study. Consequently, this bibliography does not cover all the literature on subjects such as Americans in foreign universities or the detailed history of the American colleges.

PRIMARY SOURCES

I. COLLECTIONS OF PAPERS ASSOCIATED WITH INDIVIDUAL MEN

UNPUBLISHED

Joel Barlow papers. In the Houghton Library, Harvard University.
Henry Barnard papers. In the New York University Library, Washington Square.
T. Romeyn Beck papers. In the New York State Library.
Joseph C. Cabell papers. In the University of Virginia Library.

James D. Dana papers. In the Yale University Library.
Day family letters. In the Yale University Library.
Jeremiah Day papers. In the Yale University Library.
Delafield papers. In the New York University Library, University Heights.
Edward Everett letter-books. In the Massachusetts Historical Society.
Albert Gallatin papers. In the New-York Historical Society.
Francis W. Gilmer papers. In the University of Virginia Library.
James Hall papers. In the New York State Museum.
Thomas Jefferson papers. In the Library of Congress.
Thomas Jefferson papers. In the University of Virginia Library.
Correspondence of Francis Lieber. In the Library of Congress.
Benjamin Peirce papers. In the American Academy of Arts and Sciences.
Benjamin Peirce papers. In the Harvard University Archives.
Josiah Quincy papers. In the Harvard University Archives.
Benjamin Silliman, Sr., papers. In the Yale University Library.
Joseph Story papers. In the Massachusetts Historical Society.
Charles Sumner papers. In the Houghton Library, Harvard University.
Henry P. Tappan papers. In the possession of Mrs. Louis Faulkner. Microfilm copies in the University of Michigan Historical Room.
Henry P. Tappan papers. In the University of Michigan Historical Room.
Thacher family papers. In the Bowdoin College Library.
George Ticknor letters. In the Boston Public Library.
George Ticknor papers. In the Harvard University Archives.

PUBLISHED

"The Jefferson Papers," *Collections of the Massachusetts Historical Society*, 7th Ser., I (1900), 1–377.

II. DIARIES

UNPUBLISHED

EVERETT, EDWARD. Diary, 1845–49. In the Massachusetts Historical Society.
[HOWARD, OLIVER O.]. "A Journal Kept by Oliver O. Howard," 1847–55. In the Oliver O. Howard papers, Bowdoin College Library.
Pearson diary, 1854–56. At Union College.
PIERCE, JOHN. Memoirs, Vol. IV: 1823–27. In the Massachusetts Historical Society.
SIBLEY, JOHN L. Private journal. In the Harvard University Archives.
STRONG, GEORGE T. Diary, 1850–60. Enlarged microfilm prints in the Columbiana Room, Columbia University.

PUBLISHED

HAMMOND, WILLIAM G. *Remembrance of Amherst: An Undergraduate's Diary, 1846–1848*. Edited by GEORGE F. WHICHER. New York, 1946.
STRONG, GEORGE T. *Diary*. Edited by ALLAN NEVINS and MILTON HALSEY THOMAS. 4 vols. New York, 1952.

III. INSTITUTIONAL RECORDS

Columbia University

Minutes

Columbia College, Minutes of the Trustees of Columbia College, 1850–63, Vols. IV², V¹, V². Typed copy in the Columbiana Room, Columbia University.

Reports

Report of a Committee of the Trustees of Columbia College, Appointed To Inquire into the Condition of the Institution, and To Consider Such Measures as Might Be Judged Expedient To Increase Its Efficiency and Usefulness. New York, 1858.

Miscellaneous Official Documents

UNPUBLISHED

College Papers, 1854, 1857. In the Columbiana Room, Columbia University.

PUBLISHED

[COMMITTEE OF SEVEN]. *Circular Questionnaire.* December, 1852. Copy in the Columbiana Room, Columbia University.
Letter to Faculty Members of Columbia College from Committee on College Course. Printed circular, March 22, 1854.
Statements, Opinions, and Testimony Taken by the Committee of Inquiry, Appointed by the Trustees of Columbia College. New York, 1857.

Unofficial Writings

[RUGGLES, SAMUEL B.]. *The Duty of Columbia College to the Community, and Its Right To Exclude Unitarians from its Professorships of Physical Science.* New York, 1854.

Harvard University

Minutes

College Records, 1819–27, 1827–36, 1836–47, 1857–66. 4 vols. In the Harvard University Archives.
[Lawrence Scientific School]. Faculty Records, 1848–71. In the Harvard University Archives.
Records of the Overseers of Harvard College, 1830–47. In the Harvard University Archives.

Reports

UNPUBLISHED

Condition of College, 1821 and 1824. In the Harvard University Archives.
Report of Committee Appointed To Enquire into the Income and Expenses of the College, December 26, 1826. In the George Ticknor papers, 1819–35, Harvard University Archives.
Reports to the Overseers, 1831–33. In the Harvard University Archives.

PUBLISHED

KIRKLAND, JOHN T., for the Committee of the Corporation. *Statement of the Income of Harvard College and of the Manner in Which It Is Applied.* 1824.
[STORY, JOSEPH]. *Report.* Harvard University. This is the report of the committee of inquiry appointed July 24, 1823; report made on May 4, 1824.
[LOWELL, JOHN]. *Report of a Committee of the Overseers of Harvard College, January 6, 1825.* Cambridge, 1825.
Printed annual reports of the President of Harvard College, usually appearing in *Annual Reports of the President and Treasurer of Harvard College, 1830–61.* Cambridge.
[EVERETT, EDWARD]. *Report of the Committee of the Overseers of Harvard College Appointed To Visit the Lawrence Scientific School, in 1849.* Cambridge, 1850.

Statutes

Laws of Harvard College. Cambridge, 1820.

Statutes and Laws of the University in Cambridge, Massachusetts. Cambridge, 1825.

A Revision of the Statutes and Laws of the University at Cambridge. Cambridge, 1847.

A Revision of the Statutes and Laws of the University at Cambridge, Prepared To Be Submitted to the Corporation, for Whose Use It Is Privately Printed. Cambridge, 1848.

Catalogues

A Catalogue of the Officers and Students . . . 1846–47. Cambridge.

Miscellaneous Official Documents

College letters, 1846–47, 1848–49. EDWARD EVERETT. 2 vols. In the Harvard University Archives.

Corporation Papers, 1816–19 and 1846. 2 vols. In the Harvard University Archives.

Harvard College Papers, Vol. VIII, 1815–19. In the Harvard University Archives.

Harvard College Papers, 1831–33. In the Harvard University Archives.

Harvard College Papers, 2d Ser., 1831–33, 1845–46, 1846–47, 1847–48. (Vols. V, XIII–XV.) In the Harvard University Archives.

Outline of Rules and Regulations for a Philological Department. In the Harvard College Papers, 1831–33. In the Harvard University Archives.

Unofficial Writings

UNPUBLISHED

[BECK, CHARLES]. Recommendation and Plan of a Seminary for Classical Learning. In the Benjamin Peirce papers, American Academy of Arts and Sciences.

PEIRCE, BENJAMIN. Plan of a School of Practical & Theoretical Science, February 27, 1846. In the Harvard College Papers, 2d Ser., 1845–46 (Vol. XIII). In the Harvard University Archives.

TICKNOR, GEORGE. Remarks on College, August 20, 1823. In the George Ticknor papers, 1819–35. In the Harvard University Archives.

[TICKNOR, GEORGE]. Remarks Read by Mr. Ticknor at the Meeting, July 23, 1823. In the George Ticknor papers, 1819–35. In the Harvard University Archives.

PUBLISHED

[NORTON, ANDREWS]. *Remarks on a Report of a Committee of the Overseers of Harvard College Proposing Certain Changes, Relating to the Instruction and Discipline of the College.* Cambridge, 1824.

NORTON, ANDREWS. *Speech Delivered before the Overseers of Harvard College, February 3, 1825, in Behalf of the Resident Instructers [sic] of the College, with an Introduction.* Boston, 1825.

TICKNOR, GEORGE. *Remarks on Changes Lately Proposed or Adopted, in Harvard University.* Boston, 1825.

Union College

Minutes

Trustees Minutes, 1851–62. In the Union College Library.

Catalogues

Catalogue of the Officers and Students in Union College. . . . 1852–63. Schenectady.

Miscellaneous Official Documents

Trust Deed from Eliphalet Nott and Wife, to the Trustees of Union College. Dated Schenectady, January 28, 1854. In Union College Library.

University of Albany

Catalogues

Circular of the Scientific Department, Courses of Instruction for 1852. Albany, 1851.

Miscellaneous Official Documents

[BECK, T. ROMEYN, and KENNEDY, DUNCAN]. *Memorial Presented to the Legislature of the State of New-York, on Behalf of the Scientific Commission Convened at the Capitol, in the City of Albany, on the 19th Day of February, 1852, in Relation to a National University To Be Established in the State of New-York.*

University of the City of New York [New York University]

Minutes

Minutes of the First Meetings in Relation to a University, December–January, 1829–30. Typed copy in the New York University Library, University Heights.
Minutes of the Council of the University of the City of New York. Typed copy in the New York University Library, University Heights.

Reports

Reports of Chancellors, to 1838. In the New York University Library, University Heights.
Reports to New York State Regents, 1834–38. In the New York University Library, University Heights.

Statutes

The Constitution and Statutes for the Present Government of the University of the City of New York. First version. New York, 1831.
The Constitution and Statutes for the Present Government of the University of the City of New York. Revised version. New York, 1831.
The Statutes of the University of the City of New York. New York, 1832.
The Act of Incorporation with the Ordinances and By-Laws of the University of the City of New York, 1849.
The Charter, Ordinances, and By-Laws of the University of the City of New York. New York, 1849.

Catalogues

Announcements, University of the City of New-York, 1835, 1836, 1837. Copies in the New York University Library, University Heights.
Catalogue of the Officers, Alumni, and Statutes, of the University of the City of New York, 1839–1840. New York, 1840.
General Alumni Catalogue of New York University, 1833–1905. New York, 1906.

Miscellaneous Official Documents

UNPUBLISHED

[Council of the University of the City of New York.] [Petition] To the Honourable the Legislature of the State of New York in Senate and Assembly Convened. [The petition for an act of incorporation, which was passed in 1831.]

PUBLISHED

An Act Incorporating the University of the City of New York, Passed April 18, 1831. New York, 1831.

Circular, University of the City of New York. 1830.

Unofficial Writings

UNPUBLISHED

NOYES, WILLIAM C. Notes on Testimony before a Committee of Regents, 1839. In the New York University Library, University Heights.

PUBLISHED

GALLATIN, ALBERT. *The Writings of Albert Gallatin.* Edited by HENRY ADAMS. 3 vols. Philadelphia, 1879.

"New York University," *American Annals of Education and Instruction,* I (1831), 105–9.

"New York University," *American Annals of Education and Instruction,* II (1832), 531–35.

[NOYES, WILLIAM C.]. *An Exposition by the Council of the University of the City of New York, Respecting the Late Measures of Retrenchment Adopted in That Institution, and Which Led to the Dismissal of Some of the Professors in the Faculty of Science and Letters.* New York, 1838.

PROFESSORS OF THE FACULTY OF SCIENCE AND LETTERS. *History of the Controversy in the University of the City of New-York; with Original Documents and an Appendix.* New York, 1838.

[PROFESSORS OF THE FACULTY OF SCIENCE AND LETTERS]. *A Letter to the Councillors of the University of the City of New York: From the Professors of the Faculty of Science and Letters.* New York, 1838.

VETHAKE, HENRY; MULLIGAN, JOHN; and TORREY, JOHN. *An Exposition of the Reasons for the Resignation of Some of the Professors in the University of the City of New York.* New York, 1833.

[WAINWRIGHT, JONATHAN M.]. *Considerations upon the Expediency and the Means of Establishing a University in the City of New-York.* New York, 1830.

University of Michigan

Minutes

Faculty Minutes, 1852–59. 2 vols. In Michigan Historical Collections, Ann Arbor.

Reports

TAPPAN, HENRY P. *Report to the Board of Regents of the University of Michigan, Made November 15, 1853.* Ann Arbor, 1853.

University of Michigan Regents' Proceedings, with Appendixes and Index, 1837–1864. Ann Arbor, 1915.

Statutes

By-Laws of the Department of Science, Literature, and the Arts, Adopted by the Board of Regents, and Ordered Printed, June 25th, 1855. Ann Arbor, 1855.

Code of Rules and Regulations, for the Government of the University of Michigan, Adopted by the Board of Regents, July 19, 1848.

General Rules and Regulations, and By-Laws of the University of Michigan. Detroit, 1859.

Laws, Ordinances, By-Laws, and Regulations for the Government of the University of Michigan. Detroit, 1861.

Catalogues

Catalogue of the Corporation, Officers, and Students in the Departments of Medicine, Arts, and Sciences, of the University of Michigan, 1852–1853. Detroit, 1853.

Catalogue of the Officers and Students. . . . 1839–64. Ann Arbor.

University of Pennsylvania

Unofficial Writings

[ALLEN, GEORGE]. *Professor Allen's Remarks on the Letter and By-Law Reported November 3, 1852.* n.d.

FRAZER, JOHN F. Printed letter from John F. Frazer, University of Pennsylvania, to Alonzo Potter, January 1, 1853. Copy in the University of Pennsylvania Library.

[POTTER, ALONZO]. *Objections to a Re-organization of the University Considered.* Philadelphia, 1853.

POTTER, ALONZO. Printed letter from Alonzo Potter, Philadelphia, to Joseph R. Ingersoll, July 8, 1852. Copy in the University of Pennsylvania Library.

VETHAKE, HENRY. Printed letter from Henry Vethake, Philadelphia, to William M. Meredith, November 27, 1852. Copy in the University of Pennsylvania Library.

University of the South

Reports and Formal Appeals

Address of the Commissioners for Raising the Endowment of the University of the South. New Orleans, 1859.

An Address to the Members and Friends of the Protestant Episcopal Church in the Southern and South-western States. Philadelphia, 1856.

Report of the Committee of the Board of Trustees of the University of the South, Appointed To Prepare the Draft of a Constitution and Code of Statutes for the University. New Orleans, 1860.

Unofficial Writings

"Central Southern University," *DeBow's Review*, XXIII (1857), 490–503, 575–87.

"The Southern University," *DeBow's Review*, XXVIII (1860), 726–29. [Contains extract from *Mobile Register*.]

University of Virginia

Minutes

UNPUBLISHED

Minutes of the Faculty of the University of Virginia, Vol. I: April 12, 1825—July, 1827. Typed copy in the University of Virginia Library.

PUBLISHED

"An Exact Transcript of the Minutes of the Board of Visitors of the University of Virginia during the Rectorship of Thomas Jefferson," *Writings of Thomas Jefferson*, pp. 361–499. Edited by ALBERT E. BERGH. Washington, 1907.

Miscellaneous Official Documents

Sundry Documents on the Subject of a System of Public Education for the State of Virginia. Published by the President and Directors of the Literary Fund. Richmond, 1817.

Unofficial Writings

[CABELL, NATHANIEL F.]. *Early History of the University of Virginia, as Contained in the Letters of Thomas Jefferson and Joseph C. Cabell.* Richmond, 1856.

Correspondence of Thomas Jefferson and Francis Walker Gilmer, 1814–1826. Edited by RICHARD B. DAVIS. Columbia, S.C., 1946.

Western Reserve University

Minutes

Faculty Record, 1847. In the President's office, Western Reserve University.

Catalogues

Catalogue of the Officers and Students in the Western Reserve College. . . . 1847–52. Hudson, Ohio.

Yale University

Minutes

Corporation Records. [(1) Yale Corporation Records, Vol. I, to 1858. (2) Records of Corporation, Yale College, 1858——]. In Woodbridge Hall, Yale University.

Records of the Prudential Committee of the Corporation of Yale College, 1806–51. In Woodbridge Hall.

Reports

UNPUBLISHED

Prudential Committee Reports, 1852–1906. In Woodbridge Hall.

PUBLISHED

"Original Papers in Relation to a Course of Liberal Education," *American Journal of Science and Arts,* XV (1829), 297–351. [These papers constitute the bulk of the Yale report of 1828.]

Annual Report of the Visitors of the Sheffield Scientific School. 1865–71. New Haven. [The titles of individual reports vary.]

Catalogues

Catalogue of the Officers and Students in Yale College. . . . 1847–66. New Haven.

Miscellaneous Official Documents

UNPUBLISHED

Funds for Professorships, etc. [Apparently an extract from the Corporation Records for September, 1824.] In the Yale Memorabilia Room, Yale University Library.

Sheffield Scientific School, miscellaneous MSS. In the Rare Book Room, Yale University Library.

PUBLISHED

Proposed Plan for a Complete Organization of the School of Science, Connected with Yale College. New Haven, 1856.

WOOLSEY, THEODORE D., *et al. Appeal in Behalf of the Yale Scientific School, with an Appendix.* New Haven, 1856. [Contains as an appendix a reprint of DANIEL C. GILMAN, "Scientific Schools in Europe."]

Unofficial Writings

"Department of Philosophy and the Arts in Yale College," *American Journal of Education*, I (1855–56), 359–63.

SILLIMAN, BENJAMIN, [SR.]. "Notice of the Late Sheldon Clark, Esq., of Oxford, Connecticut," *American Journal of Science and Arts*, XLI (1841), 217–31.

IV. ADDRESSES, ESSAYS, AND SIMILAR WORKS ON HIGHER EDUCATION

UNPUBLISHED

QUINCY, JOSIAH. Inaugural Address. In the Harvard University Archives.

PUBLISHED

Addresses at the Inauguration of Daniel C. Gilman, as President of the Johns Hopkins University, Baltimore, February 22, 1876. Baltimore, 1876.

Addresses at the Inauguration of Mr. Charles King as President of Columbia College, New-York, on Wednesday, November 28, 1849, in the College Chapel. New York, 1849.

Addresses of the Newly-appointed Professors of Columbia College. New York, 1858. [Addresses by William Betts, Charles A. Joy, Francis Lieber, Charles Davies, Charles M. Nairne.]

AN ALABAMIAN. "An American University," *American Journal of Education*, III (1857), 213–16.

BACHE, ALEXANDER D. *Anniversary Address before the American Institute, of the City of New-York, at the Tabernacle, October 28th, 1856, during the Twenty-eighth Annual Fair.* New York, 1857.

BACHE, ALEXANDER D. "A National University," *American Journal of Education*, I (1855–56), 477–79.

[BARLOW, JOEL]. *Prospectus of a National Institution To Be Established in the United States.* Washington, 1806.

BARNARD, FREDERICK A. P. "Improvements Practicable in American Colleges," *Proceedings of the Fifth Session of the American Association for the Advancement of Education, Held at the City of New York, August 28th, 29th, 30th, and 31st, A.D. 1855*, pp. 55–82. Hartford, 1856.

BARNARD, FREDERICK A. P. *Letter to the Honorable, the Board of Trustees of the University of Mississippi.* Oxford, [Miss.], 1858.

BARNARD, FREDERICK A. P., and PRATT, JOHN W. *Report on a Proposition to Modify the Plan of Instruction in the University of Alabama, Made to the Faculty of the University.* New York, 1855.

BRISTED, CHARLES A. *Five Years in an English University.* 2 vols. New York, 1852.

DANA, JAMES D., "Science and Scientific Schools," *American Journal of Education*, II (1856), 349–74.

Discourses and Addresses at the Ordination of the Rev. Theodore Dwight Woolsey, LL.D. to the Ministry of the Gospel, and His Inauguration as President of Yale College, October 21, 1846. New Haven, 1846.

ELIOT, CHARLES W. "National University," *The Addresses and Journal of Proceedings of the National Educational Association, Session of the Year 1873, at Elmira, New York*, pp. 107–20. Peoria, 1873.

[ELIOT, CHARLES W.]. "The New Education: Its Organization," *Atlantic Monthly*, XXIII (1869), 203–20.

The English Universities in the North American Review. Albany, 1854.

EVERETT, EDWARD. "University Education," *Orations and Speeches on Various Occasions*, II, 493–518. Boston, 1865. [Everett's inaugural address at Harvard, 1846.]

[FENNO, JOHN]. "Importance of a proper system of education—Establishment of a federal university recommended," *American Museum*, VI (1789), 290–91.

GILMAN, DANIEL C. "Scientific Schools in Europe," *American Journal of Education*, I (1855–56), 315–28.

KNOX, SAMUEL. *An Essay on the Best System of Liberal Education, Adapted to the Genius of the Government of the United States*. Baltimore, 1799.

LINDSLEY, PHILIP. *An Address, Delivered in Nashville, January 12, 1825, at the Inauguration of the President of Cumberland College*.

LINDSLEY, PHILIP. *Speech in Behalf of the University of Nashville, Delivered on the Day of the Anniversary Commencement, October 4, 1837*. Nashville, 1837.

MERCER, CHARLES F. *A Discourse on Popular Education; Delivered in the Church at Princeton, the Evening before the Annual Commencement of the College of New Jersey, September 26, 1826*. Princeton, 1826.

PEIRCE, BENJAMIN. *Working Plan for the Foundation of a University*. [Cambridge], 1856.

PEIRCE, BENJAMIN, et al. "Remarks on a National University," *Proceedings of the Fifth Session of the American Association for the Advancement of Education, Held at the City of New York, August 28th, 29th, 30th, and 31st, A.D. 1855*, pp. 22–28. Hartford, 1856. [More easily available in *American Journal of Education*, II (1856), 86–92.]

POPKIN, JOHN S. *Three Lectures on Liberal Education*. Cambridge, 1836.

RUGGLES, SAMUEL B., et al. *Speeches in Behalf of the University of Albany*. Albany, 1852.

RUSH, BENJAMIN. "Address to the people of the united states [*sic*]," *American Museum*, I (1787; 3d ed., 1790), 8–11.

[RUSH, BENJAMIN]. *A Plan for the Establishment of Public Schools and Diffusion of Knowledge in Pennsylvania; to Which Are Added Thoughts upon the Mode of Education, Proper in a Republic*. Philadelphia, 1786.

RUSH, BENJAMIN. "Plan of a federal university," *American Museum*, IV (1788), 442–44.

SMITH, GOLDWIN. "University Education," *Journal of Social Science*, I (1869), 24–55.

SMITH, SAMUEL H. *Remarks on Education*. Philadelphia, 1798.

STORRS, RICHARD S., JR. "Colleges: A Power in Civilization, To Be Used for Christ," *American Journal of Education and College Review*, I (1856), 523–44.

TAPPAN, HENRY P. *A Discourse Delivered by Henry P. Tappan, D.D., at Ann Arbor, Mich., on the Occasion of His Inauguration as Chancellor of the University of Michigan, December 21st, 1852*. Detroit, 1852.

TAPPAN, HENRY P. *The Growth of Cities: A Discourse Delivered before the New York Geographical Society, on the Evening of March 15th, 1855*. New York, 1855.

TAPPAN, HENRY P. *The Progress of Educational Development: A Discourse Delivered before the Literary Societies of the University of Michigan, on Monday Evening, June 25, 1855*. Ann Arbor, 1855.

TAPPAN, HENRY P. "Progress of Educational Development in Europe," *Proceedings of the Fifth Session of the American Association for the Advancement of Education, Held at the City of New York, August 28th, 29th, 30th, and 31st,*

A.D. 1855, pp. 29–54. Hartford, 1856.

TAPPAN, HENRY P. *Public Education: An Address Delivered in the Hall of the House of Representatives, in the Capitol at Lansing, on the Evening of January 28th, 1857.* Detroit, 1857.

TAPPAN, HENRY P. *University Education.* New York, 1851.

TAPPAN, HENRY P. *The University: Its Constitution and Its Relations, Political and Religious: A Discourse Delivered June 22d, 1858, at the Request of the Christian Library Association.* Ann Arbor, 1858.

[WAYLAND, FRANCIS]. *Report to the Corporation of Brown University, on Changes in the System of Collegiate Education, Read March 28, 1850.* Providence, 1850.

WAYLAND, FRANCIS. *Thoughts on the Present Collegiate System in the United States.* Boston, 1842.

V. CRITICAL REVIEWS

[COGSWELL, JOSEPH]. Review of *On the Principles of English University Education* (William Whewell) and of Other Works. *New York Review*, VII (1840), 109–36.

"College-Instruction and Discipline," *American Quarterly Review*, IX (1831), 283–314.

[EVERETT, EDWARD]. Review of *Proceedings and Report of the Commissioners of the University of Virginia, Presented 8th December, 1818*, in *North American Review*, X (1820; 3d ed., 1822), 115–37.

"German Review of the Literary Convention at New York," *American Annals of Education and Instruction*, I (1831), 454–57.

[GILMAN, DANIEL C.]. "Four College Inaugurals, White, McCosh, Eliot, Porter, by a Graduate of Yale," *Christian Union*, V (January 31, 1872), 119–20.

[KINGSLEY, JAMES L.]. "Review of Dwight's *Travels in the North of Germany*," *Quarterly Christian Spectator*, I (1829), 631–74.

"Literary Institutions—University," *North American Review*, VII (1818), 270–78.

MÜNCHE, PROFESSOR. "On the Organization of Universities," translated from *Heidelberger Jahrbücher der Literatur*, No. 37, *American Annals of Education and Instruction*, I (1831), 457–61.

[PACKARD, ALPHEUS S.]. Review of *The Substance of Two Reports of the Faculty of Amherst College to the Board of Trustees, with the Doings of the Board Thereon*, in *North American Review*, XXVIII (new ser.; 1829), 294–311.

Review of CHARLES A. BRISTED, *Five Years in an English University*, in *North American Review*, LXXV (1852), 47–83.

Review of JOHN RUSSELL, *A Tour in Germany and Some of the Southern Provinces of the Austrian Empire, in the Years 1820, 1821, 1822*, in *North American Review*, XXVII (new ser.; 1828), 317–37.

[THORNWELL, JAMES H.]. "Barnard on American Colleges," *Southern Quarterly Review*, I (new ser.; 1856), 168–88.

VI. EDUCATIONAL PERIODICALS AND SERIAL PROCEEDINGS

American Annals of Education and Instruction (Boston). 1831–39. [A continuation of *American Journal of Education* (Boston), 1826–30.]

American Journal of Education (Boston). 1826–30.

American Journal of Education. Edited by HENRY BARNARD (Hartford). 1855–63.

American Journal of Education and College Review (New York). Vol. I (1855), edited by ABSALOM PETERS and HENRY BARNARD. Vol. II (1856), edited by ABSALOM PETERS.

American Quarterly Register (Boston). 1838–42.

Proceedings of the American Association for the Advancement of Education. 1851–55. 5 vols. Philadelphia, Newark, and Hartford, 1852–56.

VII. NEWSPAPERS

Albany Argus. 1851–53.
Albany Evening Atlas. 1851–53.
Albany Evening Journal. 1851–53.
New York American. 1829–30.
New York Commercial-Advertiser. 1830–33.

VIII. PUBLIC DOCUMENTS

"Bequest of James Smithson," *House of Representatives Executive Documents* (25th Cong., 3d sess.), II, No. 11 (December 10, 1838), 1–18.

Documents of the Board of Aldermen, of the City of New York, Vol. XXIII, Doc. No. 31 (July 7, 1856).

New York Assembly Journal. 1851–53.
New York Senate Journal. 1851–53.

IX. MISCELLANEOUS PRIMARY SOURCES

BACHE, ALEXANDER D. *Report on Education in Europe, to the Trustees of the Girard College for Orphans.* Philadelphia, 1839.

BLODGET, SAMUEL, JR. *Economica: A Statistical Manual for the United States of America, with Additions to the Beginning of the Year 1810.* Washington, 1810.

CALVERT, GEORGE H. *First Years in Europe.* Boston, 1866.

CHANNING, WILLIAM E. "Address on the Present Age," *Works of William E. Channing, D.D.* (8th ed.), VI, 145–82. Boston, 1848. [This address was originally delivered in 1841.]

[COLLEGE OF CALIFORNIA TRUSTEES AND HORACE BUSHNELL]. *Movement for a University in California.—A Statement to the Public, by the Trustees of the College of California, and an Appeal, by Dr. Bushnell.* San Francisco, 1857.

[COLUMBIAN COLLEGE]. *A Catalogue of the Officers and Students of Columbian College, District of Columbia. . . .* 1855–61. Washington. [The catalogue for 1855–56 indicates requirements for an earned M.A. degree.]

DWIGHT, HENRY E. *Travels in the North of Germany, in the Years 1825 and 1826.* New York, 1829.

GREENE, BENJAMIN F. *The Rensselaer Polytechnic Institute. Its Reorganization in 1849–50; Its Condition at the Present Time; Its Plans and Hopes for the Future.* Troy, New York, 1855.

HALL, BASIL. *Travels in North America in the Years 1827 and 1828.* 3 vols. Edinburgh, 1829.

Journal of the Proceedings of a Convention of Literary and Scientific Gentlemen, Held in the Common Council Chamber of the City of New York, October, 1830. New York, 1933; facsimile of edition of 1831.

LYELL, SIR CHARLES. *Travels in North America; with Geological Observations on the United States, Canada, and Nova Scotia.* 2 vols. New York, 1845.

[MOTLEY, JOHN L.]. *Morton's Hope; or the Memoirs of a Provincial.* 2 vols. New York, 1829.

"New-Haven Gymnasium," *American Journal of Education,* III (1828), 115–16.

Proceedings of the American Association for the Advancement of Science, Sixth Meeting, Held at Albany (N.Y.), August, 1851. Washington, 1852.

RHEES, WILLIAM J. (ed.). *The Smithsonian Institution: Documents Relative to Its Origin and History*. 2 vols. Washington, 1901.

TOCQUEVILLE, ALEXIS DE. *Democracy in America*. Edited by PHILLIPS BRADLEY. 2 vols. New York, 1945.

[UNIVERSITY OF ROCHESTER]. *Report to the Board of Trustees of the University of Rochester on the Plan of Instruction To Be Pursued in the Collegiate Department*. September 16, 1850. Rochester, N.Y., 1850.

Washington Directory. Compiled by JUDAH DELANO. Washington, 1822.

SECONDARY SOURCES

I. GRADUATE EDUCATION

CAPEN, SAMUEL P., and ZOOK, GEORGE F. *Opportunities for Study at American Graduate Schools*. Washington, 1921.

DEFERRARI, ROY J. "The Origin and Development of Graduate Studies under Catholic Auspices." In ROY J. DEFERRARI (ed.), *Essays on Catholic Education in the United States*, 195–215. Washington, 1942.

HOLLIS, ERNEST V. *Toward Improving Ph.D. Programs*. Washington, 1945.

HORTON, BYRNE J. *The Graduate School (Its Origin and Administrative Development)*. New York, 1940.

JOHN, WALTON C. *Graduate Study in Universities and Colleges in the United States*. Washington, 1935.

KRAUS, CHARLES A. "The Evolution of the American Graduate School," *American Association of University Professors Bulletin*, XXVII (1951), 497–505.

PIERSON, MARY B. *Graduate Work in the South*. Chapel Hill, N.C., 1947. [This book refers to several pre–Civil War provisions for graduate work in the South which it has not been possible to study for the purposes of this book.]

PIERSON, W. W. "The Past, Present, and Future of the Graduate School," *The Graduate School of the University of North Carolina Research and Publications*, pp. 3–55. Edited by EDGAR W. KNIGHT and AGATHA B. ADAMS. Chapel Hill, N.C., 1946.

RYAN, W. CARSON. *Studies in Early Graduate Education: The Johns Hopkins, Clark University, the University of Chicago*. New York, 1939.

II. HISTORIES OF COLLEGES AND UNIVERSITIES

UNPUBLISHED

BOWDITCH, NATHANIEL. [Harvard] College History. In the Harvard University Archives.

PUBLISHED

ADAMS, ELIZABETH S. "The Administration of Henry Philip Tappan," *The University of Michigan: An Encyclopedic Survey*, Part I, pp. 39–52. Edited by WILFRED B. SHAW. Ann Arbor, 1941.

BAKER, RAY P. *A Chapter in American Education; Rensselaer Polytechnic Institute, 1824–1924*. New York, 1925.

BALDWIN, EBENEZER. *Annals of Yale College, in New Haven, Connecticut, from Its Foundation, to the Year 1831*. New Haven, 1831.

BECKER, CARL L. *Cornell University: Founders and the Founding*. Ithaca, 1943.

BRONSON, WALTER C. *The History of Brown University, 1764–1914*. Providence, 1914.

BRUCE, PHILIP A. *History of the University of Virginia, 1819–1919; the Lengthened Shadow of One Man*. 5 vols. New York, 1920–22.

CHEYNEY, EDWARD P. *History of the University of Pennsylvania, 1740–1940.* Philadelphia, 1940.

CHITTENDEN, RUSSELL H. *History of the Sheffield Scientific School of Yale University, 1846–1922.* 2 vols. New Haven, 1928.

COON, HORACE. *Columbia, Colossus on the Hudson.* New York, 1947.

DEXTER, BENJAMIN F. *Biographical Sketches of the Graduates of Yale College, with Annals of the College History.* 6 vols. New Haven, 1912.

DEXTER, FRANKLIN B. *Sketch of the History of Yale University.* New York, 1887.

DUTCHER, GEORGE M. *An Historical and Critical Survey of the Curriculum of Wesleyan University and Related Subjects.* Middletown, Conn., 1948.

ELLIS, JOHN T. *The Formative Years of the Catholic University of America.* Washington, 1946.

FAIRBANKS, GEORGE R. *History of the University of the South, at Sewanee, Tennessee, from Its Founding by the Southern Bishops, Clergy, and Laity of the Episcopal Church in 1857 to the Year 1905.* Jacksonville, 1905.

FARRAND, ELIZABETH M. *History of the University of Michigan.* Ann Arbor, 1885.

FRENCH, JOHN C. *A History of the University Founded by Johns Hopkins.* Baltimore, 1946.

FUESS, CLAUDE M. *Amherst.* Boston, 1935.

GILMAN, DANIEL C. *The Sheffield Scientific School of Yale University: A Semicentennial Historical Discourse, October 28, 1897.* New Haven, 1897.

GREEN, EDWIN L. *A History of the University of South Carolina.* Columbia, 1916.

HASKINS, CHARLES H. "The Graduate School of Arts and Sciences, 1872–1929." In SAMUEL E. MORISON (ed.), *The Development of Harvard University since the Inauguration of President Eliot, 1869–1929,* pp. 449–62. Cambridge, 1930.

HASKINS, DAVID G. *A Brief Account of the University of the South.* New York, 1877.

A History of Columbia University, 1754–1904. New York, 1904.

JONES, THEODORE F., *et al. New York University, 1832: 1932.* New York, 1933. [Jones is the author of the chapters on the founding of the University, and its early years.]

KEPPEL, FREDERICK P. *Columbia.* New York, 1914.

KINGSLEY, WILLIAM L. *Yale College: A Sketch of Its History, with Notices of Its Several Departments, Instructors, and Benefactors, Together with Some Account of Student Life and Amusement.* 2 vols. New York, 1879.

MORISON, SAMUEL E. *The Founding of Harvard College.* Cambridge, 1935.

MORISON, SAMUEL E. *Harvard College in the Seventeenth Century.* 2 vols. Cambridge, 1936.

MORISON, SAMUEL E. *Three Centuries of Harvard, 1636–1936.* Cambridge, 1936.

QUINCY, JOSIAH. *The History of Harvard University.* 2 vols. Cambridge, 1840.

RUDY, S. WILLIS. *The College of the City of New York: A History, 1847–1947.* New York, 1949.

RUSSELL, WILLIAM F. (ed.). *The Rise of a University,* Vol. I. New York, 1937.

SHAW, WILFRED B. *The University of Michigan.* New York, 1920.

STEINER, BERNARD C. *The History of Education in Connecticut.* Washington, 1893.

TEN BROOK, ANDREW. *American State Universities, Their Origin and Progress: A History of Congressional University Land Grants, a Particular Account of the Rise and Development of the University of Michigan, and Hints toward the Future of the American University System.* Cincinnati, 1875.

WAITE, FREDERICK C. *Western Reserve University: The Hudson Era.* Cleveland, 1943.

WARREN, CHARLES H. "The Sheffield Scientific School from 1847 to 1947." In GEORGE A. BAITSELL (ed.), The Centennial of the Sheffield Scientific School, pp. 156–67. New Haven, 1950.

WERTENBAKER, THOMAS J. Princeton, 1746–1896. Princeton, 1946.

III. BIOGRAPHIES, AUTOBIOGRAPHIES, AND MEMOIRS

UNPUBLISHED

DUNAWAY, WAYLAND F. "Charles Fenton Mercer." A Master's degree thesis, Department of History, University of Chicago, 1917.

PUBLISHED

BURGESS, JOHN W. Reminiscences of an American Scholar: The Beginnings of Columbia University. New York, 1934.

CLARKE, JOHN M. James Hall of Albany, Geologist and Palaeontologist, 1811–1898. Albany, 1921.

CROSS, WILBUR L. Connecticut Yankee: An Autobiography. New Haven, 1943.

CUNNINGHAM, CHARLES E. Timothy Dwight, 1752–1817: A Biography. New York, 1942.

DAVIS, RICHARD B. Francis Walker Gilmer: Life and Learning in Jefferson's Virginia. Richmond, 1939.

DORFMAN, JOSEPH, and TUGWELL, REXFORD G. "Francis Lieber: German Scholar in America," Columbia University Quarterly, XXX (1938), 159–90, 265–93.

DORFMAN, JOSEPH, and TUGWELL, REXFORD G. "Henry Vethake: A Chapter in the Development of the Higher Learning in the United States," Columbia University Quarterly, XXV (1933), 335–64.

DWIGHT, TIMOTHY. Memories of Yale Life and Men, 1845–1899. New York, 1903.

FISHER, GEORGE P. Life of Benjamin Silliman, M.D., LL.D., Late Professor of Chemistry, Mineralogy, and Geology in Yale College. Chiefly from His Manuscript Reminiscences, Diaries, and Correspondence. 2 vols. New York, 1866.

FLEXNER, ABRAHAM. Daniel Coit Gilman, Creator of the American Type of University. New York, 1946.

FRANKLIN, FABIAN. The Life of Daniel Coit Gilman. New York, 1910.

"Frederick A. P. Barnard," American Journal of Education, V (1858), 753–80.

FREIDEL, FRANK. Francis Lieber, Nineteenth-Century Liberal. Baton Rouge, 1947.

FRIEZE, HENRY S. A Memorial Discourse on the Life and Services of Rev. Henry Philip Tappan, D.D., LL.D., President of the University from 1852 to 1863. [Ann Arbor], 1882.

FROTHINGHAM, PAUL R. Edward Everett, Orator and Statesman. Boston and New York, 1925.

FULTON, JOHN. Memoirs of Frederick A. P. Barnard. New York, 1896.

FULTON, JOHN F., and THOMSON, ELIZABETH H. Benjamin Silliman, 1779–1864, Pathfinder in American Science. New York, 1947.

[GILMAN, DANIEL C.] "James L. Kingsley, LL.D.," Congregational Quarterly, V (1863), 117–30.

GILMAN, DANIEL C. The Life of James Dwight Dana, Scientific Explorer, Mineralogist, Geologist, Zoölogist, Professor in Yale University. New York, 1899.

GOOD, HARRY G. Benjamin Rush and His Services to American Education. Berne, Ind., 1918.

GOODMAN, NATHAN G. Benjamin Rush, Physician and Citizen, 1746–1813. Philadelphia, 1934.

GOULD, BENJAMIN A., JR. An Address in Commemoration of Alexander Dallas Bache, Delivered August 6, 1868, before the American Association for the Advancement of Science. Salem, Mass., 1868.

HARLEY, LEWIS R. *Francis Lieber, His Life and Political Philosophy.* New York, 1899.

HILLARD, GEORGE S. *Life, Letters, and Journals of George Ticknor.* 2 vols. 8th ed. Boston, 1876.

HONEYWELL, ROY J. *The Educational Work of Thomas Jefferson.* Cambridge, 1931. [The appendixes of this work reproduce much documentary material.]

HOWE, M. A. DE WOLFE. *Classic Shades: Five Leaders of Learning and Their Colleges.* Boston, 1928. [Timothy Dwight, the elder; Mary Lyon; Mark Hopkins; James McCosh; Charles W. Eliot.]

HOWE, M. A. DE WOLFE. *Memoirs of the Life and Services of the Rt. Rev. Alonzo Potter, D.D., LL.D., Bishop of the Protestant Episcopal Church in the Diocese of Pennsylvania.* Philadelphia, 1871.

JAMES, HENRY, *Charles W. Eliot, President of Harvard University, 1869–1909.* 2 vols. Boston and New York, 1930.

LAND, WILLIAM G. *Thomas Hill, Twentieth President of Harvard.* Cambridge, 1933.

MATHEWS, JAMES M. *Recollections of Persons and Places, Chiefly in the City of New York; Being Selections from His Journal.* New York, 1865.

ODGERS, MERLE M. *Alexander Dallas Bache, Scientist and Educator, 1806–1867.* Philadelphia, 1947.

PALMER, B. M. *The Life and Letters of James Henry Thornwell, D.D., LL.D., Ex-president of the South Carolina College, Late Professor of Theology in the Theological Seminary at Columbia, South Carolina.* Richmond, 1875.

PARSONS, FRANCIS. *Six Men of Yale.* New Haven, 1939.

PEABODY, ANDREW P. *Harvard Reminiscences.* Boston, 1888.

PERRY, CHARLES M. *Henry Philip Tappan, Philosopher and University President.* Ann Arbor, 1933.

POLK, WILLIAM M. *Leonidas Polk, Bishop and General.* 2 vols. New York, 1893. [This biography contains transcripts of much original material on the University of the South.]

RAYMOND, ROSSITER W. *Peter Cooper.* Boston, 1901.

ROELKER, WILLIAM G. *Francis Wayland, a Neglected Pioneer of Higher Education.* Worcester, 1944.

ROGERS, WALTER P. *Andrew D. White and the Modern University.* Ithaca, 1942.

THOMPSON, D. G. BRINTON. *Ruggles of New York: A Life of Samuel B. Ruggles.* New York, 1946.

WHITE, ANDREW D. *Autobiography of Andrew Dickson White.* 2 vols. New York, 1905.

WOOLSEY, THEODORE S. "Theodore Dwight Woolsey—a Biographical Sketch," *Yale Review*, I (1912), 239–60, 453–70, 620–38.

IV. MISCELLANEOUS SECONDARY SOURCES

UNPUBLISHED

BOATFIELD, HELEN C., and PIERSON, GEORGE W. "Scholars of the House." A report presented to the Yale College Course of Study Committee, 1944.

PUBLISHED

BENNETT, CHARLES A. *History of Manual and Industrial Education up to 1870.* Peoria, 1926.

BUTTS, R. FREEMAN. *The College Charts Its Course: Historical Conceptions and Current Proposals.* New York, 1939.

COHEN, I. BERNARD. "Harvard and the Scientific Spirit," *Harvard Alumni Bulletin*, L (1948), 393–98.

Cowley, W. H. "The University in the United States of America." In Edward Brady (ed.), *The University outside Europe: Essays on the Development of University Institutions in Fourteen Countries.* Oxford, 1939.

Faust, Albert B. *The German Element in the United States, with Special Reference to Its Political, Moral, Social, and Educational Influence.* New York, 1927. [Vol. II, chap. v, "The German Influence on Education in the United States."]

Fox, Dixon R. "The Rise of Scientific Interests in New York." In Alexander C. Frick (ed.), *History of the State of New York,* Vol. IX. New York, 1937.

Gildersleeve, Basil L. "University Work in America and Classical Philology," *Essays and Studies, Educational and Literary,* pp. 87–123. Baltimore, 1890.

Gilman, Daniel C. "Bishop Berkeley's Gifts to Yale College," *Papers of the New Haven Colony Historical Society,* I (1865), 147–70. [Here Gilman presents several documents bearing on Bishop Berkeley's benefaction.]

Gilman, Daniel C. "Scientific Schools," *Johnson's (Revised) Universal Cyclopaedia* (1886 ed.), VII, 86–89.

Gilman, Daniel C. "University," *Johnson's Universal Cyclopaedia* (1895 ed.), VIII, 388–95.

Hansen, Allen O. *Liberalism and American Education in the Eighteenth Century.* New York, 1926.

Hinsdale, Burke A. "Notes on the History of Foreign Influence upon Education in the United States," *Report of the [United States] Commissioner of Education for the Year 1897–98,* I, 591–629. Washington, 1899.

Le Duc, Thomas H. A. *Piety and Intellect at Amherst College, 1865–1912.* New York, 1946.

Long, Orie W. *Literary Pioneers: Early American Explorers of European Culture.* Cambridge, 1935.

Quintard, Charles T. *An Address Delivered in St. Augustine's Chapel, Sewanee, Tenn., at the Meeting of the Board of Trustees of the University of the South on Thursday, July 31st, 1890.* New York, 1890.

Royce, Josiah. "Present Ideals of American University Life," *Scribner's Magazine,* X (1891), 376–88.

Schmidt, George P. "Intellectual Crosscurrents in American Colleges, 1825–1855," *American Historical Review,* XLII (1936–37), 46–67.

Schmidt, George P. *The Old Time College President.* New York, 1930.

Sears, Jesse B. *Philanthropy in the History of American Higher Education.* Washington, 1922. [Department of the Interior, Bureau of Education, Bull. 26 (1922).]

Snow, Louis F. *The College Curriculum in the United States.* New York, 1907.

Struik, Dirk J. *Yankee Science in the Making.* Boston, 1948.

Tewksbury, Donald G. *The Founding of American Colleges and Universities before the Civil War, with Particular Reference to the Religious Influences Bearing upon the College Movement.* New York, 1932.

Thwing, Charles F. *The American and the German University.* New York, 1928.

Thwing, Charles F., *A History of Higher Education in America.* New York, 1906.

Tuedt, Carl W. "A Brief History of the National University," *School and Society,* XXXIII (1931), 42–47.

Walz, John A. *German Influence in American Education and Culture.* Philadelphia, 1936.

Wills, Elbert V. *The Growth of American Higher Education.* Philadelphia, 1936.

Notes

CHAPTER I
THE SHORTCOMINGS OF THE COLLEGE

1. This accepted practice was not universal. For instance, the Georgetown University prospectus of 1822 stated: "If he [the Bachelor of Arts] remain longer, and study the higher branches of mathematics and philosophy, with success, he may take the degree of Master of Arts" (*The Washington Directory* [1822], p. 131). This quotation was copied through the courtesy of Father W. C. Repetti, S.J., archivist of Georgetown University. It may be significant that the earned M.A. appeared in the announcement of an institution which did not have its taproots in the English universities.

St. Louis University offered an M.A. degree in 1861–62 to those, presumably alumni, who devoted a second year to the study of philosophy in the institution, as well as to those who had spent two years in a learned profession (see John T. Ellis, *The Formative Years of the Catholic University of America* [Washington, D.C., 1946], p. 23; and also Roy J. Deferrari, "The Origin and Development of Graduate Studies under Catholic Auspices," in Roy J. Deferrari [ed.], *Essays on Catholic Education in the United States* [Washington, D.C., 1942], p. 199).

2. This is not the place to examine the merits of the attack on the pre–Civil War college, perhaps the best-known instance of which is Andrew D. White's description of "gerund grinding" at Yale (see Andrew D. White, *Autobiography of Andrew Dickson White* [New York, 1905], I, 27). For a more recent account of the old-fashioned college read Walter P. Rogers, *Andrew D. White and the Modern University* (Ithaca, N.Y., 1942), pp. 18–45. There is some evidence that the charges have not been entirely fair, although they may approximate the truth. See George F. Whicher's remarks on the belittling of the college in his prologue to William G. Hammond, *Remembrance of Amherst: An Undergraduate's Diary, 1846–1848* (New York, 1946), pp. 1–2. The intellectual and social history of the United States would be enriched by an extensive and objective study of the early nineteenth-century college.

3. *Catalogue of the Officers and Students in Yale College, 1845–6* (New Haven, 1845), p. 31.

4. Samuel E. Morison, *The Founding of Harvard College* (Cambridge, 1935), pp. 307–12.

5. Bishop Berkeley's conveyance of the Whitehall Farm to Yale College, reproduced in Daniel C. Gilman, "Bishop Berkeley's Gifts to Yale College," *Papers of the New Haven Colony Historical Society*, I (1865), 154–56. "Scholars of the House" are discussed at length in a report, bearing that title, made to the Yale College Course of Study Committee, 1944, by Helen C. Boatfield and George W. Pierson.

6. Timothy Dwight, *Memories of Yale Life and Men, 1845–1899* (New York, 1903), p. 98.

7. [Oliver O. Howard], "A Journal Kept by Oliver O. Howard," entry for June 16, 1847, in the Oliver O. Howard papers, Bowdoin College Library.

8. "Original Papers in Relation to a Course of Liberal Education," *American Journal of Science and Arts*, XV (1829), 300. The paper from which the quotation is taken is an 1828 report of the Yale College faculty and is presumed to have been written by President Jeremiah Day.

9. Letter from Peter Thacher, Bowdoin College, to Stephen Thacher, May 7, 1829, and letter from Stephen Thacher, Lubec, Maine, to Peter Thacher, May 14, 1829, in the Thacher family papers, Bowdoin College Library.

10. See Thomas Le Duc, *Piety and Intellect at Amherst College, 1865–1912* (New York, 1946), particularly pp. 22 ff. In *Cornell University: Founders and the Founding* (Ithaca, 1943), Lecture I, Carl L. Becker, too, discusses the close relation between religion and education in America.

11. See George P. Schmidt, *The Old Time College President* (New York, 1930), *passim*, for a description of the college president as an intellectual influence.

12. "Original Papers in Relation to a Course of Liberal Education," p. 305.

13. *Ibid.*, p. 342.

14. John S. Popkin, *Three Lectures on Liberal Education* (Cambridge, 1836), p. 16.

15. Henry E. Dwight, *Travels in the North of Germany, in the Years 1825 and 1826* (New York, 1829), p. 191.

16. *Ibid.*, marginal comment in Bowdoin College Library copy.

17. For one account of the effect of ordinary college teaching on the instructor, see [Francis Wayland], *Report to the Corporation of Brown University, on Changes in the System of Collegiate Education, Read March 28, 1850* (Providence, 1850), p. 19.

18. See letter from George Ticknor, Boston, to Thomas Jefferson, March 28, 1825, in the Thomas Jefferson papers, Library of Congress. Ticknor writes explicitly of the multiplication of colleges in New England and of the competition between them.

19. Jesse B. Sears, *Philanthropy in the History of American Higher Education* (Washington, 1922), p. 39.

20. [Edward Everett], Review of *Proceedings and Report of the Commissioners of the University of Virginia, Presented 8th of December, 1818*, in *North American Review*, X (1820; 3d ed., 1822), 136. The rich were certainly urged to endow colleges. In 1837, Philip Lindsley, president of the University of Nashville, expressed the opinion that, "of all the ways of expending wealth, the least harmful and obtrusive is precisely this of building colleges" (Philip Lindsley, *Speech in Behalf of the University of Nashville, Delivered on the Day of the Anniversary Commencement, October 4, 1837* [Nashville, 1837], pp. 10–11).

21. [John L. Motley], *Morton's Hope: or the Memoirs of a Provincial* (New York, 1839).

22. Review of Dwight's *Travels in the North of Germany*, *Quarterly Christian Spectator*, I (1829), 653. This review is attributed to James L. Kingsley in [Daniel C. Gilman], "James L. Kingsley, LL.D.," *Congregational Quarterly*, V (1863), 127.

23. Report of the substance of an address by Albert Gallatin, October 22, 1830, in facsimile *Journal of the Proceedings of a Convention of Literary and Scientific Gentlemen, Held in the Common Council Chamber of the City of New York, October, 1830* (New York, 1831), p. 176.

24. Lindsley, *op. cit.*, p. 18.

25. "Literary Institutions—University," *North American Review*, VII (1818), 271–77.

26. *Ibid.*, p. 276.

27. *Ibid.,* p. 277. The *Review* was inclined to believe that the expansion of colleges, Harvard being one, in several sections of the country was to be preferred to the erection of a national university.

CHAPTER II
"The Revolution Is Not Over"

1. Benjamin Rush, "Address to the people of the united states [*sic*]," *American Museum,* I (1787; 3d ed., 1790), 11. The chapter title is Rush's own sentence.

2. Benjamin Rush, "Plan of a federal university," *American Museum,* IV (1788), 444.

3. [John]Fenno, "Importance of a proper system of education—Establishment of a federal university recommended," *American Museum,* VI (1789), 290–91.

4. [Benjamin Rush], *A Plan for the Establishment of Public Schools and Diffusion of Knowledge in Pennsylvania; to Which Are Added Thoughts upon the Mode of Education, Proper in a Republic* (Philadelphia, 1786), pp. 4 ff. This plan is the earliest I have found in which college study is treated as a prerequisite of university work.

5. Rush, *American Museum,* I, 10.

6. Samuel Knox, *An Essay on the Best System of Liberal Education* (Baltimore, 1799), pp. 83, 163–64.

7. Samuel H. Smith, *Remarks on Education* (Philadelphia, 1798), quoted in Allen O. Hansen, *Liberalism and American Education in the Eighteenth Century* (New York, 1926), pp. 164–65.

8. Fenno, *op. cit.,* p. 290.

9. Smith, *op. cit.,* quoted in Hansen, *op. cit.,* p. 165.

10. Rush, *American Museum,* IV, 443–44.

11. *Ibid.,* pp. 442–43. As Rush discussed them in 1788, the general subjects to be taught at the university should be government, history, agriculture, principles and practice of manufactures, commerce, mathematics, natural philosophy and chemistry, natural history, philology, German and French, and athletic exercises.

12. Knox, op. cit., pp. 147–48.

13. *Ibid.,* pp. 164–65.

14. *Ibid.,* p. 148. Knox was particularly emphatic that university students should be college graduates (*ibid.,* p. 159). Because of the neglect of the principle of suitable preparation, many European universities, he thought, had been ineffectual and fruitless in their general operation. "Such as attend after a proper preparatory course, have reaped all that advantage from them they have expected; while such as were admitted when destitute of due qualifications, have passed through the systems of instruction, and remained nearly as ignorant as when they commenced" (*ibid.,* p. 148). In his plan Knox specified professorships of classical learning or belles-lettres and composition; Latin and Roman antiquities; Greek and Grecian antiquities; Hebrew and oriental languages; rhetoric, logic, moral philosophy; natural philosophy; mathematics; astronomy; history and chronology; law and principles of government; elocution and oratory, plus professorships in a medical department and of various ornamental arts.

15. Josiah Meigs apparently used this expression in discussing institutions designed to improve society. See letter from Joel Barlow, Paris, to Josiah Meigs, August 26, 1801. A copy of this letter, made by Meigs's daughter, is in the Joel Barlow papers, Houghton Library.

16. Rush, *American Museum*, I, 10. This figure is derived from Rush's suggestion that Congress, instead of spending one-half million dollars on a federal city, should appropriate one-quarter of that sum to found a university.

17. Charles F. Mercer, *A Discourse on Popular Education; Delivered in the Church at Princeton, the Evening before the Annual Commencement of the College of New Jersey September 26, 1826* (Princeton, 1826), Appendix, n. XVIII.

18. *Ibid.*, p. 74.

19. "Report of the President and Directors of the Literary Fund, to the General Assembly in December, 1816," printed in *Sundry Documents on the Subject of a System of Public Education for the State of Virginia*, published by the President and Directors of the Literary Fund (Richmond, 1817), p. 27.

20. *Ibid.*, p. 32.

21. *Ibid.*

22. Mercer, *op. cit.*, Appendix, n. XVIII.

23. Wayland F. Dunaway, "Charles Fenton Mercer," MS thesis for the M.A. degree (University of Chicago, 1917), pp. 10–17. Dunaway gives an account of Mercer's educational activities.

24. Roy J. Honeywell, *The Educational Work of Thomas Jefferson* (Cambridge, 1931), p. 17. Also undated MS in Joseph C. Cabell papers, University of Virginia Library. On the back is written, "Early legislation concerning The University." The handwriting seems to be Cabell's. See, too, Philip A. Bruce, *History of the University of Virginia, 1819–1919*, I (New York, 1920), 89.

25. *A Bill for Establishing a System of Public Education*, reproduced in Honeywell, *op. cit.*, pp. 233–43.

26. *Ibid.*, p. 241.

27. *Ibid.*, pp. 242–43.

28. Letter from Thomas Jefferson, Monticello, to Governor Wilson C. Nicholas, April 2, 1816, partially reproduced in Honeywell, *op. cit.*, p. 231.

29. Letter from Thomas Jefferson, Monticello, to Joseph C. Cabell, January 25, 1822, reproduced in [Nathaniel F. Cabell], *Early History of the University of Virginia, as Contained in the Letters of Thomas Jefferson and Joseph C. Cabell* (Richmond, 1856), p. 239.

30. In this connection it is interesting that Thomas Cooper wrote to Jefferson of a college as a place furnishing instruction in every branch of knowledge that a well-educated gentleman is expected to possess. This would seem to have been the typical conception (letter from Thomas Cooper, Carlisle, to Thomas Jefferson, September 22, 1814, in the Thomas Jefferson papers, Library of Congress).

31. Joel Barlow, who corresponded with Jefferson on the subject of higher education, was much concerned with the state of learning and education. As early as September 15, 1800, he suggested a national university to Jefferson and had in mind at the time the fact that the contemporary state of knowledge presented little more than a confused idea of the immense void of the unknown (letter from Joel Barlow, Paris, to Thomas Jefferson, September 15, 1800, in the Thomas Jefferson papers, Library of Congress; this may be a copy of the original letter). Barlow proposed a "Polysophic Society," one object of which was to extend the limits of general science. In 1806 he prepared a *Prospectus of a National Institution To Be Established in the United States* (Washington, D.C., 1806) with the aim of advancing knowledge by the association of learned men as well as of disseminating the rudiments of knowledge through the instruction of youth.

32. Letter from Thomas Jefferson, Monticello, to Thomas Cooper, August 25, 1814, in the Thomas Jefferson papers, Library of Congress.

33. See two undated MSS on the education bills in the Joseph C. Cabell papers, University of Virginia Library. One of these accounts is marked on the back, "Early legislation concerning The University"; the other bears no title of any sort. Both seem to be in Cabell's handwriting. See also Honeywell, *op. cit.*, pp. 19–21; and Bruce, *op. cit.*, I, 89 ff. While Jefferson did not, of course, take part in the legislative debates, he was not inactive. He even went so far as to ask President James Monroe to support the university bill (letter from Thomas Jefferson, Poplar Forest, to James Monroe, December 13, 1817, in the Thomas Jefferson papers, University of Virginia Library).

34. "Report of the Commissioners Appointed To Fix the Site of the University of Virginia, &c." (Rockfish Gap, August 4, 1818), reproduced in Honeywell, *op. cit.*, pp. 250–51.

35. *Ibid.*, p. 251. In 1805 Jefferson had flatly stated that "science is progressive" (letter from Thomas Jefferson, Washington, to a Tazewell, January 5, 1805, in the Thomas Jefferson papers, University of Virginia Library).

36. Rockfish Gap report, Honeywell, *op. cit.*, pp. 252–53.

37. Letter from H. Lee, Washington, to Thomas Jefferson, June 23, 1825, in the Thomas Jefferson papers, Library of Congress.

38. Letter from Thomas Jefferson, Monticello, to H. Lee, June 28, 1825, in the Thomas Jefferson papers, Library of Congress.

39. Letter from John A. Smith, Williamsburg, to Joseph C. Cabell, November 10, 1818, in the Joseph C. Cabell papers, University of Virginia Library.

40. Letter from Thomas Jefferson, Monticello, to John Taylor, February 14, 1821, printed in the *Collections of the Massachusetts Historical Society*, 7th ser., I (1900), 306.

41. Rockfish Gap report, Honeywell, *op. cit.*, p. 254.

42. Letter from Thomas Jefferson, Monticello, to Thomas Cooper, April 2, 1819, in the Thomas Jefferson papers, University of Virginia Library.

43. Honeywell, *op. cit.*, p. 50.

44. Letter from Timothy Dwight, New Haven, to Governor Wilson C. Nicholas, August 16, 1816, printed in *Sundry Documents*, p. 69. In connection with the fact that Jefferson was not a professional educator, note this comment made by Dwight: "If I am not deceived, a considerable number of *American* colleges have failed of success, from defects in their original establishment; defects, derived from the want of an experimental acquaintance with such an institution, in those under whose direction their several systems began their operations" (*ibid.*).

45. The later history of the University of Virginia is not discussed in this essay, but it should be noted that an earned M.A. degree was authorized in 1831. Unlike the requirements for the conventional Master's degree, those in force at Virginia did not call for a B.A. In fact, the faculty was not empowered to bestow a B.A. until 1848. See Bruce, *op. cit.*, II (New York, 1920), 140, and III (New York, 1921), 64. According to Bruce (*ibid.*, III, 37), a postgraduate department was created in the session of 1859–60. It gave advanced students an opportunity to study those Greek classics which were not suited in form or subject for the regular courses. Bruce also reports that instruction was offered in the Hebrew language, but he does not say explicitly that this was a graduate course. Presumably, advanced Greek studies were introduced in order to take advantage of the talents and attainments of the professor of Greek, Basil L. Gildersleeve.

CHAPTER III

GERMAN INFLUENCES

1. Letter from Thomas Jefferson, Monticello, to Thomas Cooper, March 9, 1822, in the Thomas Jefferson papers, Library of Congress.

2. Letter from George Ticknor, Boston, to Francis W. Gilmer, April 2, 1815, in the Francis W. Gilmer papers, University of Virginia Library. Gilmer did not, in fact, go abroad in 1815 but remained in Virginia, his home, to become a lawyer. Ten years later, as Jefferson's agent, he went to Europe to recruit a faculty for the University of Virginia.

3. Letter from George Ticknor, Göttingen, to Francis W. Gilmer, May 31, 1816, in the Francis W. Gilmer papers, University of Virginia Library.

4. *Ibid.*

5. Letter from George Ticknor, Göttingen, to Thomas Jefferson, April 23, 1816, in the Thomas Jefferson papers, Library of Congress.

6. Letter from George Ticknor, Göttingen, to Stephen Higginson, May 20, 1816, in the Boston Public Library.

7. *Ibid.*

8. In 1825, Ticknor referred to a written plan which he had prepared when or before he began teaching at Harvard. His letter to Savage may have been that plan. See letter from George Ticknor to N. A. Haven, October 26, 1825, quoted in George S. Hillard, *Life, Letters, and Journals of George Ticknor* (8th ed.; Boston, 1877), I, 354.

9. Letter from John T. Kirkland, Cambridge, to George Ticknor, November 8, 1816, in the George Ticknor papers, 1819–35, Harvard University Archives.

10. *Ibid.*

11. Draft of a letter from John T. Kirkland, Cambridge, to George Ticknor, October 26, 1816, in the Harvard College Corporation Papers, 1816–19, Harvard University Archives. As an alternative to this arrangement, Kirkland suggests that, if the college should provide an option of studies within certain limits, the more advanced undergraduates might be allowed into seminaria or that unmatriculated students might be admitted to particular branches. These possibilities were all raised in connection with the offer of a Harvard chair to Ticknor.

12. Letter from Edward Everett, Cambridge, to Joseph Story, April 13, 1821, in the Joseph Story papers, Massachusetts Historical Society.

13. [Edward Everett], review of *Proceedings and Report of the Commissioners of the University of Virginia, Presented 8th December, 1818*, in *North American Review*, X (1820; 3d ed., 1822), 127.

14. *Ibid.*, p. 131. Everett believed that private means were not great enough to support universities.

15. *Ibid.*, p. 133.

16. George Otis, statement dated May 6, 1822, in papers on Condition of College, 1821 and 1824, Harvard University Archives. Otis considered Harvard a school but suggested "established fellowships" for destitute men of fair promise who looked to literature rather than to the professions.

17. Letter from George Ticknor to N. A. Haven, October 26, 1825, quoted in Hillard, *op. cit.*, I, 355. Norton, Frisbie, and Ware were all satisfied with Ticknor's letter to Prescott (*ibid.*).

18. Letter from George Ticknor to William Prescott, July 31, 1821, in the George Ticknor papers, 1819–35, Harvard University Archives.

19. Letter from George Ticknor to N. A. Haven, October 26, 1825, quoted in Hillard, *op. cit.,* I, 355–56; notations in Ticknor's hand on the folders containing his papers on Harvard reform in the George Ticknor papers, 1819–35, Harvard University Archives. Ticknor at some time sorted his Harvard papers, apparently for his own or the University files, and added occasional explanations on the face of the folders.

20. Letter from George Ticknor to N. A. Haven, October 26, 1825, quoted in Hillard, *op. cit.,* I, 356.

21. Copy of a letter from James Jackson to John Lowell, [1823], in papers on Condition of College, 1821 and 1824, Harvard University Archives.

22. George Ticknor, *Remarks on Changes, Lately Proposed or Adopted in Harvard University* ([Boston], 1825), p. 33; handwritten marginal comment in Ticknor's own copy, Harvard University Archives.

23. Hillard, *op. cit.,* I, 356 n. See also George Ticknor's MS notes about the meeting of July 23, 1823, in George Ticknor papers, 1819–35, Harvard University Archives.

24. Letter from George Ticknor to N. A. Haven, October 26, 1825, quoted in Hillard, *op. cit.,* I, 359.

25. [George Ticknor], Remarks read by Mr. Ticknor at the meeting, July 23, 1823, p. 16, in the George Ticknor papers, 1819–35, Harvard University Archives.

26. *Ibid.*

27. *Ibid., passim.*

28. See Hillard, *op. cit.,* for a different and what seems to be an erroneous account of Ticknor's remarks. Hillard reproduces "extracts" from Ticknor's paper of July 23, 1823. Several of these quotations cannot be found in the text preserved in the George Ticknor papers, 1819–35, Harvard University Archives. What Hillard produces gives the impression that Ticknor largely elaborated on his Prescott letter. Consequently, the development of Ticknor's thought is obscured. Curiously enough, Hillard, quoting what seems rightly to be a part of the Prescott letter, uses asterisks just after Ticknor mentions medicine, law, and theology as graduate studies. Reading Hillard at the time of copyright, 1876, one would not have known that Ticknor spoke of general learning in connection with graduate study. Yet 1876 was the year in which the Johns Hopkins University opened its graduate school of arts and sciences.

29. *Ibid.,* pp. 9–10.

30. *Ibid.*

31. *Ibid.,* p. 12. Like Everett, Ticknor feared the creation of a school for special branches of learning. Harvard might avoid this, he said in August, 1823, by approaching more closely the liberal system of a university (see George Ticknor, Remarks on College, August 20, 1823, in the George Ticknor papers, 1819–35, Harvard University Archives).

32. Letter from George Ticknor, Boston, to Thomas Jefferson, December 25, 1823, in the Thomas Jefferson papers, Library of Congress.

33. Letter from George Ticknor to N. A. Haven, October 26, 1825, quoted in Hillard, *op. cit.,* I, 359–60.

34. Letter from John Pickering, Salem, to George Ticknor, September 30, 1823, in the George Ticknor papers, 1819–35, Harvard University Archives.

35. *Ibid.*

36. Joseph Story [chairman of the committee of inquiry appointed July 24, 1823], *Report* (Harvard University), p. 3. Report made May 4, 1824.

37. *Ibid.,* pp. 5–7.

38. J. Pierce, "Memoirs," Vol. IV, "1823–1827," entry for January 6, 1825, in the Massachusetts Historical Society.

39. *Statutes and Laws of the University in Cambridge Massachusetts* (Cambridge, 1825), arts. 58, 63, 151. Ticknor's hopes went further than the laws of 1825. He wanted abolition of the classes at the College; division in each branch solely according to merit; fixed minimal requirements for admission, for a degree, and for residence; and a maximum choice of studies. See letter from George Ticknor to John T. Kirkland, October 26, 1825, in the George Ticknor letters, 1816–28, Harvard University Archives.

40. [Andrews Norton], *Remarks on a Report of a Committee of the Overseers of Harvard College Proposing Certain Changes, Relating to the Instruction and Discipline of the College* (Cambridge, 1824), p. 3.

41. Andrews Norton, *Speech Delivered before the Overseers of Harvard College, February 3, 1825* (Boston, 1825), p. 19.

42. *Ibid.*, p. 20.

43. Letter from Andrews Norton, Cambridge, to Dr. Channing, September 10, 1824, in the George Ticknor papers, 1819–35, Harvard University Archives.

44. [Norton], *Remarks*, p. 10.

45. *Ibid.*

46. See George Ticknor, *Remarks on Changes, Lately Proposed or Adopted in Harvard University* ([Boston], 1825), pp. 11 ff. Ticknor went from a discussion of reform to an attack on the faculty's view of the issue of college government.

47. Norton, *Remarks*, pp. 11–12.

48. MS statements by members of the Harvard faculty in a file entitled "Condition of College, 1821 and 1824," in the Harvard University Archives. For further evidence on the attitude of the faculty, see "Report of the Immediate Government, May 21, 1825," [Harvard] College Records, 1819–27, in the Harvard University Archives.

49. See Samuel E. Morison, *Three Centuries of Harvard, 1636–1936* (Cambridge, 1937), pp. 233–36, for an account of faculty opposition to the laws of 1825, in particular to law 61 calling for division of sections by proficiency.

50. John T. Kirkland for the Committee of the Corporation, *Statement of the Income of Harvard College and of the Manner in Which It Is Applied* (1824), p. 4. This statement was made on February 16, 1824.

51. Report of committee appointed to inquire into the income and expenses of the College, December 26, 1826, in the George Ticknor papers, 1819–35, Harvard University Archives.

52. *Ibid.* Earlier Gray had opposed parts of the Story report. See J. Pierce, "Memoirs," Vol. IV, "1823–1827," entry for January 6, 1825, in the Massachusetts Historical Society.

53. Letter from George Ticknor to Harvard College Corporation, December 30, 1826, in the George Ticknor papers, 1819–35, Harvard University Archives.

54. Basil Hall, *Travels in North America in the Years 1827 and 1828* (Edinburgh, 1829), II, 175.

55. Philip Lindsley, *An Address, Delivered in Nashville, January 12, 1825, at the Inauguration of the President of Cumberland College* (Nashville, 1825), p. 46.

56. The institutions in question were what we would call seminars, not seminaries, considered either as schools in the generic sense or as theological schools.

57. Review of John Russell, *A Tour in Germany, and Some of the Southern*

Provinces of the Austrian Empire, in the Years 1820, 1821, 1822, in *North American Review,* XXVII (1828), 337.

58. Beck came to the United States for political reasons, traveling here with Charles Follen.

59. Josiah Quincy, Inaugural Address, p. 30. This is a MS in the Harvard University Archives. In a letter to William E. Channing, written from Cambridge, February 14, 1834, Quincy said that the question before the college was not how to become popular, but rather how to deserve to be popular (letter in the Josiah Quincy papers, 1834, Harvard University Archives).

60. Quincy, *op. cit.* p. 20.

61. *Ibid.,* p. 22.

62. Minutes of the Harvard Corporation, June 23, 1831, in [Harvard] College Records, 1827–36, Harvard University Archives. Beck's paper is not to be found in the Harvard University Archives; but a MS memorandum, entitled "Recommendation and Plan of a Seminary for Classical Learning" and indorsed as a copy of a Beck MS, appears with the Benjamin Peirce papers, American Academy of Arts and Sciences. The title and contents of this document suggest strongly that it is the Beck communication of June 23, 1831.

63. *Ibid.*

64. *Ibid.*

65. *Ibid.*

66. Minutes of Harvard Corporation, August 25, 1831, in [Harvard] College Records, 1827–36, Harvard University Archives.

67. *Ibid.,* October 20, 1831. The name of the department varied. Sometimes the seminary was designated by its teacher-training side, on other occasions by its philological character.

68. "Outline of Rules and Regulations for a Philological Department," in Harvard College Papers, 1831–33, pp. 53–57, Harvard University Archives. The rules carefully pointed out that for his dissertation the student could employ "all literary means within his reach, of course without committing plagiarism."

69. Report of Committee, to which was referred Communication from the Philological Department, in Harvard College Papers, 1831–33, Harvard University Archives.

70. Letter from Charles Beck to Josiah Quincy, July [?] 16, 1832, with inclosed plan for a philological seminary, in the Josiah Quincy papers, 1832, Harvard University Archives. The schedule reproduced above conforms to the original in substance but not in form.

71. Beck likened the fully developed seminary to the philosophical faculty of European universities; and the Visiting Committee report of 1833 referred to the department as a "Philosophical Seminary." The implications of such terminology are clear (see Visiting Committee report, 1833, in [Harvard] Overseers Records, 1830–47, Harvard University Archives). A draft of this report spoke of the new department as a "Philological Seminary" (see report of Visiting Committee, January 10, 1833, in Reports to Harvard Overseers, 1831–33, Harvard University Archives).

72. *Sixth Annual Report of the President of Harvard University to the Overseers on the State of the Institution, for the Academical Year 1830–31* (Cambridge, 1832), p. 5.

73. *Ibid.*

74. Six resident graduates originally enrolled in the seminary *(ibid.).*

75. Letter from Charles Beck to Harvard College Corporation, in Harvard

College Papers, 1831–33. This letter is undated, but internal evidence indicates that it was written at the end of the first term of the seminary.

76. *Ibid.*

77. Minutes of Harvard Corporation, June 27, 1832, in [Harvard] College Records, 1827–36, Harvard University Archives.

78. If the Beck experiment contributed nothing permanent to the development of graduate education at Harvard, the terminology employed throws considerable light on the academic notions of the time. Although Beck showed no confusion in his ideas, there seems to have been some uncertainty as to the most appropriate title for the thing he suggested. The names given the projected department denoted not one but three things; philosophy, philology, and education. This situation may simply have resulted from failure to pin Beck down to a single descriptive term, or it may have sprung from something deeper. In the German universities, from which Beck derived his ideas, philosophy was closely allied to philology, and the study of both was regarded as essential to the training of teachers. To Beck, who had firsthand knowledge, the German system presumably made the sense that familiar customs do; to native Americans, possessed of no profound understanding of foreign institutions, they might well have been confusing. The fact that Harvard usage varied suggests that German terminology had yet to be naturalized. Until it was, the effort to reform American institutions after the German pattern would have its semantic pitfalls.

CHAPTER IV
"The Spirit of the Age"

1. [Alpheus S. Packard], review of *The Substance of Two Reports of the Faculty of Amherst College to the Board of Trustees, with the Doings of the Board Thereon,* in *North American Review,* XXVIII, new ser. (1829), 294.

2. "Original Papers in Relation to a Course of Liberal Education," *American Journal of Science and Arts,* XV (1829), 300.

3. In Ebenezer Baldwin, *Annals of Yale College, in New Haven, Connecticut, from Its Foundation, to the Year 1831* (New Haven, 1831), p. 169, the authorship of the faculty reports is attributed to Day and Kingsley. [Daniel C. Gilman], "James L. Kingsley, LL.D.," *Congregational Quarterly,* V (1863), 125, attributes the second statement to Kingsley. As the two papers were written independently, the presumption is that Day prepared the first report.

4. "Original Papers," *American Journal of Science and Arts,* XV (1829), 297–98. In this article, Benjamin Silliman, Sr., printed a large part of the Yale report with comments.

5. For three modern discussions of the Yale report, see George P. Schmidt, "Intellectual Crosscurrents in American Colleges, 1825–1855," *American Historical Review,* XLII (1936–37), 53 ff.; R. Freeman Butts, *The College Charts Its Course* (New York, 1939), pp. 118 ff.; and Carl L. Becker, *Cornell University: Founders and the Founding* (Ithaca, 1943), p. 19.

6. Basil Hall, *Travels in North America in the Years 1827 and 1828* (Edinburgh, 1829), II, 200.

7. [Day], "Original Papers," *American Journal of Science and Arts,* XV (1829), 316.

8. *Ibid.,* p. 315.

9. *Ibid.,* p. 316.

10. See Dwight's letters as printed in Henry E. Dwight, *Travels in the North*

of Germany, in the Years 1825 and 1826 (New York, 1829), pp. 59, 184. Dwight described the University of Berlin at length, as well as Göttingen. He also devoted an entire letter to the gymnasia, which impressed him very favorably. He was pleased to discover, on his return home, that "Messrs. Coggswell [Joseph G. Cogswell] and Bancroft, in introducing the Gymnasium into the United States, have conferred a blessing on their native land" (*ibid.*, p. 392). In 1828 Dwight, with his brother Sereno, founded a boarding school for boys called the "New Haven Gymnasium" (see Franklin B. Dexter, *Biographical Sketches of the Graduates of Yale College* [New Haven, 1912], VI, 747; "New-Haven Gymnasium," *American Journal of Education,* III [1828], 115–16).

11. Day's reaction to the idea that American higher education might be made to resemble German universities seems quite sympathetic in comparison with Kingsley's (see [James L. Kingsley], review of Dwight's *Travels, Quarterly Christian Spectator,* I [1829], 631–74). Although he admitted that American collegiate education was not perfect, Kingsley defended it stoutly against Dwight's criticism and carried the battle onto the enemy's ground by associating a German "disposition to extravagant speculation and manifest licentiousness both in principle and practice" with the universities ([Kingsley], *op. cit.*, pp. 651–52). He did not attribute the decline of faith exclusively to them, but he considered them to be in the first rank of the agents of evil against good. In short, Kingsley simply disapproved of German universities and saw no reason to be gentle to those like Dwight who proclaimed their virtues. Had Kingsley written the first faculty statement, it might have been very different from what it was.

12. Benjamin Silliman, [Sr.], "Notice of the Late Sheldon Clark, Esq. of Oxford, Connecticut," *American Journal of Science and Arts,* XLI (1841), 217–31.

13. Paper on Funds for Professorships, etc., in Yale Memorabilia Room. The paper is apparently an extract from the Corporation records for September, 1824.

14. Timothy Dwight, *Memories of Yale Life and Men, 1845–1899* (New York, 1903), pp. 97 ff.

15. Letter by "S," *New York American,* February 16, 1830.

16. Theodore F. Jones *et al., New York University 1832:1932* (New York, 1933), pp. 11–13.

17. *Considerations upon the Expediency and the Means of Establishing a University in the City of New-York* (New York, 1830), *passim.* Theodore F. Jones, historian of New York University, believes that Jonathan M. Wainwright wrote the *Considerations* (see Jones, *op. cit.*, p. 12).

18. Typed copy of Minutes of the First Meetings in Relation to a University, entry for January 14, 1830, in the New York University Library, University Heights.

19. *Ibid.*, entry for March 1, 1830.

20. In the fall of 1830, Albert Gallatin said that completion of studies commenced in college was one of the two generally accepted aims of the University. Facsimile reprint of *Journal of the Proceedings of a Convention of Literary and Scientific Gentlemen* (New York, 1831), p. 170. A contemporary newspaper (the *New York Commercial-Advertiser,* January 20, 1830) implied that friends of the University saw a need for regular provision for college graduates. Moreover, James M. Mathews, first chancellor of the University, recollected later—but perhaps without complete accuracy—that one consideration in founding the University was the demand for higher branches of learning, not usually taught in the colleges and sought of necessity abroad. James M. Mathews, *Recollections of*

Persons and Places, Chiefly in the City of New York: Beings Selections from His Journal (New York, 1865), p. 190.

21. Letter by "Academist" [Joseph Leo Wolf], in the *New York American,* January 8, 1830. This newspaper correspondence appears in the *New York American,* Wolf contributing on December 24, 1829, and January 8, 1830; Hassler on December 25, 1829, and January 13, 1830.

22. *New York American,* October 14, 1830.

23. Facsimile reprint of *Journal of the Proceedings of a Convention of Literary and Scientific Gentlemen* (New York, 1831), pp. 9–12.

24. "College-Instruction and Discipline," *American Quarterly Review,* IX (1831), 285–86.

25. *Journal of Proceedings,* p. 78.

26. *Ibid.,* p. 116.

27. *Ibid.,* p. 132. Keating explicitly left West Point out of the question.

28. *Ibid.,* p. 141.

29. *Ibid.,* p. 139.

30. *Ibid.,* pp. 247–48. Commenting on the journal of the convention, Professor Münche of Heidelberg said that Leo Wolf's essay contained imperfect statements. It is unclear whether or not Münche had the quoted section in mind. See account of Münche's remarks (original in *Heidelberger Jahrbücher der Literatur,* No. 37) in "German Review of the Literary Convention at New York," *American Annals of Education and Instruction,* I (1831), 456. In a letter to several members of the convention, Moses Stuart did not refer to German models but did express the hope "that you will have a side [of the proposed university] that is *deeply & radically learned*—in law—in medicine—in Classic & Oriental languages." He also said: "A *University completes* scholars—does not *begin* them. This idea is radical in your whole plan—at least it seems to me that it should be so. I do entreat of you not to let the solid part be *half made, half furnished,* an *ephemeral affair,* which will disappear in a few years, as every superficial thing must. Everything will depend on your *commander in chief*—i.e. your President, when clothed with adequate powers" (letter from Moses Stuart, Andover, to Mathews, Wainwright, and Delafield, October 18, 1830, in the Delafield papers, New York University Library, University Heights).

31. Although it was generally critical of the convention, the *American Quarterly Review* called this speech excellent (see "College-Instruction and Discipline," *American Quarterly Review,* IX [1831], 286).

32. *Journal of the Proceedings,* p. 170.

33. *Ibid.,* p. 171.

34. Letter from Albert Gallatin to Josiah Quincy, December 9, 1830, published in *The Writings of Albert Gallatin,* ed. Henry Adams (Philadelphia, 1879), II, 445.

35. *Journal of the Proceedings,* p. 173.

36. Typed copy of Minutes of the Council of the University of the City of New York, entries from October 30, 1830, to January 28, 1831, in the New York University Library, University Heights. The Minutes for January 28, 1831, report adoption of the Constitution and Statutes; but Jones, *op. cit.,* p. 27, gives the date as January 31.

37. *The Constitution and Statutes for the Present Government of the University of the City of New York* (New York, 1831), p. 13.

38. *Journal of the Proceedings,* p. 174.

39. *The Constitution and Statutes,* p. 13. Commenting on the Constitution and

Statutes, the editor of *American Annals of Education and Instruction* noted that the intent, in part, was to combine "*a University*, in the European sense of the term, with *a College for Classical Instruction*, on the usual plan of our colleges, and *an English College*, whose students shall attend only to science and modern literature" (see "New York University," *Annals*, I [1831], 108).

40. Gallatin did not take exception to the classical course; but he hoped that it could be kept separate from the other course. His reaction to the Statutes is revealed in his marginal comments on a printed copy of the unamended version, now in the New York University Room, New York University Library, University Heights, and in a letter from Albert Gallatin to John Delafield, probably January 10, 1831, in the Delafield papers, in the same depository. Gallatin's sharpest comments on the unamended Statutes were reserved for the office of Chancellor: "As to the Chancellor [he wrote Delafield], I cannot think of the office with temper. He is made a perfect Monarch, and I do not like Monarchy. We have no man of such acknowledged superiority, as that Professors would submit to his Government, unless they wanted bread." That Gallatin should have written in this manner is interesting in the light of later difficulties between the Chancellor and the faculty. Gallatin believed that the utility and the reputation of any university depended exclusively on the qualifications of the professors. In his eyes, their "susceptibility" had to be respected, a detailed synopsis of courses was not to be demanded of them. Note the contrast between this attitude and that of another member of the Council, James Tallmadge, who wrote of the "known tendency of Professors to combine and beget feuds with their Principals" (letter from James Tallmadge to the professors of the University, August 31, 1838, reprinted in Professors of the Faculty of Science and Letters, *History of the Controversy in the University of the City of New-York* [New York, 1838], p. 38).

41. Gallatin chaired the committee which drafted the petition; but Theodore F. Jones doubts that he was the author (see Jones, *op. cit.*, p. 28).

42. [Petition] to the Honourable the Legislature of the State of New York in Senate and Assembly Convened, in the New York University Archives.

43. The petitioners anticipated that "men of Science," employed in New York as instructors, writers, or otherwise, would study at the University. This can possibly be taken to mean that the Council did have "gradute students" in mind (see *ibid.*).

44. Minutes of the Council, February 7, 1831, to March 13, 1832.

45. Minutes of the Council, April 19, 1832.

46. "New York University," *American Annals of Education and Instruction*, II (1832), 533.

47. James Milnor's address at the inauguration of professors, 1832, reproduced in Mathews, *op. cit.*, pp. 209–10.

48. For an explanation of Gallatin's retirement from University affairs, see Jones, *op. cit.*, pp. 29–30.

49. Professors of the Faculty of Science and Letters, *op. cit.*, p. 5.

50. Henry Vethake, John Mulligan, and John Torrey, *An Exposition of the Reasons for the Resignation of Some of the Professors in the University of the City of New York* (New York, 1833), pp. 1–2.

51. Report of Committee of Advice on Professor of Geology & Mineralogy and of a Lecturer on Education, in Mathew's handwriting, in Reports of Chancellors. New York University Archives. This paper is marked as the report of the Chancellor.

52. For the kind of men chosen as professors, see Jones, *op. cit., passim.*

53. Mathews, *op. cit.,* p. 230.

54. *Journal of the Proceedings,* p. 15.

55. *University of the City of New-York* [an announcement for the year] (New York, 1835), pp. 5 ff.

56. *Ibid.,* pp. 12–13.

57. Report to Regents, 1837 [New York State] Senate Doc. No. 52, II (1838), Martin Collection, New York University Library, University Heights.

58. Report of Finance Committee, Minutes of the Council, June 5, 1838.

59. Minutes of the Council for years mentioned.

60. Minutes of the Council, *passim.*

61. Report of Finance Committee, Minutes of the Council, November 21, 1837.

62. Joint report of Finance and Advice Committees, Minutes of the Council, November 29, 1837.

63. Minutes of the Council, March 8, 1838.

64. Report of Chancellor, Minutes of the Council, May 3, 1838.

65. *Ibid.*

66. *Ibid.*

67. *Ibid.,* May 17, 1838.

68. Report of Finance Committee, Minutes of the Council, June 5, 1838.

69. Minutes of the Council, August 30, 1838.

70. Jones, *op. cit.,* p. 49.

71. *Ibid.,* p. 50.

72. John Davis in the U.S. Senate, April 30, 1836, reproduced in *The Smithsonian Institution, Documents Relative to Its Origin and History,* ed. William J. Rhees (Washington, D.C., 1901), I, 140.

73. Thomas Cooper, Columbia, South Carolina, to [Secretary of State John Forsyth], July 20, 1838, in *House of Representatives Executive Documents* (25th Cong., 3d sess.), II (Doc. No. 11), 10–11.

74. Francis Wayland, Providence, to Secretary of State John Forsyth, October 2, 1838, in *House of Representatives Executive Documents* (25th Cong., 3d sess.), II (Doc. No. 11), 8.

75. *Ibid.*

76. *Ibid.*

77. This list of subjects, presented by Wayland as an extension of the college course, seems to cover an inordinate amount of ground. It is conceivable, however, that Wayland or other professors at Brown at least touched on all these subjects in a rudimentary form or that he did not mean to say that *every* part of his list had a counterpart in the undergraduate curriculum.

CHAPTER V

THE EXPANSION OF LEARNING

1. Edward Everett, diary, November 18, 1845, MS in the Massachusetts Historical Society.

2. Letter from Edward Everett, Cambridge, to Charles Sumner, June 8, 1846, in the Charles Sumner papers, Houghton Library.

3. Letter from Edward Everett, Cambridge, to Dr. Holland of England, December 11, 1848, in the Edward Everett letter-books, Massachusetts Historical Society. Unless otherwise stated, this is the location of the Everett letters referred to hereafter.

4. Letter from Edward Everett, Cambridge, to Alexander H. Everett, April 8, 1846.

5. Everett, diary, January 16, 1848. This remark was made in connection with an article in the *North British Review* on the subject of reform at Oxford University.

6. [Edward Everett], review of *Proceedings and Reports of the Commissioners of the University of Virginia*, in *North American Review*, X (1820; 3d ed., 1822), 125.

7. Edward Everett, "University Education," *Orations and Speeches on Various Occasions* (Boston, 1865), pp. 496–97.

8. Letter from Edward Everett, Cambridge, to Samuel A. Eliot, November 24, 1846.

9. Letter from Edward Everett, Cambridge, to Amos Lawrence, September 2, 1847.

10. Everett's address evidently had very general approval. Samuel A. Eliot, Treasurer of the College, noted a unanimous opinion that the doctrines of the address be understood as those of the College (see letter from Samuel A. Eliot, Boston, to Edward Everett, May 1, 1846, in the Harvard College Corporation Papers, 1846, Harvard University Archives). John L. Sibley wrote in his Private Journal, Vol. I, April 30, 1846: "There was but one general enthusiastic feeling, that Mr. Everett was *the* man for the place & the expectations of the audience were in every respect fully realized. Nothing more could have been desired." This journal is in the Harvard University Archives.

11. These faculty statements, dated September 26 to October 10, 1846, are in the Harvard College Papers, 2d ser., Vol. XIV, Harvard University Archives.

12. Letter from Edward Everett, Cambridge, to Abbott Lawrence, August 19, 1847, in [Harvard] College Letters, Vol. I, 1846–47, Edward Everett, Harvard University Archives.

13. Minutes of the Harvard Corporation, December 27, 1845, in [Harvard] College Records, 1836–47, Harvard University Archives.

14. Everett, diary, July 27, 1846.

15. The substance of Peirce's thought is to be ascertained from an extant plan which he prepared at about this time and which is presumably the one for which Everett had asked. See "Plan of a School of Practical & Theoretical Science," February 27, 1846, in Harvard College Papers, 1845–46, 2d ser., Vol. XIII, Harvard University Archives. The date is rather early, but it is possibly inexact.

16. Minutes of the Harvard Corporation, November 28, 1846, in the [Harvard] College Records, 1836–47, Harvard University Archives.

17. Letter from Edward Everett, Cambridge, to Abbott Lawrence, August 19, 1847, in the [Harvard] College Letters, Vol. I, 1846–47, Edward Everett, Harvard University Archives.

18. Everett, diary, January 27, 1847.

19. *Ibid.*, February 13 and 18, 1847.

20. *A Catalogue of the Officers and Students of the University at Cambridge, for the Academical Year 1846–47, Second Term* (Cambridge, 1847), p. 60; also Minutes of the Harvard Corporation, February 13, 1847.

21. Minutes of the Harvard Corporation, February 27, 1846, in [Harvard] College Records, 1836–47, Harvard University Archives.

22. *A Catalogue of the Officers and Students of the University at Cambridge, 1846–47*, p. 59.

23. *Twenty-second Annual Report of the President of the University at Cam-*

bridge to the Overseers, Exhibiting the State of the Institution for the Academical Year 1846–47 (Cambridge, 1848), p. 7.

24. Letter from Edward Everett, Cambridge, to Jared Sparks, May 13, 1847, in [Harvard] College Letters, 1846–47, Vol. I, Edward Everett, Harvard University Archives. When Sparks counseled delay in establishing a history course, Everett was distinctly annoyed, writing in his diary, May 28, 1847: "Anglicé [Sparks] won't take the trouble & risk of the experiment, but has no objection if it succeeds to share the fruits."

25. Letter from Edward Everett, Cambridge, to Dr. Holland of England, July 30, 1847. In the same letter Everett claimed that the experiment of the new school was undertaken as a result of an idea thrown out in his inaugural address.

26. Letter from Edward Everett, Cambridge, to Alexander H. Everett, August 9, 1847.

27. Letter from Edward Everett, Cambridge, to Dr. Holland, May 14, 1847.

28. Letter from Edward Everett, Cambridge, to George Ticknor, May 21, 1847.

29. Everett, diary, May 29, 1847.

30. *Twenty-second Annual Report of the President of the University at Cambridge*, 1846–47 (Cambridge, 1884), p. 8.

31. Letter from Edward Everett, Cambridge, to Jared Sparks, June 1, 1847, in the [Harvard] College Letters, 1846–47, Vol. I, Edward Everett, Harvard University Archives.

32. Everett, diary, June 9, 1847. Everett's biographer, Paul R. Frothingham, gives the credit for securing the Lawrence gift to the President (see Paul R. Frothingham, *Edward Everett, Orator and Statesman* [Boston and New York, 1925], p. 290).

33. Minutes of the Harvard Corporation, July 12 to August 25, 1847, in [Harvard] College Records, 1836–47, Harvard University Archives.

34. Letter from Charles Beck, Cambridge, to Edward Everett, January 14, 1848, in Harvard College Papers, 2d ser., Vol. XV, 1847–48, Harvard University Archives.

35. Letter from James Walker to Edward Everett, June 20, [1847], in Harvard College Papers, 2d ser., Vol. XIV, 1846–47, Harvard University Archives.

36. Letter from Edward Everett, Cambridge, to Samuel A. Eliot, January 21, 1848, in [Harvard] College Letters, Vol. II, 1848–49, Edward Everett, Harvard University Archives.

37. *Ibid.*

38. Letter from Samuel A. Eliot, Boston, to Edward Everett, January 21, 1848, in Harvard College Papers, 2d ser., Vol. XV, 1847–48, Harvard University Archives.

39. Letter from Edward Everett, Cambridge, to Samuel A. Eliot, January 27, 1848. Everett was now a sick and unhappy man. Speaking of the Lawrence School, he wrote in his diary, January 17, 1848: "Had I twenty years more on my side, I could do something." In this frame of mind, he was not willing to undertake a long crusade.

40. Letter from Edward Everett, Cambridge, to Francis J. Child, February 11, 1848.

41. Letter from Edward Everett, Cambridge, to Charles Beck and Cornelius C. Felton, January 31, 1848.

42. *Revision of the Statutes and Laws of the University at Cambridge* (Cambridge, 1847), Title 89. For Everett's claim of authorship, see his diary, November 27, 1847. A draft of the revised laws, with a similar title, was printed but

not published in 1848. Its section 88 is identical with the paragraph above except for the use of "Professional Schools" instead of "Professional Colleges."

43. Everett, diary, September 7, 1848.

44. *Revision of the Statutes,* Title 89.

45. [Edward Everett], *Report of the Committee of the Overseers of Harvard College Appointed To Visit the Lawrence Scientific School, in 1849* (Cambridge, 1850), p. 6.

46. *Ibid.*

47. There is irony in Everett's remarks. It will be noted that he spoke as an Overseer of a "College."

48. [Everett], *Report of the Committee of the Overseers, 1849, passim.*

49. Letter from Theodore D. Woolsey, New Haven, to Cornelius C. Felton, March 6, 1840, in the Josiah Quincy papers, 1845, Harvard University Archives.

50. Theodore D. Woolsey, "The Inaugural Discourse," *Discourses and Addresses at the Ordination of the Rev. Theodore Dwight Woolsey, and His Inauguration as President of Yale College, October 21, 1846* (New Haven, 1846), p. 76.

51. Jeremiah Day, "The Inaugurating Address," *Discourses and Addresses at the Ordination of the Rev. Theodore Dwight Woolsey, and His Inauguration as President of Yale College* (New Haven, 1846), *passim.*

52. Theodore S. Woolsey, "Theodore Dwight Woolsey—a Biographical Sketch. II," *Yale Review,* I (1912), 453 ff.

53. Theodore D. Woolsey, *op. cit.,* p. 82.

54. *First Annual Report of the Visitors of the Sheffield Scientific School of Yale College* (New Haven, 1866), p. 8.

55. George P. Fisher, *Life of Benjamin Silliman, M.D., LL.D.* (New York, 1866), II, 276. See also John F. Fulton and Elizabeth H. Thomson, *Benjamin Silliman, 1779–1864* (New York, 1947), pp. 208–12.

56. Fulton and Thomson call Silliman the leading spirit of the committee of August, 1846 (*ibid.,* p. 211).

57. Resolution of the Yale Corporation, August 19, 1846, quoted in Russell H. Chittenden, *History of the Sheffield Scientific School of Yale University, 1846–1922* (New Haven, 1928), I, 40–41.

58. Committee report, reproduced in "Department of Philosophy and the Arts in Yale College," *American Journal of Education,* I (1855–56), 359–60. See Charles H. Warren, "The Sheffield Scientific School from 1847 to 1947," *The Centennial of the Sheffield Scientific School,* ed. George A. Baitsell (New Haven, 1950), p. 158. Warren states that the committee, nominally headed by President Day, was actually headed by Benjamin Silliman.

59. Committee report, reproduced in "Department of Philosophy and the Arts in Yale College," *American Journal of Education,* I (1855–56), 359.

60. *Ibid.*

61. *Catalogue of the Officers and Students in Yale College, 1847-8* (New Haven, 1847), pp. 42–43.

62. See Chittenden, *op. cit.,* I, 41–42.

63. Timothy Dwight, *Memories of Yale Life and Men, 1845–1899* (New York, 1903), p. 101.

64. See *ibid.,* p. 99.

65. These figures are derived from the Yale catalogues for the years indicated. Before 1852, the statistics are inadequate for a table of this sort.

66. Yale Corporation Records, August 17, 1847.

67. *Catalogue of the Officers and Students in Yale College, 1865–66* (New Haven, 1865), p. 4.

68. "Department of Philosophy and the Arts in Yale College," *American Journal of Education*, I, 360.

69. James D. Dana, "Science and Scientific Schools," *American Journal of Education*, II (1856), 374. This address was delivered before a group of Yale alumni in August, 1856.

70. Yale Corporation Records, July 24, 1860.

71. *Catalogue of the Officers and Students in Yale College, 1860–61* (New Haven, 1860), p. 54.

72. Charles W. Eliot, "The New Education," *Atlantic Monthly*, XXIII (1869), 208.

73. *Ibid.*

74. These figures are derived from the Yale catalogues for the years mentioned.

75. Eliot, *op. cit.*, p. 208.

76. *Ibid.*

77. *Ibid.* See Wilbur L. Cross, *Connecticut Yankee: An Autobiography* (New Haven, 1943), pp. 152 ff., for an appraisal of early graduate education at Yale by a son of Yale and a Dean of the Graduate School. Among other things, Cross comments on the withdrawal of Daniel C. Gilman in lean financial years after he had taken a prominent place in graduate instruction. One wonders what would have been the history of the University if Gilman had become dean of graduate instruction and, perhaps, president.

78. Western Reserve College Faculty Record, March 10, 1847. Excerpts were taken from this record for me by Professor John Culver, of Case Institute of Technology. Record in the President's office, Western Reserve University.

79. Faculty Record, April 14, 1847.

80. *Catalogue of the Officers and Students in the Western Reserve College, 1847–8* (Hudson, Ohio, 1847).

81. Western Reserve College catalogues, 1847–51. See also Fredrick C. Waite, *Western Reserve University: The Hudson Era* (Cleveland, 1943), p. 312. Waite writes that most of the students enrolled in the new course were recent graduates of Western Reserve College and that all of them ultimately received the degree of Master of Arts.

82. This account of the internal troubles of Western Reserve College is condensed from Waite, *op. cit.*, pp. 316 ff.

CHAPTER VI

DIAGNOSIS AND PRESCRIPTION

1. Francis Wayland [for a Brown University committee], *Report to the Corporation of Brown University, on Changes in the System of Collegiate Education, Read March 28, 1850* (Providence, 1850), pp. 11 ff. Wayland's solution to the academic problems of his time is discussed in Walter C. Bronson, *The History of Brown University, 1764–1914* (Providence, 1914), pp. 258 ff.; and in William G. Roelker, *Francis Wayland, a Neglected Pioneer of Higher Education* (Worcester, 1944), *passim*. Wayland is treated here only very briefly, not because of any intent to continue a tradition of neglect—he was certainly important in the general history of higher education—but because he does not seem to have been much interested in graduate study. In his *Thoughts on the Present Collegiate System in the United States* (Boston, 1842), p. 110, Wayland suggests that a college might be made more nearly to resemble "a real University," and in his 1850 Report, he recommends an earned M.A. degree. He does not, however, dwell on these matters.

His heart was more in his effort to draw new classes of students into the college than in the possibility of providing advanced instruction for the old ones. Perhaps a good test of Wayland's policy in regard to graduate study was his attitude toward the M.A. Bronson (*op. cit.*, p. 282) indicates that the Master's degree under the new system introduced by Wayland in 1850 required no more work than the old Bachelor's degree.

2. This work was probably the first bound volume of American authorship to be devoted almost exclusively to advanced study.

3. George T. Strong, MS diary, May 24, 1857. Enlarged microfilm prints in the Columbiana Room, Columbia University.

4. Review of Charles A. Bristed, *Five Years in an English University*, in *North American Review*, LXXV (1852), 47.

5. Henry P. Tappan, *University Education* (New York, 1851), p. 10.

6. *Ibid.*, pp. 10–11.

7. *Ibid.*, p. 11.

8. *Ibid.*, pp. 11–12.

9. *Ibid.*, p. 13.

10. This idea seems to approach the German concept of *Bildung*, and Tappan conceivably acquired it with his other Germanic enthusiasms.

11. In Charles M. Perry, *Henry Philip Tappan, Philosopher and University President* (Ann Arbor, 1933), pp. 212 ff., the architectonic character of Tappan's system is emphasized.

12. Tappan, *op. cit.*, p. 69.

13. *Ibid.*, p. 68.

14. *Ibid.*, pp. 82–83.

15. *Ibid.*, p. 43.

16. *Ibid.*, p. 44.

17. *Ibid.*, p. 45.

18. *Ibid.*, p. 50.

19. *Ibid.*, p. 51.

20. *Ibid.*, p. 67.

21. *Ibid.*, p. 64.

22. *Ibid.*, p. 61.

23. *Ibid.*, p. 65.

24. *Ibid.*, pp. 68–69.

25. *Ibid.*, p. 81.

26. *Ibid.*, p. 90. In writing here of the founding of a university, Tappan definitely had New York City in mind as its site.

27. See *ibid.*, p. 114.

28. *Ibid.*, p. 92.

29. *Ibid.*

30. *Ibid.*, p. 84.

31. *Ibid.*, p. 87.

32. *Ibid.*, p. 97.

33. *Ibid.*, p. 98.

34. Charles A. Bristed, *Five Years in an English University* (2 vols.; New York, 1852). The book is dedicated to Theodore D. Woolsey.

35. A second edition was brought out in the year of the original publication, 1852; a third revised edition appeared in 1873.

36. Bristed, *op. cit.*, I, 393–94. Bristed was not the first American to notice the English fellowship system. In 1837, for instance, Philip Lindsley had said: "Endowed fellowships [in Oxford and Cambridge] also support a certain number of

the most accomplished and promising poor scholars: who frequently remain for years in the assiduous pursuit of knowledge, and in the tranquil enjoyment of the extraordinary advantages afforded by a highly cultivated literary society and daily access to the accumulated wisdom and erudition of the illustrious dead" (Philip Lindsley, *Speech in Behalf of the University of Nashville, Delivered on the Day of the Anniversary Commencement, October 4, 1837* [Nashville, 1837], p. 13). If Lindsley thought that *only* poor scholars were eligible for fellowships, he was, of course, in error.

37. Bristed, *op. cit.*, II, 156–57.

38. *Ibid.*, p. 157.

39. *Ibid.*

40. Bristed was only preaching what he had already practiced when he urged the foundation of fellowships. In 1848 the Yale College catalogue announced that he had founded a "Scholarship," yielding about $80, which the recipient, originally a sophomore or junior, could hold until he would regularly take his second degree (see *Catalogue of the Officers and Students in Yale College, 1848–9* [New Haven, 1848], p. 37). The catalogue of 1850 stipulated, presumably with Bristed's consent, that the recipient would forfeit one-third of the "annuity" in case of non-residence (see *Catalogue of the Officers and Students of Yale College, 1850–51* [New Haven, 1850], p. 37).

41. *North American Review*, LXXV (1852), 81.

42. *Ibid.* The *North American Review* attack on *Five Years in an English University* was, in turn, attacked in a pamphlet entitled *The English Universities in the North American Review* (Albany, 1854), by an unidentified Harvard LL.B. and "Sometime Commoner of Magdalen Hall, Oxford." The essayist remarked on the fresh stimulus afforded by fellowships after the attainment of the University degree, but he placed his emphasis on the Honours system (see pp. 33–34).

43. The direct effect of Bristed's recommendation or of the *Review*'s similar statement is not traceable to any large extent. There is little positive evidence that they actually brought the fellowship idea into the forefront of university reform. Nevertheless, the apparent popularity of Bristed's book can hardly be overlooked, nor can the wide influence of the *North American Review* be denied. It is likely, therefore, that many men interested in academic matters in the early 1850's were familiar with the contents of one or both of these statements.

CHAPTER VII

Reform in New York State and Pennsylvania

1. See a letter from Benjamin Peirce, Cambridge, to Alexander D. Bache, January 27, 1855, in the Benjamin Peirce papers, Harvard University Archives. "Mrs[.] Peirce wishes me to get from you the recipe for your mode of cooking oysters. I told her, with becoming dignity, it was not *recipe* but *genius*. I burned with igneous indignation at her malignant insinuation—but nevertheless, dear Florentine, if there is a recipe sub rosâ, prey [*sic*] send it that I may fulminate it as the inspired lightening [*sic*] of genius."

2. Basil Hall, *Travels in North America in the Years 1827 and 1828* (Edinburgh, 1829), II, 172. The misspelling of the last name is in the original.

3. George T. Strong, diary, December 9, 1850. Enlarged microfilm prints in Columbiana Room, Columbia University. Ruggles' reaction was to suggest merging the undertaking with a movement to regenerate the scientific department at Columbia College.

4. Letters from Josiah D. Whitney to James Hall, January 13, 24, and 29, 1851, in the James Hall papers, New York State Museum.

5. Letter from Josiah D. Whitney, Paris, to James Hall, July 22, 1851, in the James Hall papers, New York State Museum.

6. Printed letter from Alexander D. Bache, in Virginia, to Alonzo Potter, August 2, 1852, reproduced in [Alonzo Potter], *Objections to a Re-organization of the University Considered* (Philadelphia, 1853), p. 32.

7. Letter from Josiah D. Whitney, Paris, to James Hall, July 22, 1851, in the James Hall papers, New York State Museum; letter from Benjamin Peirce, Cambridge, to [James Hall?], October 19, 1851, in the James Hall papers, New York State Museum; letter from Louis Agassiz to James Hall, August 3, [1851], quoted in John M. Clarke, *James Hall of Albany, Geologist and Palaeontologist, 1811–1898* (Albany, 1921), pp. 193–94.

8. Letter from Eben Horsford, Cambridge, to James Hall, December 25, 1851, in the James Hall papers, New York State Museum.

9. Letter from Josiah D. Whitney, Paris, to James Hall, July 22, 1851; letter from Benjamin A. Gould, Jr., Sharon Springs, July 5, 1852; letter from Benjamin Peirce, Cambridge, to [James Hall?], October 19, 1851. These letters are all in the James Hall papers, New York State Museum. Also letter from Louis Agassiz, Charleston, to James D. Dana, February 9, 1852, quoted in Daniel C. Gilman, *The Life of James Dwight Dana, Scientific Explorer, Mineralogist, Geologist, Zoölogist, Professor in Yale University* (New York, 1899), p. 321.

10. Letter from Benjamin Peirce, Cambridge, to [James Hall?], October 19, 1851, in the James Hall papers, New York State Museum.

11. Letter from John P. Norton, New Haven, to Benjamin Peirce, November 19, 1851, in the Benjamin Peirce papers, American Academy of Arts and Sciences.

12. [University of Albany], *Circular of the Scientific Department: Courses of Instruction for 1852* (Albany, 1851).

13. T. Romeyn Beck's remarks as reported in a letter from James Hall to Louis Agassiz, October 27, 1851, quoted in Clarke, *op. cit.*, pp. 196–97.

14. *Memorial Presented to the Legislature of the State of New York, on Behalf of the Scientific Commission Convened at the Capitol, in the City of Albany, on the 19th Day of February, 1852, in Relation to a National University To Be Established in the State of New York.*

15. Judgments on the success of the meetings differed. The *Albany Evening Journal*, March 11, 1852, was enthusiastic. Bache exclaimed over the "pretty botch they made of the last meetings" (letter from Alexander D. Bache to Benjamin Peirce, February 24, 1853, in the Benjamin Peirce papers, Harvard University Archives).

16. *New York Senate Journal*, March 9, 1852.

17. For an account of Ruggles' career see D. G. Brinton Thompson, *Ruggles of New York: A Life of Samuel B. Ruggles* (New York, 1946).

18. Samuel B. Ruggles *et al.*, *Speeches in Behalf of the University of Albany* (Albany, 1852), p. 7.

19. *Ibid.*

20. *Ibid.*, pp. 21–22.

21. *Ibid.*, p. 23.

22. *Ibid.*, p. 31.

23. *Memorial Presented to the Legislature of the State of New York* (1852). The patriotic note was struck again by State Senator Azor Taber, who referred to the necessity of foreign study for the completion of education. This, he said, exposed one's son to more or less corrupting influences. He would probably return,

"half cockney and half monarchist, to the discharge of the earnest duties of a republican citizen" (see extracts from Taber's speech in Ruggles *et al.*, *op. cit.*, p. 36).

24. The New York State Senate received several petitions in support of the Albany University (see *New York Senate Journal*, March 31, 1852).

25. Senator Pierce's speeches of March 11 and 13, 1852, on colonization and college appropriation bills, reported in the *Albany Evening Journal*, March 15, 1852.

26. *New York Senate Journal*, February 28, 1852, to April 16, 1852, and January 10, 1853. When a resolution was introduced on January 26, 1853, to grant the use of the Senate chamber to a scientific convention assembled to discuss the establishment of a state university, the decision went to the negative after a tie vote.

27. Letter from Josiah D. Whitney, Northampton, to James Hall, January 28, 1852, in the James Hall papers, New York State Museum.

28. Letter from Benjamin Peirce, Albany, to his wife, undated, in the Benjamin Peirce papers, Harvard University Archives.

29. Letter from Benjamin A. Gould, Jr., Sharon Springs, to James Hall, June 29, 1852, in the James Hall papers, New York State Museum.

30. *Ibid.*

31. This list is derived from an article on the National University Association in the *Albany Evening Journal*, February 26, 1853.

32. Letter from Benjamin Peirce, Cambridge, to James Hall, March 30, 1853, in the James Hall papers, New York State Museum. Clarke (*op. cit.*, pp. 198–99) attributes this letter to E[duard] Desor. The signature is indeed poorly written, but the hand is a crabbed one like that of Peirce's other correspondence rather than the clear one of Desor. The month is indicated by a Roman numeral, the year by the last two figures, in Peirce's characteristic manner. Just two days before, James Hall had written to Peirce of the founding of the Association, by a resolution offered by Gibbs; of the opportunity for action; of control being in the right hands; and of Hall's belief that the legislature would not do anything that year or in any other. The suggestion which is attributed to Peirce above might well have been in answer to this letter of Hall's (see letter from James Hall, Albany, to Benjamin Peirce, March 28, 1853, in the Benjamin Peirce papers, American Academy of Arts and Sciences).

33. Letter from Samuel B. Ruggles, New York, to Benjamin Peirce, August 2, 1853, in the Benjamin Peirce papers, Harvard University Archives. Ruggles called attention to the most gratifying effect of $30 prizes offered in a theological seminary and asked what might not be expected from five hundred prizes of $100 each.

34. Letter from Josiah D. Whitney to James Hall, December 18, 1853, in the James Hall papers, New York State Museum.

35. Letter from Benjamin Peirce, Cambridge, to Alexander D. Bache, December 17, 1855, in the Benjamin Peirce papers, Harvard University Archives. Peirce and Bache had agreed somewhat earlier that the Albany group had done badly (see letter from Alexander D. Bache, Dixmont, to Benjamin Peirce, September 27, 1855, in the Benjamin Peirce papers, Harvard University Archives).

36. Letter from Benjamin Peirce, Cambridge, to Alexander D. Bache, December 17, 1855, in the Benjamin Peirce papers, Harvard University Archives.

37. Benjamin Peirce, *Working Plan for the Foundation of a University* (Cambridge, 1856). A MS draft of this plan, placing the university at Albany, is in the Benjamin Peirce papers, American Academy of Arts and Sciences. Writing to Peirce on November 1, 1856, Bache referred to "our Albany friends" in connection

with a university of arts and sciences but doubted that they could carry it (see letter from Alexander D. Bache, New York, to Benjamin Peirce, November 1, [1856]).

38. *Catalogue of the Officers and Students in Union College, during the Third Term, 1852* (2d ed.; Schenectady, 1852), pp. 20–21. The graduate and "University" programs were distinct. Students in the "University" program did not have to be graduates.

39. *Catalogue of the Officers and Students in Union College, during the Third Term, 1853* (Schenectady, 1853), p. 20.

40. *Ibid.*

41. *Ibid.*, p. 21.

42. *Ibid.*, p. 20.

43. Trust Deed from Eliphalet Nott and Wife, to the Trustees of Union College, dated Schenectady, January 28, 1854, Art. IV, sec. 24, Sixth, in Union College Library.

44. *Ibid.*, Art. VIII, secs. 75 and 76.

45. See [Alonzo Potter], *Objections to a Re-organization of the University Considered* (Philadelphia, 1853), p. 26. Potter referred here to devoting a large sum at Union to enabling graduates to reside in the college and to study under active and regular supervision.

46. Union College Trustees Minutes, July 25, 1854, in Union College.

47. *Catalogue of the Officers and Students in Union College, during the Third Term, 1854* (Schenectady, 1854), p. 22.

48. [Potter], *op. cit.*, p. 29.

49. *Ibid.*, p. 40. This quotation comes from Appendix C, an extract from the proceedings of the first session of the American Association for the Advancement of Education, August, 1851.

50. Printed letter from Alonzo Potter, Philadelphia, to Joseph R. Ingersoll, July 8, 1852, p. 3. There is a copy of this letter in the University of Pennsylvania Library.

51. *Ibid.*, p. 4. Potter was perfectly aware that student subsidies would necessitate additional funds, but he was confident that the money would be forthcoming. Like some of the supporters of the University of the City of New York, he sought to provide adult and graduate education simultaneously. In discussing his "open university," he did not distinguish between an institution suited to the needs of the ambitious but under-educated craftsman and one designed to satisfy the B.A. in search of higher learning. As these divergent interests seem to call for separate departments, which could hardly have been established without greater expense than Potter contemplated, his optimism over finances appears ill-founded.

52. *By-Law of Instruction*, printed with the letter from Potter to Ingersoll, p. 8.

53. Edward P. Cheyney, *History of the University of Pennsylvania, 1740–1940* (Philadelphia, 1940), p. 248.

54. See M. A. DeWolfe Howe, *Memoirs of the Life and Services of the Rt. Rev. Alonzo Potter, D.D., LL.D., Bishop of the Protestant Episcopal Church in the Diocese of Pennsylvania* (Philadelphia, 1871), pp. 202–5. Howe says of the reception of Potter's proposals: "For so brave an advance, it was at length determined the time had not yet come" (p. 205).

55. Letter from Alexander D. Bache, Virginia, to Alonzo Potter, August 2, 1852, reproduced in [Potter], *Objections*, p. 33.

56. Merle M. Odgers, *Alexander Dallas Bache, Scientist and Educator, 1806–1867* (Philadelphia, 1947), p. 152. Frazer seems to have been a member of the Lazzaroni (see *ibid.*, p. 158).

57. Printed letter from John F. Frazer, University of Pennsylvania, to Alonzo Potter, January 1, 1853, p. 2. A copy of this letter is in the University of Pennsylvania Library.

58. *Ibid.*

59. *Ibid.*

60. Printed letter from Henry Vethake, Philadelphia, to William M. Meredith, November 27, 1852, pp. 4–5. There is a copy of this letter in the University of Pennsylvania Library.

61. *Ibid.*, p. 8.

62. [George Allen], *Professor Allen's Remarks on the Letter and By-Law Reported November 3, 1852* (n.d.), pp. 3–4.

63. *Ibid.*, p. 4.

64. *Ibid.*, p. 9.

65. *Ibid.*

66. [Potter], *Objections*, p. 12.

CHAPTER VIII

A GREAT UNIVERSITY FOR NEW YORK CITY

1. Henry P. Tappan, *The Growth of Cities: A Discourse Delivered before the New York Geographical Society* (New York, 1855), p. 19.

2. *Ibid.*, *passim.* Some of Tappan's remarks appear in the appendix to the address.

3. Alexander D. Bache, "A National University," *American Journal of Education,* I (1855–56), 477.

4. *Ibid.*, p. 478.

5. *Ibid.*

6. *Ibid.*

7. *Ibid.*

8. Francis Lieber advocated concentration, saying that with easy communication the talents of one man might be secured by two or three colleges at once. He pointed out that something of the sort had happened in the case of Agassiz (see letter from Francis Lieber, Columbia, S.C., to Samuel B. Ruggles, January 20, 1856, in the correspondence of Francis Lieber, Library of Congress).

Lieber should be mentioned in connection with the movement described in this chapter; but what seems to be his contribution—two unnamed, undated pages on the subject—cannot be placed exactly enough to stand without question beside the work of Tappan, Peirce, and Bache. Lieber had a personal interest in the project, which offered him escape from his post at South Carolina College. In the spring of 1856, Lieber expressed his curiosity concerning the "Cooperion," as he called the Cooper Union, and wrote to Ruggles: "The name has a strikingly Chinese air. You know their taverns have such signs, as: The Union of Celestial Felicity and the Five Social Duties. A *name* is a *name*. How can you name that thing? The *Union?* It will take a long time before that word palpably precipitates[.] However, the old gentleman, I suppose, must be humored" (letter from Francis Lieber, Columbia, S.C., to Samuel B. Ruggles, March 10, 1856, in the correspondence of Francis Lieber, Library of Congress). Here Lieber was condescending, but in his undated statement he had positive suggestions to make. Real learning and the highest science, as well as information, ought to be the object of the New York City University, which should be for America what Buffon had been in France for natural philosophy. The direction of the institution should be in the hands of a few men, the head not to be an *ex officio* member such as the Mayor. Yet there ought to be a strong tie between the enterprise, the city as such, and its people. The lecturers should be (1) professors with salaries and fees; (2) lecturers or second-class professors with smaller salaries and fees; (3) licentiates, receiving fees but no salaries; and (4) invited or occasional lecturers. The professors with some other officers should constitute a senate for the immediate government of the university. Anyone would be eligible for admission upon the payment of fees, but degrees would be granted only on examination. Prizes and rewards in the form of loans should be given, especially to facilitate European travel for a period of two or three years (see undated, two-page statement on a New York City university, in the correspondence of Francis Lieber, Library of Congress).

9. Henry P. Tappan, "Progress of Educational Development in Europe," *Proceedings of the Fifth Session of the American Association for the Advancement of Education, Held at the City of New York, August 28th, 29th, 30th, and 31st, A.D. 1855* (Hartford, 1856), pp. 52–53.

10. Benjamin Peirce *et al.*, "Remarks on a National University," *Proceedings of the Fifth Session of the American Association for the Advancement of Education*, p. 26.

11. Letter from Henry P. Tappan, University of Michigan, to Samuel B. Ruggles, February 19, 1856, in the University of Michigan Historical Room.

12. Letter from Henry P. Tappan, Frankfort, to his daughter [Rebecca Tappan Brünnow], March 20, 1871. The original is in the possession of Mrs. Louis Faulkner; a copy is in the University of Michigan Historical Room.

13. *Ibid.*

14. Letter from Henry P. Tappan, University of Michigan, to Samuel B. Ruggles, February 20, 1856, in the University of Michigan Historical Room.

15. See Benjamin Peirce *et al.*, "Remarks on a National University," *American Journal of Education*, II (1856), 89. Peirce refers to "the Coopers, of our race."

16. Charles Astor Bristed was a nephew of William Astor, the controlling influence of the Astor Library; but there is no available evidence that Bristed played any part in the New York university movement.

17. Letter from Henry P. Tappan, University of Michigan, to Samuel B. Ruggles, January 29, 1856, in the University of Michigan Historical Room.

18. As early as September 20, 1855, Francis Lieber had written to Samuel B. Ruggles that he, Lieber, was to see Cooper in the evening on some important business, the nature of which he did not specify. This may have been the first effort to approach Cooper on behalf of the university project (see letter from Francis Lieber, Bordentown, to Samuel B. Ruggles, September 20, 1855, in the correspondence of Francis Lieber, Library of Congress).

19. Letter from Henry P. Tappan to Peter Cooper, as reported in a letter from Henry P. Tappan, University of Michigan, to Samuel B. Ruggles, January 29, 1856, in the University of Michigan Historical Room. The use here of "union" may have suggested the word to Cooper as the name for his institution.

20. Draft of a letter from Henry P. Tappan, University of Michigan, to William Astor, February 18, 1856. The original is in the possession of Mrs. Louis Faulkner; a copy is in the University of Michigan Historical Room. This is Tappan's draft of the letter. It seems safe to assume that it represents the ideas, if not the actual wording, used in the copy mailed to Astor.

21. How Astor reacted to these particular arguments has not been discovered. One can wonder whether his definition of "necessity" would have corresponded with Tappan's and whether he was much impressed by the historical evidence marshaled for his benefit. To the final portion of the brief, the son of John Jacob

Astor might perhaps have said: That is all very fine, Mr. Tappan, but a lack of taste for beaver hats was no reason for expanding the American Fur Company.

22. *Ibid.*

23. *Ibid.*

24. *Ibid.*

25. Letter from Henry P. Tappan, University of Michigan, to Samuel B. Ruggles, March 3, 1856, in the University of Michigan Historical Room. Tappan also had a private reason for avoiding any appearance of participation in the university project except as an adviser. He did not wish to arouse suspicions in Michigan, where he had lately been under sharp fire from his critics (see letter from Henry P. Tappan, University of Michigan, to Samuel B. Ruggles, February 11, 1856, in the University of Michigan Historical Room).

26. Letter from Henry P. Tappan, University of Michigan, to Samuel B. Ruggles, February 19, 1856, in the University of Michigan Historical Room.

27. Letter from Henry P. Tappan, University of Michigan, to Benjamin Peirce, April 5, 1856, in the Benjamin Peirce papers, Harvard University Archives.

28. Letter from Henry P. Tappan, University of Michigan, to Samuel B. Ruggles, February 23, 1856, in the University of Michigan Historical Room.

29. Letter from Henry P. Tappan, University of Michigan, to Samuel B. Ruggles, March 3, 1856, in the University of Michigan Historical Room.

30. Tappan flatly refused to consider the proposal that the Free Academy be converted into a university as rapidly as possible (see letter from Henry P. Tappan, University of Michigan, to Samuel B. Ruggles, March 17, 1856, in the University of Michigan Historical Room).

31. Letter from Henry P. Tappan, University of Michigan, to Samuel B. Ruggles, April 2, 1856, in the University of Michigan Historical Room.

32. *Ibid.*

33. Benjamin Peirce, as quoted in a letter from Henry P. Tappan, University of Michigan, to Samuel B. Ruggles, March 17, 1856, in the University of Michigan Historical Room.

34. Letter from Henry P. Tappan, University of Michigan, to Benjamin Peirce, April 5, 1856, in the Benjamin Peirce papers, Harvard University Archives.

35. Letter from Henry P. Tappan, University of Michigan, to Benjamin Peirce, June 19 [?], 1856, in the Benjamin Peirce papers, Harvard University Archives.

36. *Documents of the Board of Aldermen, of the City of New York*, Vol. XXIII, Doc. No. 31, July 7, 1856, *passim*. This communication from the Mayor on establishing a university was referred to the Committee on Arts and Sciences. Speaking of a potential student body, he said that the city's five academies (presumably meaning Columbia and the University of the City of New York, among others) and the nation's many colleges would send students to the university. He predicted, furthermore, that two hundred Americans in foreign universities would be provided for at home and that the number of students would be increased by the fact that there was a university to receive them.

37. Letter from Henry P. Tappan, Frankfort, to his daughter [Rebecca Tappan Brünnow], March 20, 1871. The original is in the possession of Mrs. Louis Faulkner; a copy is in the University of Michigan Historical Room.

38. This is conjectural, but it is clear that Gould was not entirely friendly toward Brünnow, believing him to be indifferent to the Dudley Observatory, of which Gould was the director (see letter from [Benjamin A. Gould, Jr.], New York, to Benjamin Peirce, January 20, 1856, in the Benjamin Peirce papers, Harvard University Archives.

39. See S. Willis Rudy, *The College of the City of New York: A History, 1847–1947* (New York, 1949), p. 40. Rudy suggests the possibility that Wood was interested in the university only as a means of regaining a reputation for integrity.

40. Peirce originally conceived of his *Working Plan* in connection with Albany. See draft of a plan for a university in the Benjamin Peirce papers, American Academy of Arts and Sciences, in which "Albany" appears in the text.

41. Benjamin Peirce, *Working Plan for the Foundation of a University* (Cambridge, 1856), pp. 1–2.

42. *Ibid.*, pp. 2 ff. Although the *Working Plan* was marked "confidential," it was rather widely known. Bache used it; Peirce received several letters in regard to it; and Chancellor Isaac Ferris of the University of the City of New York, President Benjamin Hale of Hobart College, and President Daniel C. Gilman of the Johns Hopkins University all were familiar with Peirce's proposals.

43. *Ibid.*, pp. 3–4.

44. Letter from G[eorge] J. Adler, Boston, to Benjamin Peirce, December 10, 1857, in the Benjamin Peirce papers, Harvard University Archives. Adler remarked: "I myself have read a good deal on the subject of universities."

45. Letter from Alexander D. Bache, New York, to Benjamin Peirce, October 15, 1856, in the Benjamin Peirce papers, Harvard University Archives.

46. Alexander D. Bache, *Anniversary Address before the American Institute, of the City of New-York, at the Tabernacle, October 28th, 1856, during the Twenty-eighth Annual Fair* (New York, 1857), p. 13.

47. *Ibid.*

48. *Ibid.*, p. 41.

49. *Ibid.*, p. 46. Bache believed that sixty courses in literature, arts, and science might be offered.

50. *Ibid.*, pp. 55 ff.

51. Letter from Alexander D. Bache, New York, to Benjamin Peirce, November 1, [1856], in the Benjamin Peirce papers, Harvard University Archives.

52. Letters from Benjamin Peirce, Washington, D.C., to Sarah Peirce, January 30, 1857, and February 2, 1857, in the Benjamin Peirce papers, Harvard University Archives. Peirce may have been visiting Bache in Washington while Cooper was being entertained there.

53. Letter from Benjamin Peirce, New York, to Sarah Peirce, February 9, 1857, in the Benjamin Peirce papers, Harvard University Archives.

54. George T. Strong, MS diary, June 1, 1857. Enlarged microfilm prints in the Columbiana Room, Columbia University Library.

55. *Ibid.*

56. Minutes of the Trustees of Columbia College, June 15, 1857. A typed copy of these minutes is in the Columbiana Room, Columbia University Library. Curiously enough, Ruggles was not a member of this committee.

57. Strong, diary, July 4, 1857.

58. Alexis de Tocqueville, *Democracy in America*, ed. Phillips Bradley (New York, 1945), II, 110.

CHAPTER IX

COLUMBIA UNIVERSITY

1. Letter from Benjamin A. Gould, Jr., Sharon Springs, to James Hall, June 29, 1852, in the James Hall papers, New York State Museum.

2. George T. Strong, MS diary, November 13, 1850. Enlarged microfilm prints in the Columbiana Room, Columbia University Library.

3. Minutes of the Trustees of Columbia College, October 4, 1852. A typed copy of these minutes is in the Columbiana Room, Columbia University Library. Hereafter in this chapter they will be referred to as "Trustees' Minutes."

4. *New York American*, December 2, 1829.

5. For a general view of Ruggles' work as a trustee of Columbia, see D. G. Brinton Thompson, *Ruggles of New York* (New York, 1946). Ruggles' term of service extended from 1836 to 1881.

6. Strong, diary, August 16, 1852. Strong reported that Peirce suggested that professors be prevented from becoming drones by requiring them to produce, every six months or a year, something in the nature of a memoir, an essay, or an investigation. In this entry Strong uses "Pierce," but he probably meant Peirce, as Ruggles was soon corresponding with him on university matters (see n. 7).

7. Letter from Samuel B. Ruggles, New York, to Benjamin Peirce, September 25, 1852, in the Benjamin Peirce papers, Harvard University Archives.

8. Letter from Samuel B. Ruggles to Benjamin Peirce, October 23, 1852, in the Benjamin Peirce papers, Harvard University Archives.

9. [Columbia College, Committee of Seven], *Circular Questionnaire* (December, 1852). There is a copy of the *Circular* in the Columbiana Room, Columbia University Library.

10. *Ibid.* The following year the Committee on the College Course estimated that the change in site would net the College $15,000 annually (see Trustees' Minutes, November 7, 1853).

11. Trustees' Minutes, December 13, 1852.

12. *Ibid.*, January 3, 1853.

13. *Ibid.*, February 7, 1853.

14. Strong, diary, January 3, 1853.

15. Letter from Francis Lieber to Samuel B. Ruggles, February 24, 1853, in the Correspondence of Francis Lieber, Library of Congress.

16. Report of the Committee on the Subject of Professorship of Experimental and Natural Philosophy, as entered in Trustees' Minutes, October 3, 1853.

17. Trustees' Minutes, October 3, 1853. Several similar committee designations —College Course, Collegiate Course, and Course—appear in the Trustees' Minutes. They apparently refer to a single committee for which the title Committee on the College Course is used here, since that is the most frequently employed term of the three. On December 19, 1853, the Rev. John Knox replaced Fish on the Committee (see Trustees' Minutes, December 19, 1853).

18. Report of the Committee on the College Course, November 2, 1853, as entered in Trustees' Minutes, November 7, 1853.

19. *Ibid.*

20. Letter from Benjamin A. Gould, Jr., Washington, D.C., to James Hall, December 8, 1853, in the James Hall papers, New York State Museum.

21. A review of the Gibbs controversy may be found in Thompson, *op. cit.*, pp. 77–89. Milton Halsey Thomas is the authority on the Gibbs affair, having written a thesis on it, Columbia University, 1942.

22. Strong, diary, April 1, 1854.

23. [Samuel B. Ruggles], *The Duty of Columbia College to the Community* (New York, 1854), *passim.* The quotation comes from p. 17. In his *Columbia, Colossus on the Hudson* (New York, 1947), p. 74, Horace Coon refers to this pamphlet as historic. He states that Ruggles attributed the founding of Columbia and Göttingen to George III. Ruggles did not, in fact, confuse the reigns.

24. [Ruggles], *op. cit.*, p. 17.

25. Printed circular letter from the Committee on the College Course to faculty members of Columbia College, March 22, 1854, in the Columbiana Room, Columbia University Library.

26. Letter from John McVickar to William Betts, chairman of the Committee [on the College Course], April, 1854, in College Papers, 1854, Columbiana Room, Columbia University Library.

27. Letter from Charles W. Hackley to the Committee on the College Course, undated, in College Papers, 1854, Columbiana Room, Columbia University Library.

28. Letter from Henry Drisler, Jr., to the Committee on the College Course, undated, in College Papers, 1854, Columbiana Room, Columbia University Library.

29. Trustees' Minutes, April 3, 1854.

30. Report of the Committee on the College Course, as entered in Trustees' Minutes, July 24, 1854.

31. *Ibid.*

32. Strong, diary, July 26, 1854.

33. Trustees' Minutes, September 14, 1854.

34. Ruggles may have been prompted to act by a recommendation of the Committee on the College Course to the effect that the existing program be continued until the College revenue permitted the inauguration of the co-ordinate course and that the Board consider new professorships to provide for this contingency (see resolution submitted by the Committee on the College Course, as entered in Trustees' Minutes, November 6, 1854).

35. Resolutions offered by Samuel B. Ruggles, as entered in Trustees' Minutes, November 23, 1854.

36. *Ibid.*

37. *Ibid.*, December 4, 1854.

38. Strong, diary, December 13, 1854.

39. See p. 104.

40. Letter from Richard S. McCulloh, Columbia College, to Benjamin Peirce, December 18, 1856, in the Benjamin Peirce papers, Harvard University Archives. McCulloh had accepted the post for which Gibbs had been nominated.

41. Letter from Richard S. McCulloh, Columbia College, to Benjamin Peirce, December 24, 1856, in the Benjamin Peirce papers, Harvard University Archives.

42. Letter from Richard S. McCulloh, Columbia College, to Benjamin Peirce, January 7, 1857, in the Benjamin Peirce papers, Harvard University Archives.

43. Strong, diary, December 1, 1856.

44. The other members of the Committee of Inquiry were Henry J. Anderson, William Betts, A. W. Bradford, and Benjamin I. Haight (see *Report of a Committee of the Trustees of Columbia College, Appointed To Inquire into the Condition of the Institution, and To Consider Such Measures as Might Be Judged Expedient To Increase Its Efficiency and Usefulness* [New York, 1858], p. 67). Hereafter in this chapter this report will be referred to simply as *"Report of the Committee of Inquiry."*

45. Although there is no record of a Trustees' meeting of September 10, 1856, the Committee, in seeming error, stated that it was appointed on that day and received the authorization here described on a subsequent date (*ibid.*, pp. 3–4).

46. Trustees' Minutes, July 7, 1856.

47. "Communications of Gentlemen Not Officers of the College," *Statements, Opinions, and Testimony Taken by the Committee of Inquiry, Appointed by the*

Trustees of Columbia College (New York, 1857), statement of Henry Vethake, pp. 132–36. Hereafter in this chapter this volume will be known simply as *"Statements."*

48. *Ibid.,* statement of Henry P. Tappan, p. 61.

49. *Ibid.,* statement of Mark Hopkins, p. 140.

50. *Ibid.,* statement of Benjamin Hale, p. 110.

51. *Ibid.,* "The Statement of Henry Drisler, Jr.," p. 96.

52. *Ibid.,* p. 52.

53. *Ibid.,* statement of W. H. N. Stewart, p. 68.

54. *Ibid.,* "Communication of Mr. George T. Strong," February 3, 1857, p. 19.

55. *Ibid.*

56. *Ibid.,* pp. 19–20.

57. *Ibid.,* p. 20.

58. *Ibid.,* p. 24. Francis Lieber apparently suggested fellowships for Columbia as early as March 1, 1856. It is not unlikely that Strong saw the paper in which this point was made. See letter from Francis Lieber, Columbia, S.C., to [Samuel B. Ruggles], March 1, 1856, in the Correspondence of Francis Lieber, Library of Congress.

59. *Statements,* "Communication of Mr. George T. Strong," p. 20.

60. *Ibid.*

61. *Ibid.,* pp. 22–23.

62. *Ibid.,* p. 23.

63. *Ibid.,* p. 24. Strong did not himself specify the sources from which his ideas were derived; but similarities between his recommendations and the thinking of other men are evident. Like the Yale authorities of 1828, he insisted that reform should not outrun means. In his description of the third higher course, he approached the faculty of philosophy advocated by Henry P. Tappan. When he suggested that professors be allowed to have outside occupations and that eminent men resident elsewhere be invited to take part in teaching and lecturing at the University, he was in agreement with the principles of Peirce's *Working Plan.* In a MS, "Suggestions Columbia University," February, 1857, in the Correspondence of Francis Lieber, Library of Congress, Lieber emphasized growth and organic expansion from small beginnings as good policy. With one academic planner Strong took issue. He did not share Chancellor Mathews' enthusiasm for architectural grandeur as a starting point of reform. Until the institution had taken on definite shape, he felt that outward signs of dignity would be inappropriate. "Academic shades and cloisters seem out of the question at present, but they may come in time, provided we do not attempt to begin with them" (see "Communication of Mr. George T. Strong," *Statements,* p. 26).

64. William Betts, "Introductory Address," *Addresses of the Newly-appointed Professors of Columbia College* (New York, 1858), pp. 3–5.

65. Trustees' Minutes, January 12, 1857; Betts, *op. cit.,* p. 11.

66. Trustees' Minutes, February 2, 1857.

67. *Ibid.*

68. See a communication from the Faculty to the Trustees, dated 1857 in pencil, in College Papers, January–March, 1857, Columbiana Room, Columbia University Library. This paper suggested that the faculty wanted the university course to be a continuation of the college course.

69. Trustees' Minutes, March 2, 1857.

70. *Ibid.*

71. *Ibid.,* March 30, 1857.

72. Strong, diary, March 11, 1857.

73. *Ibid.*, May 18, 1857.

74. Trustees' Minutes, May 11, 1857, June 15, 1857, and July 6, 1857. The University Course of Study was: in the School of Letters—moral and mental philosophy, aesthetics, the history of philosophy, Greek and Roman literature, oriental and modern languages, comparative philology, ethnology; in the School of Science —mechanics and physics, astronomy, chemistry and mineralogy, geology and paleontology, engineering, mining and metallurgy, arts of design, history of science, natural history, physical geography; in the School of Jurisprudence—history, political economy, political philosophy, and various aspects of the law.

75. *Ibid.*, June 15, 1857.

76. *Ibid.*, July 6, 1857.

77. Strong, diary, September 28, 1857.

78. Trustees' Minutes, June 1 and 8, 1857.

79. Strong, diary, June 15, 1857.

80. *Report of the Committee of Inquiry*, p. 40. The Committee recommended the establishment of three prizes of $300 and three of $200, payable annually for two years, one prize of each amount to be awarded in each of the three schools. It also suggested that the title of Fellow be given to the recipients of the honors at graduation. These men would have preference for employment as tutors when places fell open. All awards were to be made following special examinations (*ibid.*, pp. 41–42).

81. See Frank Freidel, *Francis Lieber, Nineteenth-Century Liberal* (Baton Rouge, 1947), pp. 292 ff., for an account of Lieber's career in New York. See also Joseph Dorfman and Rexford G. Tugwell, "Francis Lieber: German Scholar in America. II," *Columbia University Quarterly*, XXX (1938), 272 ff.

82. Charles A. Joy, "Chemistry: An Inaugural Address," *Addresses of the Newly-appointed Professors of Columbia College* (New York, 1858), pp. 50–51.

83. Francis Lieber, "Inaugural Address," *Addresses of the Newly-appointed Professors of Columbia College*, p. 59.

84. *Ibid.*, pp. 115–16.

85. Charles Davies, "Mathematics: Inaugural Address," *Addresses of the Newly-appointed Professors of Columbia College*, pp. 119, 134–35.

86. Charles M. Nairne, "Inaugural Discourse," *Addresses of the Newly-appointed Professors of Columbia College*, p. 179.

87. Trustees' Minutes, September 17, 1857.

88. Strong, diary, February 21, 1858.

89. *Ibid.*, March 3, 1858.

90. *Ibid.*, March 8, 1858; Trustees' Minutes, March 8, 1858.

91. Trustees' Minutes, April 5, 1858. These recommendations paralleled in several details those made to the Committee of Inquiry by Ruggles' friend, Francis Lieber, who urged the immediate opening of the University on a limited scale and the charging of fees (see "Communications of Gentlemen Not Officers of the College," *Statements*, statement of Francis Lieber, pp. 26–27).

92. Trustees' Minutes, April 5, 1858.

93. *Ibid.*, May 3, 1858.

94. Strong, diary, May 3, 1858.

95. *Ibid.*

96. *Ibid.*, May 17, 1858.

97. Trustees' Minutes, June 21, 1858. See these minutes for the details of Ruggles' report, which called for frequent examination, payment of fees, etc. The resolutions are reproduced in full in Thompson, *op. cit.*, pp. 201–2.

98. Lieber's influence may have been responsible for the new appointment policy. In his estimation, the teaching of eminent men was essential to a university, and he argued that only on a part-time basis could the services of such men be secured by Columbia (see "Communications of Gentlemen Not Officers of the College," *Statements*, statement of Francis Lieber, pp. 25 and 27). It is also worth noting that part-time teaching by outstanding men was a feature of the university plan which Peirce had circulated privately in 1856. Since we know that Peirce and Ruggles were friends in the movement for academic reform, it is probably safe to assume that Ruggles had been impressed by the advantages of part-time instructors at least two years before the matter came up for action at Columbia.

99. Strong, diary, June 24, 1858.

100. *Ibid.*, June 29, 1858.

101. *Ibid.*, June 24, 1858.

102. Thompson, *op. cit.*, p. 94.

103. Trustees' Minutes, November 1, 1858. The fee for each course was set at $5 for persons not graduates of Columbia College and at $3 for alumni. See Thompson, *op. cit.*, p. 94, for the suggestion that the energy of the Board may be traced to the fact that Ruggles acted as chairman during part of 1858 and most of 1859. By October, 1858, it had become clear that James D. Dana could not come to Columbia for that academic year. See Strong, diary, October 12, 1858.

104. Report to the Regents, as entered in Trustees' Minutes, December 5, 1859.

105. Trustees' Minutes, June 6, 1859.

106. Strong, diary, June 22, 1859.

107. Letter from Francis Lieber to [illegible] August——, 1859, in the Correspondence of Francis Lieber, Library of Congress.

108. Trustees' Minutes, October 3, 1859.

109. Strong, diary, July 6, 1859.

110. *Ibid.*, December 21, 1859.

111. *Ibid.*, November 5, 1860.

112. *Ibid.*, March 4, 1860.

113. *Ibid.*, June 6 and 22, 1859, and June 4, 21, July 10, 11, 19, 1860.

114. Trustees' Minutes, June 3, 1861.

115. *Ibid.*, June 24, 1861.

116. *Ibid.*

117. Strong, diary, May 28, 1860.

118. "Communications of Gentlemen Not Officers of the College," *Statements*, statement of Francis Lieber, p. 22.

119. *Ibid.*, statement of Henry P. Tappan, p. 54.

120. *Ibid.*, statement of Francis Lieber, p. 22.

121. Strong, diary, April 7, 1858.

CHAPTER X

Reform in the West and South

1. Wilfred B. Shaw, *The University of Michigan* (New York, 1920), pp. 30 ff.

2. Henry P. Tappan, *A Discourse Delivered by Henry P. Tappan, D.D. on the Occasion of His Inauguration as Chancellor of the University of Michigan, December 21st, 1852* (Detroit, 1852), *passim*.

3. *Catalogue of the Corporation, Officers, and Students in the Departments of Medicine, Arts, and Sciences, of the University of Michigan, 1852–1853* (Detroit, 1853), p. 21.

4. *Ibid.* The subjects proper to a university course would, in general, be: systematic philosophy; history of philosophy; history and political economy; logic; ethics and evidences of Christianity; law of nature and nations and constitutional law; the higher mathematics; astronomy; general physics; chemistry; natural history; philosophy; Greek language and literature; Latin language and literature; oriental languages; English language and literature; modern literature; rhetoric and criticism; history of fine arts; and arts of design (*ibid.*, p. 26).

5. Henry P. Tappan, *Report to the Board of Regents of the University of Michigan, Made November 15, 1853* (Ann Arbor, 1853), p. 32.

6. "Annual Report of the Chancellor of the University to the Board of Regents" (October 21, 1854), *University of Michigan Regents' Proceedings, with Appendixes and Index, 1837–1864* (Ann Arbor, 1915), p. 599. Hereafter cited as "*Regents' Proceedings.*"

7. "Report of Regents of the University of Michigan" (October 19, 1854), *ibid.*, p. 576.

8. Henry P. Tappan, *The Progress of Educational Development: A Discourse Delivered before the Literary Societies of the University of Michigan, on Monday Evening, June 25, 1855* (Ann Arbor, 1855), pp. 36–50.

9. Henry P. Tappan, quoted in Shaw, *op. cit.*, p. 51. For a discussion of Tappan's relations with students, see Charles M. Perry, *Henry Philip Tappan, Philosopher and University President* (Ann Arbor, 1933), pp. 263–65.

10. Perry, *op. cit.*, pp. 201–2.

11. W. F. Storey as quoted *ibid.*, p. 200.

12. In this paragraph I have relied heavily on Perry (*ibid.*, pp. 195 ff.).

13. Minutes of Faculty Meetings, September 24, 28, and 29, October 1, 27, 29, 1855, in the Michigan Historical Collections, University of Michigan.

14. "Report of the President of the University" (December 18, 1855), *Regents' Proceedings*, p. 617.

15. "Report of the President" (October 18, 1856), *ibid.*, p. 655.

16. *Ibid.*

17. *Ibid.*, December 23, 1858, p. 804.

18. This schedule is derived principally from *Regents' Proceedings*, December 23, 1858, pp. 805–6. The faculty which was to direct these studies contained real talent, if not genius. Tappan himself had been a serious student of philosophy and had written on the Will. Andrew D. White was, of course, to become the first president of Cornell University and the author of the monumental *History of the Warfare of Science with Theology in Christendom*. Francis Brünnow was a notable astronomer, while Alexander Winchell was one of the founders and later a president of the Geological Society of America. He was also a prolific writer on science. Henry S. Frieze, although not a very productive research scholar, was far from being a mere gerund-grinder.

19. One of these was Charles K. Adams.

20. These statistics are derived from the University of Michigan catalogues for the years mentioned.

21. Perry, *op. cit.*, pp. 295 ff.

22. Letter from Henry P. Tappan, Frankfort, to his daughter [Rebecca Tappan Brünnow], March 20, 1871. Original in the possession of Mrs. Louis Faulkner; copy in the University of Michigan Historical Room.

23. *Catalogue of the Officers and Students of the University of Michigan, with a Statement of the Course of Instruction in the Various Departments. For 1864* (Ann Arbor, 1864), p. 38.

24. James D. Dana, "Science and Scientific Schools," *American Journal of Education*, II, No. 6 (1856), 374.

25. The origins of graduate education in the arts and sciences in the South will have to be traced by someone able to spend much time in research at the Southern universities. Beyond what has been said about the University of Virginia in chap. ii and what appears in this chapter, it must suffice here to refer to Mary B. Pierson, *Graduate Work in the South* (Chapel Hill, 1947), primarily a study of current matters, with a brief preliminary historical sketch; to W. W. Pierson, "The Past, Present, and Future of the Graduate School," *Graduate School [of the University of North Carolina] Research and Publications*, ed., Edgar W. Knight and Agatha B. Adams (Chapel Hill, 1946), pp. 3–55; and to Edwin L. Green, *A History of the University of South Carolina* (Columbia, 1916). Clearly, at least one recipient of a pre–Civil War Master of Arts degree at the University of North Carolina must be classified as a graduate student within the meaning of the term as used here; and the letters written to Mary B. Pierson by officials of several Southern universities suggest that the North Carolina case was not unique. Green refers to an 1843 report by the president of South Carolina College that six resident graduates pursued a course of reading arranged for them by him. Green further states that the catalogues report that in nearly every year after 1843 there were two or more students enrolled as pursuing graduate studies in residence (see Green, *op. cit.*, pp. 50 and 196). In 1836 the laws of South Carolina College allowed a Bachelor to earn a Master's degree by residing in the College for one session, pursuing a course of study under the direction of the president, sustaining a fair character, and performing exercises assigned by the faculty. In addition, the M.A. in course was provided for (*ibid.*, pp. 195–96). Careful study of possible early graduate work in the South is very much needed.

26. Letter from Lewis H. Steiner, Baltimore, to Benjamin Peirce, September 14, 1856, in the Benjamin Peirce papers, Harvard University Archives.

27. Francis Lieber, "Inaugural Address," *Addresses of the Newly-appointed Professors of Columbia College* (New York, 1858), p. 65.

28. An Alabamian, "An American University," *American Journal of Education*, III (1857), 214.

29. *Ibid.*, p. 213.

30. "Central Southern University," *DeBow's Review*, XXIII (1857), 495. The author of this communication is identified only as "Mr. Richardson."

31. Professor Benjamin Silliman, Sr., had publicly indorsed the buying of fire-arms for the free-soil Kansas settlers, and he wrote in his diary, April 3, 1856, "it was a holy cause." See Silliman's diary, quoted in George P. Fisher, *Life of Benjamin Silliman, M.D., LL.D.* (New York, 1866), II, 242.

32. "Central Southern University," *DeBow's Review*, XXIII, 498.

33. *Ibid.*, pp. 498–99.

34. *Ibid.*, p. 499. What Richardson meant by "thorough and comprehensive" is suggested by his list of professorships: evidences of natural and revealed religion; moral and intellectual philosophy; history and geography; national and constitutional law; rhetoric and logic; political economy; oratory and belles-lettres; patriotism; English language and literature; Latin language and literature; Greek language and literature; Hebrew language and literature; French language and literature; Spanish language and literature; German language and literature; Italian language and literature; pure mathematics; applied mathematics; natural philosophy and astronomy; practical astronomy; chemistry and mineralogy; practical and analytical chemistry; theory and practice of agricul-

ture; geology; natural history and ethnology; botany; comparative anatomy; physiology and human anatomy; drawing; painting; music; law [two chairs]; medicine [four chairs]; civil engineering; mining, engineering, and metallurgy; mechanical engineering; military engineering; tactics and military art and science; and gymnastics (*ibid.*, p. 580).

35. *Ibid.*, pp. 575–76.

36. William M. Polk, *Leonidas Polk, Bishop and General* (New York, 1893), I, 191 ff. William M. Polk, son of the Bishop, reported that his father looked for permanent slavery only in the plantation states and did not desire the extension of slavery beyond the cotton belt (*ibid.*, I, 195–96).

37. Letter from Leonidas Polk, New Orleans, to Bishop Stephen Elliott, August 30, 1856, quoted *ibid.*, p. 212.

38. *Ibid.*, p. 212–14.

39. Letter from Leonidas Polk to the Southern bishops, quoted in *Address of the Commissioners for Raising the Endowment of the University of the South* (New Orleans, 1859), p. 4.

40. *An Address to the Members and Friends of the Protestant Episcopal Church in the Southern and South-western States* (Philadelphia, 1856), pp. 5–6.

41. *Ibid.*, p. 6.

42. *Ibid.*, pp. 9–10; David G. Haskins, *A Brief Account of the University of the South* (New York, 1877), pp. 31, 33.

43. *Ibid.*, pp. 33, 35; *Address of the Commissioners for Raising the Endowment of the University of the South*, pp. 7–8.

44. *Ibid.*, pp. 3–4.

45. *Ibid.*, p. 11.

46. *Ibid.*, p. 12. This appeal to Southern feeling was echoed in the final paragraph of the *Address*, in which the Bishops' thought clearly reflects Southern indignation at "the isolation in which the world is attempting to place you" (*ibid.*, p. 14).

47. *Ibid.*, pp. 12–13.

48. Polk, *op. cit.*, I, 228, n. 1.

49. Letter from Leonidas Polk, Chapel Hill, to Bishop Stephen Elliott, September 20, 1859, quoted *ibid.*, p. 228.

50. *Report of the Committee of the Board of Trustees of the University of the South, Appointed To Prepare the Draft of a Constitution and Code of Statutes for the University* (New Orleans, 1860), pp. 3–4; also Haskins, *op. cit.*, pp. 39–40.

51. *Report of the Committee*, p. 4.

52. "Statutes of the University of the South," reproduced in Polk, *op. cit.*, I, 247–50.

53. *Ibid.*, pp. 251–52.

54. *Ibid.*, pp. 254–55.

55. *Ibid.*, p. 255. Of the fellowship plan, one writer said: "We notice with pleasure . . . the provision for Fellowships. . . . a young man of limited means having diligently completed his academic education, and distinguished himself for unexceptional conduct, is assured of an honorable position and means of subsistence for the few years necessary to perfect himself in his chosen profession and to select a permanent career, and during that time continues to enjoy the facilities and advantages of the first University in America." This article contains two interesting remarks. One, reflecting the desire for pre-eminence, is to the effect that neither France, Germany, nor England would have a university equal

to that of the South if the plan became a reality and that, in less than a generation, students from the Old World might come to Sewanee. The other reveals the
influence of the institution of slavery, the writer expressing his gratification
at the establishment of a chair of ethnology and universal geography, science
"which teaches the aptitudes and comparative position of different human races,
as entitled to equal rank with the older and traditional divisions of profane
learning" (extract, apparently from the *Mobile Register,* in "The Southern University," *DeBow's Review,* XXVIII [1860], both quotations, p. 727).

56. Frederick A. P. Barnard, quoted in George R. Fairbanks, *History of the
University of the South* (Jacksonville, 1905), p. 55.

57. Bishop [William M.] Green, quoted in letter from Frederick A. P. Barnard
to Dr. Hilgard, July 1, 1859, quoted in John Fulton, *Memoirs of Frederick A. P.
Barnard* (New York, 1896), p. 239.

58. Letter from Frederick A. P. Barnard to (apparently) Dr. Hilgard, November 16, 1859, quoted in Fulton, *op. cit.,* p. 240.

59. Frederick A. P. Barnard and John W. Pratt, *Report on a Proposition To
Modify the Plan of Instruction in the University of Alabama* (New York, 1855),
pp. 79–82.

60. Frederick A. P. Barnard, "On Improvements Practicable in American
Colleges," *Proceedings of the Fifth Session of the American Association for the
Advancement of Education, 1855* (Hartford, 1856), p. 55.

61. *Ibid.*

62. *Ibid.,* pp. 64 ff.

63. Frederick A. P. Barnard, *Letter to the Honorable, the Board of Trustees
of the University of Mississippi* (Oxford [Miss.], 1858), p. 13.

64. *Ibid.,* pp. 15–16.

65. *Ibid.,* p. 16.

66. *Ibid.,* pp. 16–17. Barnard used several general arguments to buttress his
proposal for an expanded university. One was that the University was the prime
mover of the entire educational system of the state, with the character of every
school within the state determined in the end by the caliber of the University.
In the second place, God had created man in vain if intellectual wealth was not
a priceless treasure. Thirdly, a university was needed because of the usefulness
of scientific investigation. As for the University of Mississippi specifically, it
must be its aim ultimately to build itself up into a university in the largest
meaning of that term. Consequently, in the course of time, additional schools,
such as oriental learning, should be anticipated. No one student, obviously, would
be expected to cover all these fields. He would be permitted to choose between
schools and would receive the M.A. degree after exhibiting proficiency in a
prescribed number and variety of courses. Only a man so prepared would qualify
for the Master's degree. Instruction in the higher department would be through
the medium of lectures, although books were by no means to be discarded.

67. *Ibid.,* pp. 38–39.

68. *Ibid.,* p. 39.

69. See Fulton, *op. cit.,* pp. 205–8. Fulton points out that Barnard's view of
education became greatly enlarged as soon as he found himself head of a university.

70. [James H. Thornwell], "Barnard on American Colleges," *Southern Quarterly Review,* I, N.S. (1856), 176. This review is attributed here to Thornwell
because this is the only *Southern Quarterly Review* article to which Barnard
could reasonably have been referring in his *Letter* to the Mississippi Trustees,
p. 14.

71. [Thornwell], *loc. cit.*

72. *Ibid.*, pp. 176–77.

73. *Ibid.*, p. 177.

74. *Ibid.*

75. *Ibid.*, p. 178.

76. *Ibid.* Thornwell adds that those who wished to cultivate "the practical sciences" could have the privilege to do so to their hearts' content. Thornwell's views on college and university education are sketched out, with quotations from Thornwell, in B. M. Palmer, *The Life and Letters of James Henry Thornwell, D.D., LL.D., Ex-President of the South Carolina College, Late Professor of Theology in the Theological Seminary at Columbia, South Carolina* (Richmond, 1875), pp. 355–59.

CHAPTER XI

THE EARLY TRADITIONS OF GRADUATE EDUCATION

1. Goldwin Smith, "University Education," *Journal of Social Science*, I (1869), 25.

2. [James L. Kingsley], "Review of Dwight's Travels in the North of Germany," *Quarterly Christian Spectator*, I (1829), 639–40.

3. Letter from John A. Smith, Williamsburg, to Joseph C. Cabell, November 10, 1816, in the Joseph C. Cabell papers, University of Virginia Library.

4. Charles W. Eliot, "National University," *The Addresses and Journal of Proceedings of the National Educational Association, Session of the Year 1873, at Elmira, New York* (Peoria, Ill., 1873), p. 119. This was a report to the Department of Higher Education of the National Educational Association.

5. In 1871 Frederick A. P. Barnard estimated that the average age of Columbia College men at graduation was twenty-one, while there were many cases in earlier times of graduation at sixteen or seventeen (*Annual Report* of Frederick A. P. Barnard as President of Columbia College, June 5, 1871, reproduced in William F. Russell [ed.], *The Rise of a University* [New York, 1937], I, 101). Records of Harvard classes bear out Barnard's general point that the entering and leaving ages of college students were increasing.

6. Richard S. Storrs, Jr., "Colleges: A Power in Civilization, To Be Used for Christ," *American Journal of Education and College Review*, I (1856), 530.

7. "Communications of Gentlemen Not Officers of the College," *Statements, Opinions, and Testimony Taken by the Committee of Inquiry, Appointed by the Trustees of Columbia College* (New York, 1857), statement of President Benjamin Hale, p. 110.

8. Professor Münche, of Heidelberg University, "On the Organization of Universities," translation from a review in *Heidelberger Jahrbücher der Literatur*, No. 37, in *American Annals of Education and Instruction*, I (1831), 458.

9. Letter from Charles Beck to Josiah Quincy, February 17, 1845, in the Josiah Quincy papers, 1845, Harvard University Archives.

10. *Addresses at the Inauguration of Daniel C. Gilman as President of the Johns Hopkins University, Baltimore, February 22, 1876* (Baltimore, 1876), pp. 26–27.

BIBLIOGRAPHY

1. See Samuel E. Morison's comment on the tendency of historians to define "university" so as to make it possible to prove their own colleges the first universities (Samuel E. Morison, *Harvard College in the Seventeenth Century* [Cambridge, 1936], I, 72).

Index

Specific fields of study are not indexed separately; but reference to graduate course offerings, curricula, professorships, etc., appear under "Course offerings for graduates."

⎡ PRINTED ⎤
⎣ IN U·S·A· ⎦